MW00855948

DASEIN DISCLOSED

Dasein Disclosed

JOHN HAUGELAND'S HEIDEGGER

John Haugeland

EDITED BY JOSEPH ROUSE

HARVARD UNIVERSITY PRESS

Cambridge, Massachusetts, and London, England

2013

Copyright © 2013 by the President and Fellows of Harvard College
All rights reserved

Library of Congress Cataloging-in-Publication Data

Haugeland, John, 1945–2010.
    Dasein disclosed : John Haugeland's Heidegger / John Haugeland ;
edited by Joseph Rouse.
      p. cm.
    Includes bibliographical references (p.   ) and index.
    ISBN 978-0-674-07211-4 (alk. paper)
    1. Heidegger, Martin, 1889–1976.   I. Rouse, Joseph, 1952–   II. Title.

  B3279.H49H29 2013
  193—dc23   2012028995

Contents

Editor's Introduction

John Haugeland, well-known philosopher of mind and cognitive science who taught at the universities of Chicago and Pittsburgh, died unexpectedly in June 2010. This posthumously published volume combines a book manuscript that was incomplete at the time of his death with other published and unpublished papers on the early philosophical work of Martin Heidegger.

Haugeland's groundbreaking reflections on intentionality, cognitive science, and artificial intelligence formed the core of his philosophical work. He had entered philosophy just as digital computing and serious research on artificial intelligence were beginning to reshape the discipline's conceptions of mind and cognition. His books, *Artificial Intelligence: The Very Idea* (1985) and *Having Thought: Essays in the Metaphysics of Mind* (1998), and his two edited collections on mind design (1981, 1997), were instrumental in guiding philosophers and many cognitive and computer scientists toward a more mature, reflective understanding and assessment of digital computation's contribution to our self-understanding as thinking beings.

Haugeland's extensive engagement with Heidegger has been much less widely recognized or understood. Roughly once each decade throughout his distinguished career in the heartland of the "analytic" philosophical tradition, Haugeland published a paper that fundamentally challenged familiar readings of Heidegger's *Being and Time*. Beginning with "Heidegger on Being a Person" (1982) and continuing through "Dasein's Disclosedness" (1990), "Truth and Finitude" (2000), and "Letting Be" (2007), Haugeland's innovative, iconoclastic work presented a wide-ranging reinterpretation of

Heidegger's project and its philosophical significance. His papers stood out for their remarkable clarity and succinctness, their striking and often controversial divergence from familiar readings of many central concepts and claims in Heidegger, and the priority they accorded to philosophical engagement with Heidegger's project over textual exegesis. Along with his teacher, Hubert Dreyfus, Haugeland has contributed to an ongoing transformation of Heidegger's place in contemporary Anglophone philosophy. A generation ago, Heidegger's work marked one of the principal fault lines in sharply divided philosophical allegiances to "analytic" or "continental" philosophical traditions. Heidegger is now more often recognized as having done work that matters to anyone seriously engaged with contemporary issues in metaphysics or the philosophy of mind, language, or science. Yet the significance of Haugeland's interpretation, for Heideggerian scholarship and even more for contemporary philosophy generally, has yet to be widely assimilated.

One measure of this generational shift has been a change in the style and orientation of philosophical writing about Heidegger in English. For a long time, the primary mode of Anglophone philosophical engagement with Heidegger was textual exegesis in a style that often closely tracked Heidegger's own difficult technical vocabulary. The aim often seemed to be to learn to deploy that vocabulary in place of more familiar philosophical locutions and concerns, and one result was to isolate Heidegger from mainstream philosophical work in the English-speaking world. To work with or on Heidegger was to enter a terminological labyrinth largely disconnected from the primary issues addressed by other twentieth-century philosophers. One indeed cannot understand Heidegger without coming to grips with his often formidable idiom, steeped in etymology, philosophical twists on familiar, everyday German locutions, and sustained efforts to circumvent some of the philosophical commitments built into both ordinary language and technical philosophical terms. Yet Dreyfus and Haugeland helped guide a shift toward philosophical engagement with Heidegger's language and its motivating concerns in ways that have begun to bring Heidegger back into broader contemporary philosophical conversations.

Even in the context of the philosophical and stylistic rapprochement that he helped initiate, Haugeland's writing about Heidegger stands out for its clarity, concision, and force. The same rhetorical sensibility also informs his long-standing effort to rethink the English translations of Heidegger's terms and to work out detailed examples that illuminate as well as exemplify what

Heidegger had to say. Haugeland did not altogether eschew strange verbal coinages or unusual turns of phrase, but these occasions now stand out more strikingly against a background of philosophical exposition in remarkably colloquial language. This stylistic achievement was accompanied by a sustained effort to address the issues "with special consideration for readers trained mainly in recent Anglo-American traditions" (below, p. 48). The aim, as Haugeland explicitly noted, was not to domesticate Heidegger or lessen the extent of his challenge to familiar philosophical commitments and concerns but to pose the issues in his thinking in ways that could get an effective and informative grip upon those with different training and philosophical sensitivity.

For more than a decade, Haugeland was writing a book that would advance and complete his career-long philosophical engagement with Heidegger through a comprehensive reinterpretation of *Being and Time* and its contemporaneous lecture courses and articles. Neither the book he intended to write nor the present comprehensive collection of his work on Heidegger is a textual commentary. What we have instead is a thorough reconception of Heidegger's project and its significance for philosophy now; this book is not aimed solely or even primarily at philosophers already interested in Heidegger but rather at the much wider group of philosophers who have yet to realize how centrally and originally Heidegger addresses their own philosophical concerns. That is why the volume includes several papers that are not directly about Heidegger's work but instead spell out its implications for philosophical analyses of intentionality and meaning.

Haugeland intended the manuscript he was writing under the title *Dasein Disclosed* as a careful philosophical reading of Heidegger's project rather than a commentary on his texts. Although the manuscript is organized thematically roughly in accord with the sequential appearance of central themes in *Being and Time,* Haugeland gave extended attention only to those topics, concepts, phenomenological descriptions, and arguments that figured centrally in his reconstruction of Heidegger's aims and achievements. He treated other themes and passages only in passing. The aim was always a deeper understanding of Heidegger's philosophical import, and not merely exposition. Although Haugeland often engages very closely with specific passages and phenomenological descriptions, in many respects, his primary concerns reorient central aspects of the structure and aim of the book. What guides his reading is a reenvisioning of what Heidegger was doing and how he saw himself doing it.

Stylistically and philosophically, this aspiration is especially important in taking up Heidegger's work. A central theme in Heidegger's thinking is the pervasive tendency of all understanding toward "idle talk" or "bullshit"[1] (merely passing the word along with only a semblance of understanding) and "ambiguity" (obscuring any difference between idle talk and genuine understanding). Haugeland's career-long struggle to understand and articulate Heidegger's project has been a model of resistance to idle talk and ambiguity.

WHY HAUGELAND'S HEIDEGGER MATTERS TO PHILOSOPHY NOW

Heidegger is surely among the most influential and informative but also most controversial philosophers of the past century, so one might plausibly think that the appearance of an original, provocative, and carefully developed interpretation of his work needs no further justification. Yet Haugeland's long involvement with Heidegger was never just about the scholarly task of improving the secondary literature on the texts. In his own work, Haugeland repeatedly sought to take stock of the current philosophical situation so as to identify and focus the most exigent current philosophical tasks. Thus, the opening chapters of *Artificial Intelligence: The Very Idea* (1985) sought to uncover the historical-conceptual roots of the confluence of modern conceptions of the mind with the technologies of digital computation in ways that could guide a critical assessment of that productive convergence. Papers such as "The Intentionality All-Stars," "Representational Genera," or "Mind Embodied and Embedded" (1998, chapters 7, 9, 10) were written simultaneously as both a reformulation of how others had already posed certain issues and an effort to think past the limits of those prior conceptualizations.

Haugeland was likewise drawn to Heidegger because he saw *Being and Time* as anticipating and responding constructively to current philosophical concerns. His interpretation of Heidegger was thus integral to his contemporaneous philosophical work in his own voice. This introduction is not

---

1. Haugeland often used this term in conversation as a colloquial rendering of Heidegger's term, 'Gerede,' but he did not intend or develop any comparison to Frankfurt (2005).

the place to compare and contrast Haugeland's reading of Heidegger and the positions he developed in *Having Thought* and elsewhere. Yet we do need to consider how and why Haugeland saw a proper understanding and appropriation of Heidegger as enabling a more adequate response to the current philosophical situation.

Haugeland emphasizes Heidegger's aspiration to "raise anew the question of the meaning of being" (*SZ* 1).[2] This issue has long served as a barrier to serious thinking about Heidegger within analytic philosophy. Heidegger's "question of being" has been dismissed for several reasons: the early analytic hostility to metaphysics exemplified in Carnap's (1959) famous criticism of Heidegger's lecture "What Is Metaphysics?"; Quine's (1952, ch. 1) tersely dismissive slogan that to be is to be the value of a bound variable;[3] and the widespread contemporary turn to naturalism on metaphysical questions. The late twentieth-century rehabilitation of analytic concern with logical and natural necessity, as well as the normativity of meaning, has opened space for a more constructive encounter with Heidegger's question.[4] Haugeland's reading of Heidegger accords a central role to those modal concepts. Indeed, Haugeland argues that Heidegger's central philosophical distinction—between entities and the being of those entities—is modal: "disclosing the being of entities involves grasping them in terms of a distinction between what is possible and impossible for them" (Haugeland 2000, 53; below, p. 196), whereas discovering entities involves grasping what is or is not actually true of them.[5] Haugeland takes alethic and normative modalities to be closely connected in Heidegger's work. His

2. Abbreviations used to refer to Heidegger's work are listed at the beginning of the References section on p. 277.

3. Recent work (McDaniel 2009; Turner 2010) has forcefully challenged any dismissal of Heidegger's views about the plurality of "ways of being," which turns on the unrestricted unity of existential quantification. Van Inwagen (2009) presents a sustained defense of that dismissal.

4. For an overview of the so-called modal revolution, see Gendler and Hawthorne 2002 or Hale 1997. I know of no comparably compact survey of the reemergence of interest in laws of nature and counterfactual conditionals in the philosophy of science, but Carroll 2004 provides a good survey of the central issues. For the connection between the rehabilitation of modal concepts and normative concepts, see Brandom 2008, esp. pp. 92–102.

5. "Disclose" *(erschliessen)* and "discover" *(entdecken)* are technical terms for Heidegger that mark a difference between understanding the being of entities and understanding entities.

original paper on Heidegger, "Heidegger on Being a Person," was written amid a prominent reemergence of the metaphysics of normativity within Anglo-American philosophy, in Kripke's (1982) and McDowell's (1984) treatment of Wittgenstein on rule following and Brandom's (1979) reflection on "Freedom and Constraint by Norms," and was itself an important contributor to the ensuing debates. On Haugeland's reading, Heidegger's account of ontological understanding offers a novel way of thinking about what normativity and the various modes or grades of necessity amount to.

The most important intersection between Haugeland's Heidegger and the contemporary philosophical scene, however, concerns intentionality, that feature of human beings and possibly other "systems" that allow them to be meaningfully and accountably directed beyond themselves. In a recognizable earlier draft of *Being and Time* (Heidegger 1979; translation 1985) Heidegger explicitly formulated his philosophy as a phenomenological explication of intentionality, although *Being and Time* avoids the term. What matters is the issue and not the concept or the term, however. In multiple respects, Haugeland's Heidegger develops a distinctive approach to understanding intentionality, which directly engages with recent analytic philosophy while also moving in some novel and promising directions.

Along with Sellars, Davidson, Putnam, and many other recent Anglo-American philosophers, Heidegger rejected any identification of intentionality with consciousness or inner experience. Heidegger did not deny or explain away the existence of "conscious" phenomena, but he thought that philosophical conceptions of consciousness and experience uncritically unified distinct phenomena while overlooking or excluding indispensable aspects of intentionality. Moreover, he rejected the entire philosophical conception of a division between a meaning-bestowing inner experience and a mindless "external" causal nexus. It would be just as hopeless on Heidegger's view to try to understand intentionality behavioristically or in reductionist naturalistic terms. Heidegger and Haugeland are hardly alone on the contemporary philosophical scene in taking intentional directedness and its meaningfulness to cross or erase any putative boundary between mind and body or body and world. Heidegger stands out more distinctively, as Haugeland reads him, in how he displays the limitations of biological or social conceptions of intentionality.

Biology, arguably the most successful science of the twentieth century, has seemed to many philosophers today to provide at least a necessary and possibly a sufficient basis for understanding intentional directedness and accountability, thereby demonstrating a fundamental continuity between the intentional life of human beings and other animals. Organisms do comport themselves toward an environment in ways that are answerable via natural selection to the appropriateness of those comportments for maintaining and reproducing themselves. Their dynamic functioning as organisms tracks and responds to relevant features of that environment, and their own continuation as living entities with descendants is dependent upon the appropriateness of their response. Moreover, some animals track and respond to features of their environment in highly flexible and instrumentally rational ways that also change in response to the outcome of their prior responses. Haugeland nevertheless takes Heidegger to show why such complex, flexible, and subtle responsiveness to an environment is not continuous with genuinely intentional comportment toward entities as such.[6] Haugeland develops the Heideggerian idea that only an entity whose own being is at issue for it and who is capable of taking responsibility for the truthfulness of its own comportments toward entities is genuinely intentional. This argument is not just about how to use the word "intentional"; rather, it concerns what is essential to our own intentional directedness.

Haugeland's Heidegger also shows why conformity to social norms cannot ground our understanding of intentional comportments. Haugeland himself originally endorsed a social-conformist conception of intentionality and also attributed such a view to Heidegger (Haugeland 1998, ch. 7; 1982/this volume). Such an approach seems initially promising since conformity to social norms evidently can

> make it possible for current behavior and circumstances to incorporate not just "manifest" recognizabilia, but instituted statuses and roles, accrued over time. Social rank and office can be instituted in this way, as well as finer-grained actions, rights, and responsibilities, such as those contingent on whose turn it is, who owns what, which water is holy, or how the teams stand in the league. (Haugeland 1998, 312)

6. Elsewhere (Rouse 2002, forthcoming a) I argue that Haugeland's (and Heidegger's) arguments would indeed be decisive against a biological conception of intentionality if one takes for granted some familiar and widely accepted accounts of biological understanding but that a more adequate conception of human biology can circumvent these arguments.

What conformity to socially instituted norms nevertheless cannot do is to allow the entities addressed or incorporated within social practices to be authoritative over how those entities are understood by the practitioners. As I will discuss shortly, this line of argument is central to Haugeland's reading of division II of *Being and Time* and its importance within Heidegger's overall project. Moreover, these arguments address many central developments in recent Anglophone philosophy. Thus, in one of the papers included within the final part of this volume, Haugeland argues that, despite their apparent repudiation of traditional divisions between the mind and an "external" world, the well-known arguments of Nelson Goodman (1984) on "grue" and projectibility, W. V. O. Quine (1960) on the indeterminacy of translation, and Saul Kripke (1982) on rule following all exhibit a debilitating "social Cartesianism." Haugeland argues that these accounts implausibly turn on conceptions of intentional content that overlook our practical involvement with, dependence upon, and accountability to the entities that we encounter in our ordinary dealings with the world.

The import of Haugeland's Heidegger for philosophical work on intentionality is constructive and not just critical, however. His constructive account begins with the ineliminably modal character of intentional directedness. The very idea of intentionality requires *both* a distinction between entities as they are and entities as they are taken to be *and* a way to understand how the entities can be authoritative so that the way we take the entities to be is beholden to the way the entities are. We can see how difficult it is to understand these two aspects of intentionality together by noting the frequency with which philosophical accounts succeed in explicating one of these essential components of intentionality only by foreclosing any adequate account of the other.[7] Haugeland's Heidegger addresses these two aspects of the issue respectively by taking intentionality to require understanding entities in terms of their *possibilities* and being able to recognize and respond appropriately to the possibility that entities

---

7. Thus, for example, Haugeland's own critical arguments aim to show that biological conceptions of intentionality seem to account for the second task by failing in the first, while social conceptions seem to succeed in the first by failing to do justice to the second. Even these apparent successes are misleading, of course, since *intentional* content and *intentional* accountability to entities are mutually interdependent. See especially Haugeland 1998, ch. 13.

might show up in ways that have been ruled out as *impossible*. Intentional directedness thus requires at least an implicit grasp of the differences between what is possible for an entity and what is conceivable and recognizable but impossible. Otherwise, Haugeland argues, the relationship between intentional directedness and its supposed objects might be merely accidental.

Haugeland's Heidegger thereby develops a new understanding of the modality of intentionality in at least four fundamental and interlocking ways. First, the possibility or impossibility of various manifestations of entities is a holistic feature of the intelligibility of an entire domain or "region" of entities (e.g., of physical, biological, mathematical, or other domains of entities) rather than a semantic or metaphysical property of individual sentences, objects, or states of affairs. It is the intelligibility of the entire domain (in Heidegger's terms, an understanding of the being of entities in that region) that constitutes the specific possibilities or impossibilities for entities within that domain. Explicitly articulated laws are partial expressions of those possibilities and impossibilities, and genuine domains are those "totalities" of entities that are rendered intelligible by such interlocking possibilities.[8] Even in those scientific fields in which the explicit articulation of laws has been of central concern, there is arguably no example of an extensionally complete set of laws for a domain. Any understanding of entities in their possibilities thus commits us to more than we can express explicitly as laws since the laws would acquire necessity only as part of a complete and mutually interdependent set.[9]

8. A related conception of laws and necessity as holistically constitutive of intelligible domains has been developed by Marc Lange (2000, 2009) and further elaborated by John Roberts (2007) and Rouse (forthcoming a).

9. Although Haugeland does not make this point explicitly, Heidegger is thus committed both to the plurality of ontological "regions" with their own forms of necessity and possibility (e.g., logical, metaphysical, physical, biological, moral, and even various regions of equipmental necessity and possibility, as well as the region of Dasein) and to a unified conception of how such modes of possibility constitute the intelligibility in each domain. Haugeland does argue (see pp. 45–47, 59, 218–220, 240 below) that an articulation of this sense of being in general was the task of the unwritten division III of *Being and Time*. McDaniel (2009) attributes to Heidegger and defends such a conception that allows for both plurality and unity in the sense of being: "Heidegger recognizes a generic sense of 'being' that covers every entity that there is, but holds that it is not metaphysically fundamental: this generic sense represents something *akin to a mere disjunction* of the *metaphysically basic ways of being*" (2009, 306).

The second point about modality is that the modal character of any understanding of entities in their possibilities and impossibilities is normative as well as alethic. Laws[10] do not just describe how things must necessarily be but also demand of us that we refuse to accept any (apparent) violations of them. We must refuse to endorse logical contradictions or natural impossibilities, refuse to engage in or tolerate immoral actions (as violations of moral laws), not accept shoddy workmanship without repairing it or starting over, and so forth.[11] Third, the normative authority of such demands that we refuse to accept violations of the laws in a domain comes from us. It derives from our commitments to our own possible ways to be, as human beings who understand ourselves in specific ways (e.g., as thinkers [constituted as such by commitment to logical and broader rational laws], scientific knowers [similarly constituted by empirical laws in a scientific domain], skilled practitioners [constituted by the constitutive skills of a practical domain and its implicit instrumental laws], moral agents [constituted by moral laws], and so forth). How one understands one's own possibilities is thus always at stake in intentionally directing oneself toward entities.

Fourth, and finally, the preceding features of Haugeland's conception of the modality of laws implies that there is something distinctively first-personal about the normativity of the various modalities. This first-personality of intentional comportments does not consist in privileged access to their content or any qualitative immediacy to their manifestation but in a constitutive responsibility we undertake by engaging in those comportments. In taking up various possible ways to be, from science to game playing to friendship to skillful activity, we commit ourselves to be responsive to the constitutive possibilities for the domain of entities disclosed by those forms of conduct: for example, to play chess is (in part) not to tolerate a rook moving on a diagonal, and to carry out physics experiments is (in part) not to accept measurements of particle velocities that exceed the speed of light. A rook moving on a diagonal is forbidden by the laws of chess; a particle moving faster than light is forbidden by the laws of

10. For convenience, from here on I will often speak of "laws" when talking about what is possible and impossible for entities in a region, but we should always recognize that Heidegger takes Dasein's understanding of possibilities to outrun what can be explicitly stated as laws.

11. Haugeland developed this theme further in his as yet unpublished paper, "Two Dogmas of Rationalism," which will appear in Adams (forthcoming).

physics. If such things were possible, the entire domains of chess or modern physics, respectively, would be unintelligible. Any responsible individual chess player or physicist must therefore refuse to countenance them on pain of giving up the entire enterprise of chess or physics.

In conventional terms, the central theme in Haugeland's account of Heidegger would thus be objectivity as a constitutive norm for intentional directedness.[12] Haugeland instead introduces the term 'beholdenness' as a more precise replacement for 'objectivity.' He thereby emphasizes the descent of Heidegger's project from Kant's *Critique of Pure Reason* against the prevailing neo-Kantian emphasis upon epistemology; Heidegger read Kant as developing a regional ontology of the objects understood by Newtonian physics:

> The positive outcome of Kant's *Critique of Pure Reason* lies in what it has contributed towards the working out of what belongs to any Nature whatsoever, not in a 'theory' of knowledge. His transcendental logic is an *a priori* logic for the subject-matter of that area of Being called 'Nature'. (*SZ* 10–11)

Yet Heidegger sought to generalize that project to encompass not only a scientific understanding of nature but also any understanding of and comportment toward entities as entities at all. Heidegger argues there is a multiplicity of ways to be that are disclosed by different understandings of being. Where Kant sought to vindicate the objective purport and accountability of empirical science, Heidegger sought to vindicate the beholdenness of any intentional comportment to the entities disclosed through such comportment.[13] "Beholdenness," then, is Haugeland's revised and expanded

---

12. Objectivity as a norm for intentional directedness (in Heidegger's terms, for understanding entities *as entities*) should not be confused with objectivity as an epistemic norm. The latter conception of objectivity bears on the correctness or incorrectness of comportments toward entities. The former bears on the "aboutness" of both correct and incorrect comportments; indeed, epistemic norms could apply only where the norms for intentional directedness have been sufficiently satisfied.

13. Since Heidegger draws such a central distinction between entities themselves and the being of those entities, one might think that our intentional comportments toward entities would be beholden to the entities and the understanding of being that enables those comportments would be beholden to the being of those entities. Haugeland argues that that presumption is mistaken: a central task of the unwritten division III of *Being and Time* was to show how any understanding of the being of entities was beholden to those entities (see below, pp. 45–47, 59, 218–220, 240).

replacement for "objectivity"; it indicates the normative accountability of any intentional comportment to the entities disclosed through that comportment's constitutive understanding of being.

It is worth highlighting two further aspects of this account of "objective" beholdenness since each takes up issues that have often been thought to pull in opposing directions. The concept of objectivity emerged in the nineteenth century. Lorraine Daston and Peter Galison (2007) have compellingly worked through some of the conceptual history that indicates how objective understanding came to be identified with both the suppression of any affective response to what is understood and the overcoming of any finitely situated "perspective." Haugeland's Heidegger stands as a telling critical response to both supposed oppositions to objective understanding.

Consider first the affectivity of genuinely objective understanding. Haugeland had already touched on this theme in his own early suggestion that "the trouble with artificial intelligence is that computers don't give a damn" (1998, 47). In this book he shows how being affectively disposed[14] toward entities such that they matter to us is integral to Heidegger's account of the conditions for any truthful beholdenness to entities as they are. People cannot hold themselves responsible for the intelligibility of their comportments toward entities unless they find their possible unintelligibility deeply unsettling and the apparent manifestation of what is impossible intolerable. Only because we are not indifferent to apparent violations of domain-constitutive laws *are* there objective truths and necessities. The objective world is independent of the historical emergence and maintenance of human ways of understanding it, but its *intelligibility* is not thus independent. Understanding entities as entities requires a refusal to accept violations of the laws that constitute the intelligibility of that domain of entities, and such refusal requires that one care about those laws. Who I am (as physicist, chess player, etc.) must be at issue and at stake in understanding entities in ways that I "give a damn" about. Speaking in his own voice, Haugeland takes over Heidegger's account of "authentic intentional-

14. Haugeland's preferred translation of *Befindlichkeit* (rendered especially misleadingly by the standard Macquarrie and Robinson translation as "state-of-mind") is "findingness." Without his fuller exposition below, this term would be opaque here, and so I choose the alternative translation "being affectively disposed" to express the point somewhat more colloquially.

ity" as a caring, committed openness that enables our involvement in the world to be responsive to entities as they are rather than a willful imposition upon them.

Haugeland's second revision of traditional conceptions of objectivity emphasizes the finitude of all intelligibility or, better, its finite transcendence. The predominant general movement of philosophy since the mid-twentieth century has been toward some form of naturalism or historicism. This movement is marked by incredulity toward rationality not bounded by nature or history.[15] Yet a recurrent danger of this trend has been to undercut any normative authority over how we understand the world, such that there would be no intelligible sense in which our ways of life could "misfire" or "get the world wrong." "Bald" naturalism or historicism (to adopt John McDowell's 1994 phrase), which unrepentantly rejects any such normative authority, may seem to leave human life and the world bereft of meaning. Yet too many efforts toward a more moderate naturalism or historicism, which would restore our answerability to a world independent of how we take it to be, either fall short or tacitly abandon their commitment to human finitude. Haugeland's interpretation of Heidegger on the finitude of human understanding matters above all in its promise of a clearer prospect for secure passage between these two characteristic philosophical and existential failings. On Haugeland's reading, Heidegger shows how we can hold ourselves accountable to entities independent of our conceptions of them without tacitly presupposing the intelligibility of entities as they "really" are. His account of finitude demolishes the apparent exhaustiveness of two debilitating alternatives for thought and understanding, an impossibly realist grasp of "capital-R Reality" from nowhere and nowhen, on the one hand, and a merely arbitrary imposition of concepts, norms, interests, attitudes, or judgments favored by historically situated persons, communities, or cultures and subject only to norms of internal coherence, on the other. In this respect, Haugeland's reading brings out all the more clearly how and why Heidegger's work was so centrally engaged with Kant's critical project as a reflection on the finitude of human understanding.

Haugeland's Heidegger thereby radically reconceives what it is to be human. This conception also offers strikingly novel conceptions of sciences

---

15. The resurgence of nonnaturalist metaphysics in some parts of Anglo-American philosophy is of course a counterweight to the dominant trend.

and languages and more generally of intentionality as distinctively human phenomena. To see the originality and significance of the view Haugeland finds in Heidegger, consider four alternative ways of thinking about our humanity that dominate contemporary philosophical conceptions of the human. Each presents a different *kind* of entity as the most perspicuous class within which the specificity of our humanity and our capacity for intentionality most tellingly stands out. Within the horizons of these four familiar alternatives, the issue is whether intentionality characterizes us, respectively, as a distinctive kind of physical entity, biological organism, individual,[16] or community.

Haugeland's reading of Heidegger offers a striking alternative to each of these four familiar conceptions of the philosophical genus of which the human is a species. Heidegger does have a term ('others') for individual human beings, but he appropriated the word "dasein"[17] to express a different conception of what kind of entity we are. On Haugeland's reading, dasein is "a living way of life that incorporates an understanding of being." Because it refers to a way of life that many persons share, dasein is not individual (one dasein for each person). Yet dasein is also not a community or other kind of social entity, for multiple reasons. First, a "living way of life" includes the world in which it is lived and thus extends beyond the human beings who live it to incorporate everything that contributes to or matters to that way of life.[18] Second, although the way of life is shared by many, it is also crucially individuated: dasein is "in each case mine," such that this way of life exists in being lived only by persons who find themselves situated within that way of life and are called to take over responsibility for its

16. Under the headings of "individuals," I incorporate a diverse range of kinds of entity (mind, consciousness, rational agent, transcendental unity, soul, etc.), including those that are understood to be realized biologically or physically in ways that are nevertheless irreducible to their physical or biological makeup, as well as those that are conceived as intentional in ways that are not dependent upon their physical or biological constitution.

17. I follow Haugeland's choice to take over "dasein" as an English word for this entity that perspicuously realizes our humanity rather than as a German word that carries the specific etymological history exploited by Heidegger.

18. 'World' is an important technical term in *Being and Time*, which is extensively discussed in Part two, Chapters 4–5 below. For our purposes now, suffice to say that it includes all of the entities that matter to dasein's way of life in their constitutive interrelatedness as significant.

intelligibility.[19] Third, this distinctive form of normative accountability opens dasein to the possibility of having to confront its own unintelligibility: as a way of life, it is constitutively dependent upon whether other entities (including the other "cases of dasein"[20] who participate in that shared way of life) continue to behave and show themselves in the ways they must for that way of life to continue.[21] Fourth, and finally, a living way of life is temporally extended in a distinctive way. Such a way of life incorporates not merely how people actually live but also how they take up and take over their shared past in living toward a possible future, including the possible collapse of all possibilities intelligible within that way of life. Haugeland's Heidegger thus presents a conception of human life that is the antithesis of any relativism that treats human understanding as somehow enclosed within a specific conception of the world. Dasein is constitutively open to and enabling of encounters with entities as utterly recalcitrant to how we take them to be.

It is important that dasein refers only to ways of life that incorporate an understanding of being. Not just any old shared human practice *is* dasein (even though only dasein could engage in such practices). In providing the requisite independent conception of what it is to have an understanding of being, Haugeland's interpretation gives special prominence to Heidegger's insistence that sciences are entities that share dasein's way of being. His account of Heidegger's "existential conception of science" thereby offers a compelling reconceptualization of what a science is, which offers a philosophically important alternative to familiar interpretations of sciences as bodies of knowledge, methodological procedures, practices, social institutions, or contingent histories. Haugeland also calls attention to Heidegger's insistence upon a parallel reconception of what language is, but he did not live to work out that example to a comparable extent.

19. Heidegger not only takes this "call" to take over responsibility for one's life and way of life as omnipresent in human life but also believes it is a call that we mostly ignore, obscure, or evade.

20. Haugeland adapts the standard English translation of Heidegger's characteristic phrase "*je meinig*" ("in each case mine") to refer to individual persons who live a specific "living way of life" as "cases of dasein" rather than by using Heidegger's term, 'others.'

21. The opening chapter of Jonathan Lear's (2006) *Radical Hope* powerfully interprets a specific instance of Haugeland's conception of dasein as an essentially vulnerable living way of life to set the stage for his inquiry into the ethical demands and possibilities that arise in having to live through the death of one's way of life.

HAUGELAND'S INTERPRETATION OF HEIDEGGER

Haugeland's reading of Heidegger is innovative and controversial. An introduction is not intended to replicate the work done in a book, but it is important to call attention to the book's most distinctive and original accomplishments in relation to more orthodox readings of Heidegger. In what follows, I highlight some of the more provocative interpretations put forward in Haugeland's account. What I find especially striking is how all of these independently controversial claims hang together as a mutually vindicating whole. Moreover, Haugeland's interpretation does not merely address issues that primarily concern Heidegger scholars; his view also significantly changes our understanding of Heidegger's project and how it matters philosophically.

At the center of Haugeland's reading is an insistent focus upon Heidegger's aspiration to reawaken the question of the sense of being. The central project of *Being and Time* is to reawaken this question, which Heidegger argued had long been forgotten or overlooked. Yet too many readers and commentators are then content to let Heidegger's own subsequent discussions guide their conception of how to pose this question and grasp its significance. If philosophy and the sciences have long forgotten this question, trivialized its content, and avoided its existential import, then presumably we need to let Heidegger tell us what it asks and how it might once again grip us. Haugeland proceeds in the opposite direction. Everything Heidegger says must be examined in light of its contribution to posing and addressing the question of the sense of being. Only by getting a grip on this question and its bearing on the more specific topics in *Being and Time* can we adequately get a handle on what Heidegger was offering us in that book. Many of Haugeland's most provocative reinterpretations are guided by his insistent concern to advance our understanding of this issue.

Heidegger's "ontological" concern with the sense of being must be differentiated from most of what contemporary philosophy recognizes as metaphysics. Heidegger distinguishes entities from the being of entities. Entities include anything and everything there is or could be. When Wilfrid Sellars described the diverse subject matter of philosophy as encompassing "not only 'cabbages and kings', but numbers and duties, possibilities and finger snaps, aesthetic experience and death" (2007, 369), he was still listing only entities.[22] Being is not an entity of any kind even though

---

22. With his concern for how those diverse entities "hang together," however, Sellars did implicitly point toward the locus of Heidegger's conception of ontology.

being is always the being *of* some entity or other. Indeed, one of Heidegger's central critical concerns has been to avoid a mistaken identification of the being of entities (their intelligibility as entities) with a special kind of entity: minds, transcendental consciousness, meanings, languages, conceptual schemes/frameworks, and so on. Yet although the being of entities strictly speaking "is" not anything at all, there are several important distinctions concerning the being of entities that provide traction for philosophical understanding.

Haugeland makes especially extensive use of the "regional" differentiation of being. Different sorts of entities *are* differently: whether in some context "there is" or "there is not" an electron, an organism, a person, a tool, a prime number, a chess piece, a ball or a strike in baseball, or a legal statute turns on very different considerations. By examining how the being question plays out in activities such as chess or scientific inquiry, Haugeland provides illustrative alternatives to Heidegger's own familiar phenomenological descriptions of equipment and "others." Yet the being of entities in each of these domains is also articulated by differences in their *ways* of being. Most notably, Heidegger differentiates an entity's "that-being" from its "what-being" (a distinction that roughly corresponds to the traditional distinction between its existence and its essence) and both from its "thus-being" in all its other inessential determinations. These two articulations of being (regional and that/what/thus-being) are orthogonal, such that entities in any particular region have their own characteristic mode of existence[23] or nonexistence, as well as their own essential determinations as entities of that kind. Traditional metaphysics only differentiates entities or sorts them into something like regions by way of their essential properties: think of how Descartes distinguishes minds and bodies according to their essential properties of consciousness and extension, respectively. Moreover, that-being has a crucial normative dimension characteristic to its regional articulation. Thus, being-available *(Zuhandensein)* as the "that-being" of equipmental entities is not merely a matter of whether an item of equipment is spatiotemporally extant; equipment has deficient modes of unavailability, marked by Heidegger's distinctions among what is conspicuous (broken), obtrusive (missing), and obstinate (in the way). Organisms

---

23. Heidegger reserves 'existence' as a technical term for the that-being of dasein, but for the purposes of this introduction, it would be confusing to introduce a more generic substitute, and the plausible candidates (e.g., "actuality") have other problematic connotations. So for now, I am using "existence" as a colloquial substitute for "that-being."

have a different characteristic way of being or not being as living or dead. Likewise, dasein, the entity whose that-being is existence, can in each case take over responsibility for its existence as owned (*eigentlich*) or can live its life in an undifferentiated or deficient mode that avoids being responsibly. Haugeland emphasizes the normative dimension even to the that-being of those entities (e.g., "protons, planets or prehistoric lizards") whose presence or absence seems utterly independent of human life and understanding:

> Until dasein releases them, entities remain in the darkest of all prisons, the prison of utter obscurity; we let them out by bringing them to light (into the clearing). (2007, 98; below, p. 173)

Part of what it is for an entity to be is the capacity to show itself under appropriate circumstances.

One revealing consequence of Haugeland's recognition of these articulations of being is to rethink the widely noted contrast between availability and occurrence (*Vorhandensein*) as different ways of that-being. Heidegger does indeed frequently contrast these two ways of being in the course of insisting that available entities are not properly grasped as merely occurrent. Occurrence is the only mode of that-being recognized by traditional metaphysics, and so contrasting availability to occurrence strikingly illustrates Heidegger's recognition of diverse ways of that-being. Yet once that point is recognized, the two concepts do not play parallel roles in Heidegger's account. Availability and equipmental role (*Bewandtnis*) respectively characterize the that- and what-being of entities in the region of equipment. Occurrence, by contrast, does not belong to any particular region (and is consequently not paired with any characteristic mode of what-being). Haugeland calls explicit attention to this difference:

> In addition to these specifically regional concepts, Heidegger also often uses another ontological term, 'being-occurrent' (*Vorhandensein*), which is not specific to any region, but is a kind of lowest common denominator. (below, p. 57)

Other commentators have sometimes tried to identify a specific group of entities whose way of being is appropriately understood as being-occurrent, for example, those entities discovered (or properly discovered) through assertions or those entities disclosed by scientific dasein. The former effort confronts the difficulty that assertion plays a role in dasein's understanding and interpretation of all sorts of entities; while assertion is a derivative mode of interpretation, it thereby serves as an aspect of dasein's being-in as such rather than as a comportment toward some specific ontological region. The latter alternative has to override any ontological differences between scientific domains. Haugeland is skeptical of such readings of Heidegger or of the sciences. He notes, for example, that Heidegger's 1929 lecture course *The Fundamental Concepts of Metaphysics* (1995) contained an extensive regional ontology of life (which presumably should govern biological investigation of living entities), and he also notes that Heidegger distinguishes an ontological sense of "world" in which different ontological regions have their own characteristic forms of totality:

> A quite different world (though still in this first [nonexistential] sense of the term) is a totality of living things: a world investigated by biology. . . . Thus, the totality of the physical universe is understood in terms of the unity of space-time, as a dynamic mereological sum of all matter and material forces. The totality and unity of a biological world, by contrast, is intelligible primarily in terms of ecological interactions, forming a relatively self-contained whole of interdependent needs, resources, and "strategies." (below, pp. 99–100)

Moreover, although the supposed systematic contrast between availability and occurrence is thereby undercut, Haugeland calls attention to a different parallel that plays an important role in division I of *Being and Time*. Heidegger's phenomenology of the being of equipmental entities in chapter 3 is immediately followed in chapter 4 by a phenomenology of a different kind of intraworldly entity, "others" (individual human beings). Each kind of entity is familiar as salient elements in dasein's everyday world. Both are clearly differentiated from dasein itself and from one another.

A central concern in Haugeland's account is a third ontological articulation, the "truth-character" of being. Truth is not specific to any region or way of being but is instead a general ontological determination of entities as such. It expresses the beholdenness of any claims about or other comportment toward entities to the entities themselves. Heidegger famously generalizes the concept of truth from a semantic concept governing assertions or sentences to an ontological concept relevant to any comportment toward entities. A wide range of practical activities can also be true to entities (or not), discovering them as they are or mistaking them for some deficient "appearance." Falsehood is thus uncovered in the practical recognition of an entity as unsuitable for hammering or in "deficient" modes of caringness *(Fürsorge)* for others, as well as in uttering false sentences. More centrally, Heidegger distinguishes ontological truth—the truthfulness of an understanding of being—from ontical truth as a correct comportment toward an entity, thereby discovering it as it is. Both forms of truth are dependent upon dasein, "the entity that we ourselves in each case are," which is importantly part of why Heidegger's inquiry into the meaning of being in general had to proceed via an existential analytic of dasein. Thus, Heidegger famously concludes division I with a discussion of the sort of being that truth possesses and concludes, with double emphasis, that "*'there is' truth only in so far as dasein is and so long as dasein is*" (*SZ* 226).

The dependence of truth (the disclosure of being and the discovery of entities) upon dasein is nevertheless not any form of idealism.[24] The being of entities (their intelligibility as the entities they are) depends upon "existing" dasein, as does the possibility of their truthful discovery and disclosure. The entities themselves are not dependent upon us. Moreover, in the case of ontical truth as the correctness or incorrectness of various comportments toward entities, what Haugeland's Heidegger shows is *how* it is possible for those comportments to be beholden to the entities themselves and not merely to our own constructions or impositions. Because dasein understands the being of entities and because the being of entities is articulated by a set of laws or norms that govern the possible configurations and features of entities, dasein is beholden to those entities by being answerable for their intelligibility in terms of laws or norms.

Haugeland argues that the deeper problem, indeed the central problem of *Being and Time,* concerns the possibility and intelligibility of ontological truth:

> Unlike entities and ontical claims, being "is" not antecedent to and independent of our understandings of it. Being "is" *only in* how it is understood. But then how can such understandings fail or be faulty—how can they ever be *mis*-understandings? By what standard could they so much as be judged shallow, or confused, or misguided? To what are understandings of being *beholden* at all? (below, p. 59)

---

24. As we shall see later, Heidegger's view is also not any kind of realism. Heidegger's account of the finitude of any understanding of being undermines the assumptions that seem to make realism and idealism (or other forms of antirealism) opposed and exhaustive alternatives.

We have only the first two of the projected six planned divisions of *Being and Time*, and the question of the beholdenness of ontological truth is not addressed in detail in the extant publication. In this respect, Haugeland's *Dasein Disclosed* is also, to our loss, incomplete. Yet Haugeland does put forward a striking promissory note, an indication that we already know the intended thesis of the unpublished division III of part one of *Being and Time:*

> An essential aim and (unfinished) achievement of *Being and Time* is to show how—without circularity or vacuity—understandings of being are beholden to *entities:* the very same entities to which ontical claims are beholden. Exhibiting that ontological beholdenness will complete the explication of the truth-character of being. (below, p. 59)

Haugeland's reading of the book is organized to prepare the way for showing how the published divisions of *Being and Time* belong to an inquiry into the finite beholdenness of ontological truth to entities as they are.

In addressing how being and truth are dependent upon us, dasein, we confront the question of what Heidegger meant by referring to us with this technical term. Haugeland's interpretation of dasein is surely his most controversial claim among Heidegger scholars. An especially provocative version was put forward from the outset in Haugeland's first Heidegger paper, "Heidegger on Being a Person," and while it has been importantly revised and refined in his subsequent work, the issue of how to understand "dasein" is central to Haugeland's view, as I noted earlier. The orthodox view is cogently expressed by Taylor Carman in his careful study, *Heidegger's Analytic:* "The analytic of Dasein is an account of the existential structure of concrete human particulars, that is, individual persons" (2003, 42). Haugeland instead takes these entities that Carman and other commentators identify with dasein to be denoted in *Being and Time* by the term 'others,' used as a technical term that does not differentiate self from others:

> By 'others' we do not mean everyone else but me—those over against whom the "I" stands out. They are rather those from whom, for the most part, one does *not* distinguish oneself—those among whom one is too. (SZ 118)

Yet if each human person is an "other" whom one might encounter within the everyday world, what are we to make of Heidegger's use of *dasein* as a technical term that refers to us?

Haugeland answers this question by emphasizing the strange and distinctive referential apparatus that Heidegger repeatedly uses to introduce the term 'dasein': "Dasein is the entity that we in each case are." Haugeland's original attempt was too inclusive:

> We understand Dasein to be the anyone and everything instituted by it: a vast intricate pattern—generated and maintained by conformism—of norms, normal dispositions, customs, sorts, roles, referral relations, public institutions, and so on. On this reading, the anyone, the (everyday) world, and language are different coherent "subpatterns" within the grand pattern that is Dasein; they have Dasein's kind of being because each of them is Dasein (though none of them is all of Dasein). Within the anyone and all it institutes, the science of chemistry is a coherent subpattern: chemistry is Dasein—and so are philately, Christmas, and Cincinnati. (1982, 19; below, p. 9)

Thus, Haugeland's earliest reading replaced individualist conceptions of dasein with a still relatively familiar conception of dasein as a social practice.[25]

Haugeland later revised this early conception. His more refined view maintains his original concern to make sense of Heidegger's claim that the sciences, language, the world (in Heidegger's "existential" sense), and *das Man* (the "anyone") have dasein's way of being.

He emphasizes that Heidegger's referential apparatus explicitly combines the singularity ("*the* entity") of a "grand pattern" with its plural articulation ("that we in each case are"). Most of all, his refined view stresses Heidegger's identification of dasein as the entity that understands being. Haugeland at the outset had adapted Macquarrie and Robinson's translation of "*je meinig*" as "in each case mine" to distinguish dasein itself as a singular entity from individual persons as "cases" of dasein. On his later account, dasein is a living way of life that embodies an understanding of being. Such a way of life is lived by many people simultaneously and indeed must be so. Yet it exists only in and through people continuing to live in that way. That dasein's way of living incorporates an understanding of be-

---

25. Thus, in his well-known taxonomy of theories of intentionality as positions on the baseball diamond, "The Intentionality All-Stars," Haugeland (1998, ch. 7) originally positioned Heidegger at third base, along with many other contemporary philosophers from Hegel to Brandom. By the time that paper was reprinted in *Having Thought,* he had moved beyond that early interpretation and saw Heidegger in the terms that are developed later.

ing distinguishes dasein from other collective enterprises. Haugeland therefore excludes some of the examples he had originally cited as subpatterns of dasein, such as philately, Christmas, and Cincinnati; chemistry is the only example he retains from the list quoted earlier. He takes Heidegger's explicit identification of sciences and language as having dasein's way of being as a revealing clue for working out what it is to understand the being of entities. By contrast, Haugeland treats the social conformism that his early paper identified with dasein as a necessary but not sufficient characteristic of dasein. Dasein as a living way of life is lived by its constitutive "livers" ("others" understood as "cases" of dasein) in such a way as always to put forward a fundamental choice between taking over a kind of ontological responsibility for this shared way of life or falling in with it without taking it over responsibly.

In his (2003) book, Carman develops an extended argument against Haugeland's early interpretation of Dasein in "Heidegger on Being a Person" (1982, 37–42; this volume, pp. 3–16). Carman is surely right that the original account was incorrect in treating dasein as referring to any "coherent subpattern" of a shared way of life. He notes that Heidegger does on occasion use the indefinite article with 'Dasein'. He also emphasizes parallels between 'Dasein' and terms like *Bewusstsein* (consciousness) and *Mensch*, which are individuated even though they function grammatically as collective terms. Yet Haugeland's revised view largely circumvents Carman's objections. It is central to Haugeland's view of dasein as a living way of life that dasein "lives" only in continuing to be taken up together by individuals. Moreover, as we shall see, such ways of life embody an understanding of being only if it is possible for dasein in each case to take over responsibility for that way of life. So the possible individuation of dasein is integral to its constitution as a living way of life that understands being. Heidegger did not have readily available the nominalized distinction between dasein and cases of dasein, and so on occasion did refer to the latter with the term 'Dasein.' Moreover, he may well not have felt any tension in such uses of the term because both the collective and individuated character of dasein are essential to its "basic makeup" (*Grundverfassung*).[26]

---

26. In this respect, Haugeland reads 'dasein' in a way that is formally parallel to Hegel's use of "Spirit" as "the 'I' that is 'We' and the 'We' that is 'I'." I argue elsewhere (Rouse forthcoming b) that one of the unexpected strengths of Haugeland's account is that it recognizes the significance of both the parallels and the differences between Heidegger and Hegel. See nn. 27 and 28.

The more important considerations for how to understand 'dasein' are philosophical rather than just textual, however. To follow Carman and others in taking dasein as simply individuated, one dasein for each individual person, would require abandoning some of Haugeland's most revealing and transformative reconceptions of Heidegger's project. Such individualist readings must explain away not only the distinctive grammar of 'Dasein' and its *"jemeinigkeit"* but also Heidegger's explicit identification of sciences and languages as entities with dasein's way of being. Haugeland's interpretation of dasein also leads to an important reinterpretation of division II of *Being and Time*, for scholars have typically approached the latter on the assumption that dasein refers to individuals. The question of how to interpret the referential structure of 'dasein' thus turns on the larger question of how to understand the structure and argument of the entire book.

Division II begins just after Heidegger introduces his conception of ontological truth as the condition for the possibility of truth as correctness about entities. He concludes that account by asking whether the existential analytic of dasein as developed so far has thereby succeeded in bringing dasein into view as a whole. His negative answer leads him directly into a discussion of death:

> If, however, dasein's being-at-an-end in death, and therewith its being-a-whole, are to be included in the discussion of its possibly *being-a-whole*, and if this is to be done in a way which is appropriate to the phenomena, then we must have obtained an ontologically adequate conception of death—that is to say, an *existential* conception of it. (SZ 234)

The chapter-long discussion of existential death then initiates division II, which takes up the prominent "existentialist" themes of conscience, responsibility *(Schuld)*,[27] owned existence as resoluteness and then timeishness *(Zeitlichkeit* as the sense of Dasein's being as care), pointing toward temporality *(Temporalität)* as the horizon for the interpretation of being. Heidegger's discussion of death thus occupies a pivotal role in *Being and Time*. Not surprisingly, Haugeland's alternative interpretation of dasein also brings with it a radical alternative to familiar interpretations of Heidegger's characterization of dasein as "being-toward-death."

---

27. The standard translation of *Schuld* is "guilt." Haugeland's preferred translation as "responsibility" is controversial.

We have seen that, according to Haugeland, dasein is not a person, and so dasein's death cannot be the end of a person's life, experience, biography, or anything else at that level of analysis. If Haugeland is right that dasein is "a living way of life that embodies an understanding of being," then the technical term 'death' in *Being and Time* must refer to the end of *that*. A way of life can "die out" and thereby come to an end when no one lives in that way anymore. More profoundly, it can come to an end when it no longer makes sense for anyone to live in that way. These two ways of ending converge, however, because a way of life *cannot* make sense for anyone unless others also take up complementary roles that contribute to maintaining that way of life. Haugeland thus identifies Heideggerian "death" as the possible collapse into unintelligibility of an entire understanding of being and, with it, the end of the way of life that embodies that understanding.[28]

The sense of such a collapse of intelligibility emerges through the relationship between understanding being and dasein's beholdenness to entities. In understanding being and comporting itself toward entities, dasein allows entities to show themselves intelligibly in terms of what is possible and impossible for them. If dasein uncovers entities as conflicting with the constitutive laws of the domain to which they belong, it is normally the comportment, the uncovering, that must give way. That is, in the face of an apparent discovery of an entity that should have been impossible, dasein must revise or repair its comportment. If dasein should find itself unable to revise or repair its comportments suitably, however, then a fundamental conflict has emerged between its understanding of the being of the entities discovered and the entities themselves. That is why it is not just dasein's discovery of and comportment toward entities that is beholden to the entities themselves; dasein's understanding of the being of those entities is also thus beholden. Thus, *in extremis,* the discovery of entities to be in irremediable conflict with dasein's disclosive projection of those entities onto

---

28. In Rouse (forthcoming b), I argue that Hegel's repeated invocation of death as a metaphor for the contradictions that emerge within the experience of each form of consciousness in the *Phenomenology of Spirit* provides a familiar background that helps makes sense of why Heidegger might speak of the collapse into unintelligibility of an entire way of life as dasein's *death*. The parallel highlights the contrast between Hegel's conception of the finitude of these forms of consciousness as a deficiency and Heidegger's insistence that such finitude is an ineliminable condition of all understanding; it also explains why division II ends with a contrast between Hegel's and Heidegger's understandings of time. Haugeland himself does not make this connection, however.

their possibilities undermines dasein's very understanding of being, thereby also abolishing the very discovery of that apparent impossibility and any other discovery of entities as entities so understood. Further, since dasein *is* a living way of life that understands being, the dasein of that way of life would be no more.[29]

This conception of existential death foregrounds the modal character of ontological understanding. Heidegger carefully distinguishes death in his "existential" sense from the actual events of an organism's perishing or a person's demise and thus talks instead about "being-toward-death." Yet he also makes a stronger claim, that being-toward-death concerns "the possibility of the impossibility of existence at all . . . [i.e.,] of every way of comporting oneself towards anything" (*SZ* 262). If being-toward-death were only a comportment toward the ever-impending possibility of a person's ceasing to be, that would only be the possibility of a de facto absence of possibilities to press into, whereas Heidegger refers to the *impossibility* of all of dasein's possibilities. Haugeland is arguing that failing to take seriously this reference to impossibility would give insufficient consideration to what dasein is, namely the entity that understands being and thereby uncovers entities as entities. To understand an entity in its being is not just to discover how the entity actually is but also to understand (which for Heidegger means to be competent with respect to) what is *possible* or *impossible* for it as the entity that it is. Here most notably, Haugeland's interpretation is forcefully led by his commitment to understand everything Heidegger says in light of his concern to raise the question of the meaning of being.

Haugeland works out the application of this conception in the greatest detail for scientific dasein, or, as Heidegger puts it, "dasein [that] can exist in the manner of scientific research" (*SZ* 357). He thereby offers a novel approach to what Heidegger is proposing under the heading of an "existential conception of science" (ibid.), which connects it to the widespread recognition in the philosophy of science that scientific explanation requires understanding modalities. To project natural entities onto their possibili-

---

29. Elsewhere (Rouse forthcoming b), I argue that Haugeland's reading of existential death as the possibility of the unintelligibility of an understanding of being can also incorporate standard readings of existential death as an individual case of dasein's comportment toward its own mortality as a special case, one that reveals the unintelligibility of unowned dasein's understanding of being as publicness. Haugeland himself does not make this claim, however.

ties is to interpret one's dealings with them in terms of the laws that govern their behavior and their empirical manifestations. The laws articulate what entities in a scientific domain can and cannot do.[30] Yet the laws also articulate scientific dasein's commitment not to accept any apparent impossibility. When confronted with apparent violations of a law of nature, Haugeland argues, scientific dasein commits itself to resolve the apparent conflict. Typically, that means checking and rechecking the relevant measurements or other observations and the proper functioning of the instruments, procedures, skills, and "auxiliary" assumptions that contribute to the apparent discovery of entities as not in conformity to law. Normally, such checking is sufficient to discern where and how an apparent impossibility mistakenly seemed to occur. Sometimes scientists also need to refine and further develop the relevant skills and procedures or the conceptual norms embodied in the law. The possibility nevertheless remains open that no such revision or repair of scientific practice would be sufficient and that what had been disclosed as impossible has nevertheless actually occurred. With that recognition, the entire articulation of that region of scientific disclosure collapses. Such is existential death for scientific dasein in some ontological region: as a living way of life that understands being, it would be no more.[31]

This conception of existential death transforms how we should understand the structure of Heidegger's project. Hubert Dreyfus (1991) is the most prominent advocate of a widely held view that accords a certain degree of autonomy and priority to division I as an account of Dasein's disclosedness. Division I ends with Heidegger's initial discussion of the truth-character of

30. In an essay published a decade after *Being and Time*, Heidegger explicitly highlighted in a general way the role of laws in any scientific projection of entities onto their possibilities: "The fixedness of the facts and the constancy of their change as such is regularity. The constancy of change in the necessity of its course is law. Only from the perspective of regularity and law do facts become clear as what they are" (2002, 61, translation modified).

In *Being and Time*, the specific role of natural laws in what Heidegger called the mathematical projection of nature is only implicit except in his citations of Newton's laws of motion and gravity as examples.

31. Haugeland's interpretation of Heidegger on science has evident affinities to Thomas Kuhn's (1970) account of normal science, anomaly, and scientific crisis. This connection is not coincidental since Haugeland read and taught Kuhn's work and coedited a collection of his late writings (Kuhn 2000). Kuhn nevertheless does not discuss these issues in the modal terms of what is possible or impossible for entities within a (normal) scientific domain.

being and the conception of ontological truth as *a-letheia,* which is the condition of possibility for the discovery of ontical truth and falsity. Perhaps more strikingly, Heidegger explicitly characterizes the account of "unowned" dasein developed in division I as an *existentiale.* ("Existentiale" is Heidegger's term for an essential structure of dasein's way of being—comparable therefore to Aristotle's or Kant's categories that articulate the understanding of being as occurrence in traditional metaphysics.) By contrast, the possibility of "owned" existence developed in the opening chapters of division II may seem derivative and dependent:

> *Owned being-one's-self* does not rest upon an exceptional condition of the subject, a condition that has been detached from the "anyone"; *it is rather an existentiell modification of the "anyone"—of the "anyone" as an essential existentiale.* (SZ 130)

An existentiell possibility involves a particular case of dasein's comportment toward its own being as at issue for it, as opposed to a general structural character of dasein; thus, it has seemed to many, the general structure of the disclosedness of entities, of "intentionality" in the now-familiar philosophical idiom, is to be found in division I.

Haugeland's reading repudiates both the suggestion that division I offers a relatively self-contained account of intentionality as (unowned) disclosedness and the apparent philosophical priority of division I over division II. Dasein admittedly does exist "proximally and for the most part" in the unowned or undifferentiated modes discussed in division I, and owned resoluteness is thus not dasein's ordinary and familiar way of comporting itself. Moreover, owned resoluteness does not thereby uncover human possibilities or abilities-to-be that are different from those already sustained by the public practices and roles opened for "anyone." Resolute dasein takes over responsibility for the very comportments and roles that dasein mostly falls in and goes along with in an unowned, dispersed way. Yet it is only its openness to the *possibility* of owned resoluteness that sustains a living way of life as an understanding of the being of entities. Without at least a dim glimpse of and possible directedness toward such an "existentiell" modification of dasein's ordinary, everyday involvement in the world, dasein would never understand *entities* in their being but would do what one does only in utter indifference to any accountability beyond its own practices and norms.

Haugeland's reading of the central concepts in division II is entirely oriented toward this understanding of the philosophical priority of the possibility of owned existence. Being-toward-death is dasein's comportment toward entities in a way of life that might nevertheless turn out not to be intelligibly possible. Anxiety is a mood that discloses dasein as thrown into and burdened by a situation whose intelligibility is thus ungrounded. Resoluteness is a way of projecting dasein onto its possibilities in a diligent effort to make them work (to repeat them), while remaining open to giving up in the face of impossibility. Conscience is the call to tell the difference between situations that call for such diligence and those that require giving up an entire way of life and thereby to take over dasein's responsibility in each case for this way of life as a "thrown projection" of itself and entities within a concrete situation. Originary timeishness *(Zeitlichkeit)* is the temporalizing of that resolute commitment to responsibility for its own being and for its disclosure of the being of worldly entities. What is thereby most fundamentally manifest is the finitude of dasein's existence, not in the sense of its coming to a mortal end but of its dependence upon entities to let it be itself existingly. Dasein is called in each case to take responsibility not merely for its own life and possibilities but also for the entire way of life and understanding of being that allows for its particular "ability-to-be." That is why this account of division II and its philosophical priority is linked to Haugeland's conception of dasein as a "living way of life." Some of the most important recent work on division II (e.g., Kukla 2002; Crowell 2007; Blattner forthcoming) takes up and further develops Haugeland's overall conception of the book. The collective result of his and their inquiries revises familiar conceptions and stereotypes of Heidegger's philosophical orientation. Heidegger has the reputation, especially within the analytic tradition, of being hostile to reason and science. Haugeland's reading counters that reputation by emphasizing the depth of Heidegger's commitment to understanding the possibility and indispensability of objective truth and to a conception of conscience that enables us to understand "both our responsiveness to reasons and our practice of giving them" (Crowell 2007, 62).

THE COMPOSITION OF THE BOOK

Recognizing the import of Haugeland's work both for Heidegger scholarship and for contemporary philosophy more generally reminds us what was lost to philosophy from his untimely death at age 65 and his prior illness with early onset Alzheimer's disease. Only the first seven chapters of his planned Heidegger book were composed when Haugeland died in June 2010, and most of the work we have was completed before the onset of his illness earlier in the decade. The extant manuscript addresses roughly the first third of the itself-unfinished treatise of *Being and Time*. Fortunately, other contemporaneous papers and talks collectively round out Haugeland's account of Heidegger's project so as to provide a grasp of his distinctive reinterpretation. The book you have before you collects all of the significant components of Haugeland's work on Heidegger, the published and the unpublished papers together with the unfinished book manuscript and its proposed revisions to the canonical English translation of *Being and Time*. The aim is to bring together for the first time a comprehensive presentation of Haugeland's interpretation of and philosophical engagement with Heidegger.[32]

This body of work has been divided into four parts. The first part includes Haugeland's first two papers on Heidegger, which predate his efforts to compose a systematic, book-length interpretation of both the published and the unpublished portions of part one of *Being and Time*. These are the best known and most influential of Haugeland's published articles on Heidegger. In a few places, editorial notes indicate points in these papers that have been revised in subsequent work, and several of his translations of Heidegger's terms have been retroactively updated, but they otherwise stand as originally published. The second part contains the manuscript of *Dasein Disclosed* as we have it. While Haugeland had carefully worked and reworked much of the manuscript, there is no doubt that he was continuing to revise what he had already written, and some of the later chapters suggest gaps he planned to fill in. His formulations have been retained unchanged, apart from correcting clear typographical, grammatical, or orthographic errors and resolving multiple versions of the same passage into a single text. In a few other places, editorial notes call attention to is-

---

32. Some material that Haugeland had clearly abandoned is not included in the volume. Notes and presentations from his various courses or the close paraphrases of several chapters of *Being and Time* that he produced for his own use are also omitted. Haugeland held to very high standards for his own published work. Preparing this volume involved discerning an appropriate division between work to be omitted because its content was clearly unsatisfactory by his own standards and work to be included because it successfully conveys important elements of the project he had hoped to complete even though he himself would not have published it in this form without revision.

sues Haugeland would likely have addressed in subsequent revisions, including passages where he wrote marginal notes critical of the current manuscript's formulations. Since the manuscript itself is incomplete, Haugeland's successful proposal for a Guggenheim Fellowship introduces it with a clear and concise account of his overall conception of the book, including the unwritten parts (the onset of his illness coincided with the fellowship year, which he had hoped to use to complete the book). This part concludes with one version of Haugeland's glossary of his preferred retranslations of many of Heidegger's central concepts, prepared for his students in his courses on Heidegger at Chicago or Pittsburgh.

Part three of the volume is composed of published and unpublished papers or talks on Heidegger that Haugeland developed during the time that he was working on the book. The published papers are included without revision. The talks are also left intact since they were publicly presented in this form. While these papers and talks do not directly fit sequentially alongside the text of *Being and Time* to the same extent that the manuscript chapters do, they centrally address many of the components of Heidegger's text that Haugeland had not taken up in the extant book manuscript. The manuscript stops roughly two-thirds of the way through division I of *Being and Time*. The remaining parts of division I are the primary focus of "Reading Brandom Reading Heidegger" and especially "Letting Be," with some additional contributions from the earlier "Dasein's Disclosedness" in the first part. "Truth and Finitude" primarily concerns Haugeland's account of issues addressed in the first three chapters of division II, although it also reworks important aspects of the entire project. The unpublished paper "Death and Dasein" partially overlaps the discussion of existential death in "Truth and Finitude" but incorporates some other material into a succinct and colloquial formulation of one of Haugeland's most distinctive reinterpretations. The unpublished talk on "Temporality" usefully summarizes Haugeland's overall interpretation to introduce his treatment of chapter four of division II, which is also briefly addressed in the final paragraphs of "Letting Be." We have no sustained discussion of division II, chapter five on historicality, or chapter six on the relation between originary "timeishness" *(Zeitlichkeit)* and ordinary or world time. As I noted earlier, these papers, the manuscript, and the Guggenheim proposal also put forward the thesis and further tantalizing hints of Haugeland's promised reading of what Heidegger would have said in the unpublished division III of part one of *Being and Time*. The final part of the book includes two additional papers that do not directly expound Heidegger but nevertheless bring out especially clearly how Haugeland saw the broader significance for contemporary philosophy of many of the distinctive themes of his Heidegger interpretation.

The insight and depth of what was intended to be a comprehensive reconstruction of Heidegger's early philosophical project conspicuously calls attention to what might have been in the unfinished parts of the book. Yet we can also be grateful that, in these writings and their complementary relation to his constructive work in *Having Thought,* Haugeland leaves a legacy to reward serious philosophical attention for a long time to come.

REFERENCES

Adams, Zed, ed. Forthcoming. *Truth and Understanding: Essays in Honor of John Haugeland.*

Blattner, William. 1999. *Heidegger's Temporal Idealism.* Cambridge: Cambridge University Press.

―――. Forthcoming. Essential Guilt and Transcendental Conscience. In *Heidegger, Authenticity and the Self,* ed. D. McManus. New York: Routledge.

Brandom, Robert. 1979. Freedom and Constraint by Norms. *American Philosophical Quarterly* 16: 187–96.

―――. 2008. *Between Saying and Doing.* Oxford: Oxford University Press.

Carman, Taylor. 2003. *Heidegger's Analytic.* Cambridge: Cambridge University Press.

Carnap, Rudolf. 1959. The Eliminability of Metaphysics through the Logical Analysis of Language. In *Logical Positivism,* ed. A. J. Ayer, 60–81. Glencoe, IL: Free Press.

Carroll, John, ed. 2004. *Readings on Laws of Nature.* Pittsburgh: University of Pittsburgh Press.

Crowell, Steven. 2007. Conscience and Reason. In *Transcendental Heidegger,* ed. S. Crowell and J. Malpas, 43–62. Stanford, CA: Stanford University Press.

Daston, Lorraine, and Peter Galison. 2007. *Objectivity.* New York: Zone.

Dreyfus, Hubert. 1991. *Being-in-the-World.* Cambridge, MA: MIT Press.

Frankfurt, Harry. 2005. *On Bullshit.* Princeton, NJ: Princeton University Press.

Gendler, Tamar, and John Hawthorne. 2002. Introduction: Conceivability and Possibility. In *Conceivability and Possibility,* ed. T. Gendler and J. Hawthorne, 1–70. Oxford: Oxford University Press.

Goodman, Nelson. 1984. *Fact, Fiction, and Forecast*, 4th ed. Cambridge, MA: Harvard University Press.

Hale, Bob. 1997. Modality. In *A Companion to the Philosophy of Language*, ed. B. Hale and C. Wright, 487–514. Oxford: Blackwell.

Haugeland, John, ed. 1981. *Mind Design*. Cambridge, MA: MIT Press.

———. 1982. Heidegger on Being a Person. *Nous* 16: 16–26.

———. 1985. *Artificial Intelligence: The Very Idea*. Cambridge, MA: MIT Press.

———. 1989. Dasein's Disclosedness. *Southern Journal of Philosophy* 28 (suppl.): 51–73.

———, ed. 1997. *Mind Design II*. Cambridge, MA: MIT Press.

———. 1998. *Having Thought*. Cambridge, MA: Harvard University Press.

———. 2000. Truth and Finitude. In *Heidegger, Authenticity, and Modernity*, ed. J. Malpas and M. Wrathall, 43–77. Cambridge, MA: MIT Press.

———. 2007. Letting Be. In *Transcendental Heidegger*, ed. S. Crowell and J. Malpas, 93–103. Stanford, CA: Stanford University Press.

Hegel, G. W. F. 1977. *Phenomenology of Spirit*. Trans. A. Miller. Oxford: Oxford University Press.

Heidegger, Martin. 1962. *Being and Time*. Trans. J. Macquarrie and E. Robinson. New York: Harper and Row.

———. 1979. *History of the Concept of Time*. Trans. T. Kisiel. Bloomington: Indiana University Press.

———. 1995. *The Fundamental Concepts of Metaphysics*. Trans. W. McNeill and N. Walker. Bloomington: Indiana University Press.

———. 2002. *Off the Beaten Track*. Trans. J. Young. Cambridge: Cambridge University Press.

Kripke, Saul. 1982. *Wittgenstein on Rules and Private Language*. Cambridge, MA: Harvard University Press.

Kuhn, Thomas. 1970. *The Structure of Scientific Revolutions*, 2nd ed. Chicago: University of Chicago Press.

———. 2000. *The Road since Structure*, ed. James Conant and John Haugeland. Chicago: University of Chicago Press.

Kukla, Rebecca. 2002. The Ontology and Temporality of Conscience. *Continental Philosophy Review* 35: 1–34.

Kukla, Rebecca, and Mark Lance. 2009. *Yo! and Lo!* Cambridge, MA: Harvard University Press.

Lange, Marc. 2000. *Natural Laws in Scientific Practice*. Oxford: Oxford University Press.

———. 2009. *Laws and Lawmakers*. Oxford: Oxford University Press.

Lear, Jonathan. 2006. *Radical Hope*. Cambridge, MA: Harvard University Press.

McDaniel, Kris. 2009. Ways of Being. In *Metametaphysics,* ed. D. Chalmers, D. Manley, and R. Wasserman, 290–319. Oxford: Oxford University Press.

McDowell, John. 1984. Wittgenstein on Following a Rule. *Synthese* 58: 325–64.

———. 1994. *Mind and World.* Cambridge, MA: Harvard University Press.

Quine, W. V. O. 1952. *From a Logical Point of View.* Cambridge, MA: Harvard University Press.

———. 1960. *Word and Object.* Cambridge, MA: MIT Press.

Roberts, John. 2007. *The Law-Governed Universe.* Oxford: Oxford University Press.

Rouse, Joseph. 2002. *How Scientific Practices Matter.* Chicago: University of Chicago Press.

———. Forthcoming a. *Articulating the World.*

———. Forthcoming b. Love and Death. In Adams (forthcoming).

Sellars, Wilfrid. 2007. *In the Space of Reasons.* Cambridge, MA: Harvard University Press.

Turner, Jason. 2010. Ontological Pluralism. *Journal of Philosophy* 107: 5–34.

Van Inwagen, Peter. 2009. Being, Existence, and Ontological Commitment. In *Metametaphysics,* ed. D. Chalmers, D. Manley, and R. Wasserman, 472–506. Oxford: Oxford University Press.

ONE

Early Papers on Heidegger

Heidegger on Being a Person

(1982)

This paper presents a nonstandard and rather freewheeling interpretation of *Being and Time*, with emphasis on the first division. I make Heidegger out to be less like Husserl and/or Sartre than is usual and more like Dewey and (to a lesser extent) Sellars and the later Wittgenstein. My central point will be Heidegger's radical divergence from the Cartesian-Kantian tradition regarding the fundamental question: What is a person?

According to Aristotle, man is a logical or "word-using" animal, a political or "community-participating" animal, and a featherless biped. In a sense easier to appreciate than to explain, the last is only incidental, whereas the first two are important, but those two are not our only important differentia. People (and probably only people) make and use tools, play games, judge themselves and others critically, and develop cultural traditions. It may seem that apes and social insects share some of these characteristics, at least primitively; yet people are clearly quite distinctive. A satisfactory account of what it is to be a person would expose the roots of this distinction, thereby showing why certain differentia are important and others only incidental.

For instance, Christian and modern philosophers interpreted Aristotle's "logical" as "rational" and proposed this rationality as our fundamental distinction. Thus Descartes held that people can talk *because* they can ratiocinate, and he could well have said the same for making and using tools. Similarly, Hobbes tried both to explain and to justify our living in a commonwealth by showing that it is rational. I see Heidegger, on the other hand, as starting from Aristotle's second definition—trying, in effect, to ground all other important differentia in our basic communal nature.

But how can we conceive animals that are "political" in the relevant sense without presupposing that they are rational or word using? My reconstruction of Heidegger's answer to this question is the foundation of my interpretation. Imagine a community of versatile and interactive creatures, not otherwise specified except that they are *conformists*. "Conformism" here means not just imitativeness (monkey see, monkey do) but also censoriousness—that is, a positive tendency to see that one's neighbors do likewise and to suppress variation. This is to be thought of as a complicated behavioral disposition, which the creatures have by nature ("wired in"). It presupposes in them a capacity to react differentially (e.g., perception) and also some power to alter one another's dispositions more or less permanently (compare reinforcement, punishment, etc.). But it does not presuppose thought, reasoning, language, or any other "higher" faculty.[1]

The net effect of this conformism is a systematic peer pressure within the community, which can be viewed as a kind of mutual attraction among the various members' behavioral dispositions. Under its influence, these dispositions draw "closer" to each other in the sense that they become more similar; that is, the community members tend to act alike (in like circumstances). The result is analogous to that of gregariousness among range animals: given only their tendency to aggregate, they will tend also to form and maintain distinct herds. Other factors (including chance) will determine how many herds form, their sizes, and their location; gregariousness determines only that there will be herds—distinguishable, reidentifiable clusters of animals, separated by clear gaps where there are no animals (save the odd stray).

When behavioral dispositions aggregate under the force of conformism, it is not herds that coalesce, but *norms*. Other factors (including chance) will determine the number of norms, how narrow (strict) they are, and where they are in the "space" of feasible behavior; conformism determines only that there will be norms—distinct, enduring clusters of dispositions in behavioral feasibility space, separated in that space by clear gaps where there are no dispositions (save the odd stray). Like herds, norms are a kind of "emergent" entity, with an identity and a life of their own, over and above those of their constituents. New animals slowly replace the old, and thus a

---

1. Conformism is deeply related to the crucial notion of "falling"; compare also the discussion of *"Sorge um . . . Abstand"* (*SZ* 126). Abbreviations for Heidegger's texts are listed in References.

single herd can outlast many generations; likewise, though each individual's dispositions eventually pass away, they beget their successors in conformist youth, and thereby the norms are handed down to the generations.

The clusters that coalesce can be called "norms" (and not just groups or types) precisely because they are generated and maintained by censoriousness; the censure attendant on deviation automatically gives the standards (the extant clusters) a de facto normative force. Out-of-step behavior is not just atypical but also abnormal and unacceptable; it is what one is "not supposed to" do and in that sense improper. Norms should not be confused with conventions (in David Lewis's 1969 sense), which are "tacit" or "as if" agreements, where the parties have settled on a certain arranged behavior pattern for mutual benefit. Though nothing is implied about the origin of these arrangements, their persistence is explained by showing how, for each individual, it is rational to go along with whatever pattern is already established. The difference between norms and convention lies in the explanatory appeal: conformism does not depend on any rational or interest-maximizing decisions (and thus the norms themselves need not be beneficial). Also, insofar as conventions depend on rational self-interest, they forfeit the normative force of norms.

The total assemblage of norms for a conforming community largely determines the behavioral dispositions of each nondeviant member; in effect, it defines what it is to be a "normal" member of the community. Heidegger calls this assemblage the *anyone* (*das Man;* see, e.g., SZ 126f, 194, and 288).[2] (Perhaps Wittgenstein meant something similar by "forms of life.") I regard it as the pivotal notion for understanding *Being and Time*.[3]

Unlike a scatter of herds, the anyone is elaborately organized and structured because the norms that make it up are highly interdependent. It is crucial that what gets normalized are not, strictly speaking, actual instances of behavior but rather dispositions to behave, contingent on the circumstances. Thus, norms have a kind of "if-then" structure, connecting various

2. Haugeland almost invariably used abbreviations within the text for citations to the German pagination of Heidegger's books. I have preserved that practice, with a list of the abbreviations at the beginning of the list of references at the end of the book.—*Ed.*

3. Haugeland's later view (see later, especially "Truth and Finitude") takes the "anyone" only to be the pivotal notion of division I; the linked accounts of death, conscience, guilt/responsibility, and resoluteness that comprise the possibility of "owned" (*eigentlich*) existence become the core of the book.—*Ed.*

sorts of circumstances to various sorts of behavior. It follows that the con-forming community (in the differential responses of normal behavior and normal censorship) must effectively categorize both behavior and behav-ioral circumstances into various distinct sorts. We say that the anyone *in-stitutes* these sorts.

Imagine, for instance, that the rules of chess were not explicitly codified but were observed only as a body of conformists' norms—"how one acts" when in chess-playing circumstances. Thus, it is proper (socially acceptable) to move the king in any of eight directions, but only one square at a time. For this to be a norm, players and teacher/censors must be able to "tell" (respond differentially, depending on) which piece is the king, what the squares and directions are, what counts as a move, and so on. According to other norms, the king starts on a given square, must be protected whenever attacked, cannot cross a threatened square, can "castle" under certain conditions, and so on. The important point is that it is the *same* king, the same instituted sort, that is involved in each norm: hence, the norms them-selves are interrelated in depending on the same sorting of circumstances. We call a sort that is involved in many interrelated norms a *role* (e.g., the role of the king in chess). Many norms are also related through the sorting of squares, moves, threats, other kinds of pieces, and what have you; obvi-ously, in fact, all the norms and roles of chess are bound up in a deeply interdependent bundle.

Heidegger makes these points in terms of the equipment and parapherna-lia of everyday life, but the upshot is the same. Hammers, nails, boards, and drills, screwdrivers, screws, and glue are all bound together in a (large) nexus of intertwined roles, instituted by the norms of carpentry practice, and that is what makes them what they are. Consider what marks off our use of tools from the uses apes sometimes make of sticks, or ants or aphids. It is not that people use things more cleverly or more effectively or that we use them only to fashion other things, though all of these may be true. The main difference is that tools have proper uses—for each tool, there is "what it's for." If an ape uses a stick to get bananas, whether cleverly or not, whether successfully or not, it has in no sense used it either properly or improperly. You or I, on the other hand, might use a screwdriver properly to drive in screws or improperly to carve graffiti on a subway wall; either way, the pro-priety is independent of our cleverness or success. One misuses (or abuses) a screwdriver to gouge walls—that is not what screwdrivers are for. An ape could not misuse a stick, no matter what it did.

Being a screwdriver, like being a chess king, is being that which plays a certain role in relation to other things with interdetermined roles. These mutually defining role relations are constitutive of equipment or paraphernalia as such. Though Heidegger distinguishes and names quite a few varieties (especially *SZ* sections 15–17), we need only his generic term, 'referral':[4]

> Taken strictly, there never "is" *an* equipment. . . . In the structure [essential to equipment] there lies a referral of one thing to another. . . . Equipment always accords with its [own] equipmentality *by* belonging to other equipment: pen, nib, ink, blotter, table, lamp, furniture, windows, doors, room. (*SZ* 68)[5]

The totality of all paraphernalia cum referral relations is called the "referral nexus of significance," but since the term 'paraphernalia' is taken broadly enough to include practically everything with which we ordinarily work, cope, or bother (except other people), this totality is tantamount, in fact, to the everyday world.

The everyday world, of course, is not the universe or the planet Earth but rather the "world" of daily life and affairs—the world that has the business world and the wide world of sports as specialized portions.[6] It is essentially a cultural product, given determinate character by—instituted by—the norms of the conformists who live in it:

> The anyone itself . . . articulates the referral nexus of significance. (*SZ* 129)

4. *Verweisung* (translated by Macquarrie and Robinson as "reference or assignment"); the sense of the German is roughly "being sent or directed, by or away from one thing, toward another," for which English lacks a comfortable equivalent. But nuances in the original are at best a guide; a priori, it is just as likely that no German word is exactly right as that no English word is. Philosophical sense is ultimately determined not by dictionaries or etymologies but by examples and the doctrines themselves. [In later work, Haugeland translated '*Verweisung*' and '*verweisen*' as '*assignment*' and '*assign*', *rather than* '*referral*'.—Ed.*]

5. Dewey makes a similar point: "A tool is a particular thing, but it is more than a particular thing, since it is a thing in which a connection, a sequential bond of nature is embodied. It possesses an objective relation as its own defining property. . . . Its primary relationship is to other external things, as the hammer to the nail, and the plow to the soil" (1925, 103).

6. Compare *Welt*, sense 3 (*SZ* 65), and *Umwelt* (*SZ* 66).

This is a central thesis of *Being and Time,* which I venture to sum up in a memorable slogan: *all constitution is institution.*[7]

Language, not surprisingly, is entirely on a par with the (rest of the) everyday world, as fundamentally instituted and determined by conformist norms. This is one area, however, where recent "social practice" accounts are decidedly more sophisticated than *Being and Time,* so I rest with quoting two passages exhibiting the basic idea:

> But signs are above all themselves equipment, whose specific equipmental character consists in *indicating.* . . . Indicating can be defined as a species of referral. (*SZ* 77)

and

> [The referral nexus of] significance . . . harbors within itself the ontological condition for the possibility . . . [of disclosing] "signification," on which are founded in turn the possible being of word and language. (*SZ* 87; compare *SZ* 161)

The important point is that linguistic forms are understood as (special) equipment, and hence the word/object reference relations are just a special case of interequipmental referral relations—which suggests another slogan: *all intentionality is instituted referral.*[8]

We are at last in a position to address the fundamental question for any interpretation of *Being and Time:* What is Dasein?[9] According to the text,

---

7. Haugeland's later view rejects this slogan. Social institution is not sufficient for the constitution of entities as entities of an intelligible sort (via an understanding of their being) because they are constituted as entities only by the possibility of at least some persons taking responsibility for letting such socially instituted understandings remain accountable to the entities themselves. See especially "Truth and Finitude" and "Authentic Intentionality" and also "Letting Be," later in this volume.—*Ed.*

8. In his later view, merely instituted referral constitutes only what he calls "ersatz intentionality." See "Authentic Intentionality" in this volume.—*Ed.*

9. In the book manuscript of *Dasein Disclosed,* Haugeland chose to treat 'dasein' as a naturalized English word, uncapitalized. In this paper he had not yet made that choice, and his capitalization of 'Dasein' has been retained to acknowledge that later change in his thinking about how to present Heidegger in English. In some of Haugeland's other previously published papers, 'Dasein' was capitalized against his intentions, due to copyediting decisions for consistency throughout an edited volume. In those cases, the lower case 'dasein' has been restored.—*Ed.*

the anyone (*SZ* 126–30), the world (*SZ* 64, 364, and 380), language (*SZ* 166), and even the sciences (*SZ* 11) all have "Dasein's kind of being." We can make sense of this astonishing diversity if we understand Dasein to be the anyone and everything instituted by it: a vast intricate pattern—generated and maintained by conformism—of norms, normal dispositions, customs, sorts, roles, referral relations, public institutions, and so on.[10] On this reading, the anyone, the (everyday) world, and language are different coherent "subpatterns" within the grand pattern that is Dasein; they have Dasein's kind of being because each of them is Dasein (though none of them is all of Dasein). Within the anyone and all it institutes, the science of chemistry is a coherent subpattern: chemistry is Dasein—and so are philately, Christmas, and Cincinnati.

There is, however, one crucial omission from the foregoing list. According to the first sentence of the book proper (*SZ* 41), we are ourselves Dasein. But this is the most misunderstood sentence in all of Heidegger. For readers have surmised that 'Dasein' is just a newfangled term for 'person' (or 'ego' or 'mind')—in other words, that each of us is or has one Dasein, and there is a Dasein for each of us. This is wrong, and the first indication is a simple textual point. 'Person' is a count noun (we can "count" a person, several people, and so on); Dasein is (virtually) never used as a count noun.[11] On the other hand, it is not a mass noun, either (such as 'water' or 'gold'); Dasein can no more be measured out (e.g., in gallons or ounces) than it can be counted. Grammatically, 'tuberculosis' is a closer analogy. We neither count "tuberculosis" nor measure amounts of it; it comes, rather, in distinct occurrences or cases (which can, of course, be counted). A person is like an occurrence or a "case" of Dasein—except that one does not catch it, let

10. Compare this with Dewey's remark about "mind" (which he clearly distinguishes from personal consciousness): "the whole history of science, art and morals proves that the mind that appears in individuals is not as such individual mind. The former is in itself a system of belief, recognitions, and ignorances, of acceptances and rejections, of expectancies and appraisals of meaning which have been instituted under the influence of custom and tradition" (1925, 180; compare 184). [The later view identifies these subpatterns with unowned dasein rather than with dasein *tout court.*—*Ed.*]

11. The Macquarrie and Robinson translation, however, is poor in this regard; thus, they render the opening sentence (just mentioned) as follows: "We are ourselves the entities to be analyzed [i.e., Dasein]." The plural 'entities' would suggest a count noun, but the German is singular; such errors are common. (But on rare occasion, Heidegger himself seems to slip up; see e.g., *SZ* 240 and 336.)

alone get over it. Dasein is not a species of which we are specimens, a type of which we are tokens, a feature which we have, a spirit which is in us, a condition which we are in, or even a whole of which we are part (though that is closest). People are to Dasein as baseball games are to baseball, as utterances are to language, as works are to literature. Dasein is the overall phenomenon, consisting entirely of its individual "occurrences," and yet prerequisite for any of them being what it is. English lacks a convincing word for this relation, so I will settle for saying that a person is a *case* of Dasein.[12]

People are, in one sense, on a par with everything else the anyone institutes; they are identifiable coherent subpatterns within the overall pattern that is Dasein. Intuitively, each person is that pattern of normal dispositions and social roles that constitutes an individual member of the conforming community. Now, it is a fundamental requirement of the story so far that Dasein have such "member patterns" (conformists), but nothing has been said about what distinguishes these patterns either from one another or from other subpatterns of Dasein—in effect, a "top-down" version of the personal-identity problem. We can emphasize both this remarkable doctrine and the special difficulty it raises with a cryptic third slogan: *people are primordial institutions.* In other words, you and I are institutions like General Motors, marriage, and the common law, except that we are "primordial." What could that mean?

Try to imagine a conforming community whose members are (physically) like beehives; that is, each bee is just an organ or appendage of some conformist hive, and many such hives make up the group. These hives imitate and censure one another, thus sustaining norms of hive behavior. But what is hive behavior? If a particular bee visits a forbidden flower, how is that the hive's doing and not the bee's? Well, suppose, as a matter of physiological fact, that stinging any one bee would tend to suppress whatever any bees in her hive were (recently and conspicuously) engaged in; so, to keep bees away from forbidden flowers, it suffices to sting the sisters of any one that wanders. In effect, the hive as a whole is held to account for the activity of its parts, and it (the hive) is made to change its ways. Compare this with spanking a child's bottom when it (the child) steals with its fingers or blasphemes with its mouth. The whole hive, like the whole child, is one "unit

---

12. German does not have a terrific term for it, either; when Heidegger wants to speak of individuals, he qualifies it with '*je*' or '*jeweilig*,' meaning, roughly, "in each case" or "in the given case."

of accountability" and therefore the "subject" of the behavior because it is what takes the heat and learns from "its" mistakes. By the same token, it can be one member of a conforming community.

Units of accountability are as structured and multifarious as the norms to which they are held. Trivially, for instance, institutions of enduring ownership and debt require enduring owners and debtors. More important, many norms require "sorting" community members in the standard sorting of behavioral circumstances: thus, if you are a sergeant and you encounter a captain, then salute. In other words, what a unit of accountability is accountable for is a function of its official rank—or, more generally, its various social and institutional roles. There is an obvious analogy between these social roles and the roles which define equipment, but paraphernalia are never held to account (censured), no matter how badly they perform. Social roles ("offices") are roles whose players are accountable for how they play them.

Each unit of accountability, as a pattern of normal dispositions and social roles, is a subpattern of Dasein—an institution. But it is a distinctive institution in that it can have behavior as "my" behavior and can be censured if that behavior is improper: it is a case of Dasein. Moreover, institutions of this kind are essential to all others, for without accountability there would be no censorship, hence no norms, no anyone, no Dasein at all. Thus, accountable cases are "primordial" institutions. Heidegger places this structure, which he calls "in-each-case-mineness" (*Jemeinigkeit; SZ* 42), among Dasein's most fundamental characteristics.

There is more, however, to primordial cases of Dasein than conformist accountability. To see what it is, we must unpack a fourth slogan—this time, one which Heidegger himself states and emphasizes:

> *The "essence" of Dasein lies in its existence.* (*SZ* 42; italics and scare quotes in original)[13]

"Existence," of course, is one of the basic technical notions of *Being and Time;* it is not at all the same as "being real"—indeed, these are contrasted. Reality is the mode of being of the traditional *res*, the independent "thing" or substance. Dasein, it should be clear by now, is not a thing in any traditional sense; it is not real, but it exists. By the same token, electrons

---

13. Compare *SZ* 117, 12, 231, 318, and so on. [Haugeland's then-preferred translation of Existenz as "being extant" has been replaced by the usual translation, "existence," understood as a technical term in Heidegger.—*Ed.*]

and galaxies do not exist (but are real). The contrast is not invidious in either direction—there genuinely are both existing and real beings (entities). Nor, strictly speaking, is it exhaustive: mutually defining (interdependent) paraphernalia are neither real (independent things) nor existing (Dasein) but are "available," and there are other modes as well.[14]

Roughly, to exist is to be instituted, but Heidegger does not put it that way. The closest he comes to a definition is more like this: something exists if what (or "who") it is, in each case, is its own efforts to understand what (or who) it is (see, e.g., *SZ* 53, 231, and 325). Now there may be some plausibility to saying that who we are is, in part, a function of our self-understanding: I am a pacifist or a baseball fan if I think I am. But nothing I could think would make me emperor, let alone Napoleon, and much more than my self-image seems involved in my being a philosophy teacher, an electronics hobbyist, a middle-aged man, and so on.

The problem concerns the notion of "understanding"; Heidegger says:

> We sometimes use . . . the expression "understanding something" to mean "being able to manage an undertaking," "being up to it," [or] "knowing how to do something." (*SZ* 143)

Understanding something is equated with competence or know-how. So, the person who "really understands" race cars is the one who can make them go fast, whether by fine-tuning or fine driving (two ways to understand them); understanding formal mathematics amounts to mastery of the formalisms, ability to find proofs, and such like. But what, in this sense, could be meant by "self-understanding"? What would be the relevant "know-how"?

Well, it would be each individual's ability to be him- or herself, to manage his or her own life—in other words, knowing how (in each case) to be

---

14. I have been taking some liberties with the translations. 'Being real' translates *'Vorhandensein'* (M&R: presence-at-hand), which is not strictly correct, but pedagogically defensible in the context of *Being and Time*; 'being available' translates *'Zuhandensein'* (M&R: readiness-to-hand). For relevant texts, see *SZ* 42, 69, 92, 211ff, and 313f. [This note originally also mentioned Haugeland's translation of *'Existenz'* as 'being extant', which he later rejected as misleading (see note 15 above). He also later preferred 'being occurrent' to 'being real' for *Vorhandensein*, but the latter has been left unchanged in this paper, because it was not misleading in the way 'being extant' seems to be—*Ed*].

"me." And what know-how is that? According to Heidegger, any and all know-how that I may have is ipso facto some portion of my knowing how to be me. If I understood race cars in the way that mechanics do, then I would know how to be a race-car mechanic—which, in part, is what I would be. Even theoretical understanding, for example, of electrons, is a sophisticated and specialized aspect of knowing how to be a person of a certain sort: a quantum mechanic, say.

So far, however, this is only "dispersed" self-understanding in terms of separate worldly roles; it lacks any character of understanding oneself as a complete individual—as a self. Imagine a chess-playing device which can come up with a strong move for any given position but which lacks any overall sense of trying to win. The collected moves of such a device do not really add up to a complete game but are only a series of unconnected exercises; it does not really play chess. Analogically, a collection of dispersed roles does not really add up to a whole person, a complete "life." What is left out is *trying* to understand oneself (as such).

Two preliminary observations are in order before proceeding. First, every normal conformist is at the same time a unit of accountability and a censorious guardian of the tradition. Each normal disposition to do A in circumstance C is, by the very nature of conformism, paired with another disposition to censure any failures to do A in C. But these dispositions are distinct, meaning that it is possible to censure one's own failures. Thus, a conformist unit of accountability is also a potential unit of self-accountability. Second, in my pains to avoid any hidden presupposition of mentality or reason, I have spoken exclusively of dispositions, behavior, and know-how—making everything sound "mindless" and inarticulate. But of course it is not. Among Dasein's many institutions are those of language and explicit consideration. These can be particularly relevant to a serious effort at self-understanding: what I say about myself, for example, and why. Moreover, they enable a case of Dasein to judge its own dispositions without actually acting them out. It does not have to wait and see what it would do in a certain situation; it can "ask itself." And if it then disapproves, it does not have to spank its own bottom; it can "change its mind."

Invariably, a case of Dasein plays many roles. What is proper for it on any occasion will be a function of what roles these are; some priests, for instance, are not supposed to have love affairs, though other bachelors may. Also invariably, the demands of these roles will often conflict. What is appropriate for me, the breadwinner, may not be compatible with what

is appropriate for me, the aspiring artist, not to mention me, the shop fore-
man, me, the political activist, and me, the would-be adventurer, dreaming
of the Orient. This gives self-understanding, the ability to be me, a more
challenging aspect.

All these competing proprieties must somehow be juggled, and there are
basically two ways to do that. One, of course, is just to "slide," to take at each
moment the path of least resistance. That means attending to whatever
proprieties happen at that moment to be the most conspicuous or pressing,
forgetting about whatever others are temporarily out of sight. This is to remain dispersed in the worldly. The opposite possibility is to confront the
conflicts and resolve them: that is, to make up one's mind.[15] Trying to understand oneself is seeking out and positively adjudicating the conflicting
requirements of one's various roles in the exercise of a higher-level disposition which we might call "self-criticism" (I think it is close to what Heidegger means by "conscience").

A case of Dasein is genuinely self-critical when, in response to discovered tensions among its roles, it does something about them. Thus, I might
quit the priesthood and embrace my lover or decide to subordinate everything to my art. The important point is that I do not just let some dispositions override others (which may be weaker at the moment): rather, in the
light of some, I resolutely alter or eliminate others. As a unit of self-
accountability, I find and root out an inconsistency in my overall self-
understanding; instead of vacillating unwittingly between one "me" and
another, I become one of them (or perhaps a third) constantly and explicitly
and thereby achieve a "truer" self-understanding.

All self-critical adjudication is among current roles. In terms of the whole,
some may be rejected, others adjusted, but there is no external or higher
standard against which all are judged. The only end is self-constancy—a
clearer, more coherent self-understanding ability to be me. When a role
survives such critical scrutiny (perhaps adjusted), Heidegger says it is "taken
over as one's own" (*zugeeignet;* Macquarrie and Robinson translation: appropriated). It is no longer my role just because I happen to play it but mine
because I claim it by my own choice. Insofar as self-understanding critically takes over its roles, it is said to be *self-owned* (*eigentlich;* Macquarrie

---

15. Readers familiar with *Being and Time* will notice that "forgetting," "remaining
dispersed in the worldly," and "resolution" (and also several other expressions in the following paragraphs) are theoretical notions discussed at length by Heidegger.

and Robinson: authentic). Inconstant (dispersed and wavering) self-understanding is, in the same terms, *disowned* (but, of course, it is still *je meines:* in each case mine). A disowned case of Dasein does not lack a self or "personality," even a subtle and distinctive one; it is just un-self-critical. "Who" it is is still determined by its self-understanding, but this understanding remains unexamined and dispersed in the world.

The opposite of dispersal, self-ownedness, is, roughly, "getting your act together." As the resolution of conflicts that lead to wavering inconsistency, it is also *resoluteness.* Everything that is owned and everything that is gotten together or resolved upon is adopted in the first place from the anyone; except for small variations, there is no other source for ways of understanding oneself. To be self-owned ("authentic") is not to rise above the anyone, not to wash away the taint of common sense and vulgar custom but rather to embrace (some part of) what these have to offer in a particular selective way. The result is a critically realized, maximally self-constant ability to lead an individual cohesive, limited life: *mine!* This is what is at stake in trying to understand oneself.

It is also the rest of what is meant by saying that people are "primordial" institutions. Nobody is every wholly disowned or wholly self-owned; mostly, we are in between. Moreover, that is essential. The very possibility of multiple roles and thus of community and Dasein in any nontrivial sense depends on a fair measure of routine self-constancy in the member "cases." That people try to understand themselves and hence are always self-owned in some manner and degree is as much a prerequisite on the possibility of Dasein as that they are primitive loci of accountability (*je meines*). Heeding the call to this self-critical effort (conscience) and not mere conformist accountability is fully human responsibility. Thus Heidegger can say that to exist is to be that being the cases of which try to understand themselves: in being what they are, who they are is an issue to them.

Portions of these last few paragraphs may sound disconcertingly "existentialist," as, indeed, do large tracts of *Being and Time.* But, though the comparison is not empty, it is more often misleading than helpful. The central question is not how to be a "knight of faith" or a "superman," let alone a "futile passion," but rather what it is to be a person at all. I have tried to sketch an account of how our distinctively human use of tools and language, sense of custom and propriety, and capacity for self-criticism might all be grounded in our distinctive communality. According to the analysis, a person is not fundamentally a talking animal or a thinking thing but a case of Dasein: a crucial sort of subpattern in an overall pattern instituted by conformism and handed down from generation to generation. If the same account turns out also to lend an insight into the special existentialist concerns of personal integration and self-ownership . . . well then, so much the better.[16]

16. This paper would not have been possible were it not for years of close and fruitful collaboration with Bert Dreyfus. I am also grateful for comments and questions from Bob Brandom, Jerry Massey, Nick Rescher, and the audiences at Ohio State University, Yale University, and the Council for Philosophical Studies Summer Institute on Phenomenology and Existentialism, where earlier versions were read and discussed.

Dasein's Disclosedness

(1989)

Dasein is its disclosedness (*SZ* 133). This formula, while not exactly an equation, is at least an announcement that dasein cannot be understood apart from its disclosedness, nor disclosedness apart from dasein; each can be understood only with, and indeed *as*, the other. Here I will begin with an interpretation of disclosedness and use that as a guide to interpreting dasein.

Heidegger says a variety of things about disclosedness, and it is not always clear how they are connected or even mutually compatible. Since any interpretation must address this diversity, it is appropriate at the outset to list (some of) the claims:

1. Intraworldly entities can be discovered only because of or in terms of a prior disclosedness; disclosedness *makes discoveredness possible* (*SZ* 85, 137, 220, 297, 350, 437; *GP* 101ff.).
2. What is disclosed is not the same as the entities that are discovered in terms of it. According to some passages, what is disclosed is the *being* of those entities (*SZ* 357, 437; *GP* 100–102), but according to others, it is *dasein* (*SZ* 85; GP307) or even the *world* (*SZ* 85; *GP* 307). In the meantime, and despite the disclaimers, a few passages seem to speak of this or that intraworldly entity as itself disclosed (*SZ* 86, 137, 364).
3. Disclosedness is *primordial truth*, and, as such, it is the condition of the possibility of the truth of assertions (*SZ* 220ff., 297, 396; *GP* 24f, 307ff.).

17

4. *Publicness* and *resoluteness* are modes of disclosedness (*SZ* 167, 297).
5. The basic structure or makeup of disclosedness is this: *findingness, telling,* and *understanding.*[1]

According to the first thesis, disclosedness is the condition of the possibility of discovering intraworldly entities. But there might seem to be any number of such preconditions. For instance, scientific discoveries are impossible in principle without scientific evidence, and, *mutatis mutandis,* the same could be said for mathematical, criminological, geographical, and even treasure-hunting discoveries. So, to disclose may be *evidence* for. (That fits the connotations of revealing what is hidden or divulging a secret and is also related to truth.) But another undeniable prerequisite for discovery is *discoverers:* scientific discoveries are made by scientists, and even an accidental discovery of lost treasure requires someone to stumble across and recognize it. So maybe to be disclosed is to be a discoverer. That fits the suggestion that dasein is what is disclosed. And there are other possibilities: maybe to be disclosed is to be proven or provable—that would connect well with truth (and the German verb *erschliessen* can also mean 'to infer'), or maybe disclosedness is consciousness—that would fit well not only with the main strands in modern philosophy but also with Heidegger's explicit discussions of mood and understanding.

Each candidate, however, really accommodates only a fraction of what Heidegger says about disclosedness. Thus, whatever findingness, telling, and understanding are, they are unlikely prospects for the structure of evidence or provability; on the other hand, neither discoverers nor consciousness can easily be identified with primordial truth. What is worse, Heidegger's principal example of discovering is that of equipment and paraphernalia in the course of dasein's everyday taking care of business, and such discovering is precisely *not* dependent on evidence, proof, or consciousness—at least, not in any traditional senses. Finally, none of the four jibes with the suggestion that what is disclosed is the world or the being of entities. Clearly what is

---

1. *SZ* 180, 220, 295ff.; Heidegger is not consistent about this structure, however; sometimes falling is substituted for telling (*SZ* 349), and other times all four are given (*SZ* 269, 335). 'Findingness' and 'telling' are my translations of *Befindlichkeit* and *Rede;* they will be explained later. [The original version of this paper used 'so-foundness' rather than 'findingness' for *Befindlichkeit;* the latter, which Haugeland subsequently preferred, has been substituted throughout for translational consistency—*Ed.*]

called for is a more penetrating account of the preconditions on discovery, something which might at the same time account for the possibility of evidence, discoverers, proof, and even consciousness.

Consider, as a contrived but transparent example, playing chess. A player might discover, in the course of a game, a weakness in the opposing position, an unexpected opportunity, or a cunning avenue of attack. To be sure, a sort of evidence, discoverer, proof, and even consciousness are prerequisite to such discoveries—though, again, perhaps not in their traditional senses. But the most characteristic and peculiar precondition of any and all chess discoveries is the game of chess itself. In periods or places where chess is not played (e.g., before it was invented), discovering chess weaknesses or even pieces and positions would be quite impossible—because it would not make any sense. Without the game of chess, in terms of which they can make sense, there can be no such things as chess pieces or chess weaknesses, and hence they cannot be discovered. The sense that pieces and positions make is part and parcel of the sense that chess playing makes as a whole; pursuing the analogy then, it is *the game of chess,* as played, that is disclosed, and its *making sense* is its disclosedness.

The game of chess is a condition of the possibility of chess discoveries not only negatively, as a sine qua non, but also positively, as enabling or rendering possible; it is precisely in terms of the game that there *can be* such discoveries at all.[2] Chess evidence (e.g., from looking ahead), chess discoverers (canny players), chess proof (winning and losing), chess consciousness (whatever it is)—these too are positively made possible by the sense that the game and playing it make as a whole. We can even say that the game as such is the "world" within which chess discoveries are made. But does it also amount to the "being" of the entities thus discovered or anything that we might call "chess dasein" or "chess truth"? What, indeed,

2. Note that the game of chess not only positively enables actions that are otherwise impossible (such as checkmates and knight forks) but even enables the invention or discovery of possibilities that are unprecedented and hitherto unimagined (such as a new combination or a new strategy for the opening). One of the limitations of the chess example, however, is that the game does not offer the resources for its own elaboration (the introduction of new rules or practices); by contrast, *Sein und Zeit* (to take only one example) not only says unprecedented things with the resources of German but also elaborates and extends those resources themselves (through the introduction of new terminology and new uses of extant terms, e.g.). For a fuller treatment of these distinctions, see Robert Brandom (1979), "Freedom and Constraint by Norms," especially section III.

is "making sense of chess playing as a whole?" These are difficult questions that can be approached only by a longer route.

We can further work out the idea of disclosedness as making sense by turning to some examples which, though still not Heideggerian, are at least not as contrived as chess. In a series of influential articles, Donald Davidson distinguishes mental and physical events as two distinct sorts of entity.[3] The distinction between sorts of entity is made out in terms of a distinction between kinds of explanatory theory, each with a characteristic vocabulary. Explanatory theories are essentially ways to *make sense of* (render intelligible in general) some domain of entities and associated phenomena. Distinctive *kinds* of explanatory theory make distinctive kinds of sense or make sense of things in distinctive ways. Davidson carefully avoids claiming to have articulated the distinctive character of either the mental or the physical, but the tenor of his view is clear. Physical events and conditions make sense as such—hence count as *physical*—insofar as they are subsumable with others under *strict causal laws* in a closed comprehensive system of such laws. Mental events and states, by contrast, make sense as such—hence count as *mental*—insofar as they are ascribed in a holistic account that shows some individual's behavior to be generally *rational*.

It is part of Davidson's purpose to show that, because of the difference between these ways of making sense, there can be no strict laws connecting the mental and physical as such—that is, laws expressed in a mixed psychophysical vocabulary. In a revealing passage he writes:

> There are no strict psychophysical laws because of the disparate commitments of the mental and physical schemes. It is a feature of physical reality that physical change can be explained by laws that connect it with other changes and conditions physically described. It is a feature of the mental that the attribution of mental phenomena must be responsible to the background of reasons, beliefs, and intentions of the individual. There cannot be tight connections between the realms if each is to retain allegiance to its proper source of evidence. (Davidson 1980, 222)

---

3. See, for instance, [Davidson's articles] "Mental Events" (1970), "Psychology as Philosophy" (1974b), "Belief and the Basis of Meaning" (1974a), and "Thought and Talk" (1975). Of course, Davidson also maintains that every mental event is a physical event, but that is the conclusion of an argument requiring further factual and conceptual premises. It is not built in to his notions of mental and physical events per se.

The notions of "commitment," "allegiance," and "proper evidence" are used here without elaboration or defense; yet they suggest a deep (and, I think, deeply right) intuition to the effect that different schemes or realms entail different *standards* or criteria of adequacy to which descriptions of the phenomena must "live up." Or, to put it another way (accepting Davidson's connection between vocabulary and domain): entities themselves must live up to these standards if they are to count as entities in that domain at all. Thus, being rationally related to other mental states and events is a standard that any proposed candidate must meet if it is to join the mental club; being interrelated with others according to strict causal laws is the analogous entry condition for physical phenomena.

The notion of standards for entities themselves introduces the *being* of those entities. When Davidson tells us (if not quite in so many words) that *to be* a mental entity is to be rationally ascribable to a rational individual, he is telling us something about the *being* of the mental as such. Following Heidegger (and, via him, the history of philosophy), we may distinguish between the *how* of an entity's being and its *way* of being.[4] The "how" of its being is how it has a determinate character, how it is *as* it is, how it is "what it is like." In the case of things, we might say that they are determinate in general by having *intrinsic properties—those* properties which, for each particular thing, make it what it is. The "way" of an entity's being is the way or manner in which it is at all, as opposed to not. In the case of things, we might say that the way they are is by *actually occurring*, being present at particular times and places. Thus, the how concerns *what* the thing is, whereas the way concerns *that* (or *whether*) it is. In medieval ontology (oriented to the thing), this distinction shows up as that between essence and existence.

The standards for the entities in a domain effectively establish both the how and the way of their being. Thus, the standard of overall rationality establishes both how mental entities are determinate and the way that they are at all. Mental states are determinate in general as attitudes to propositions and, in each instance, by which attitude it is to which proposition.[5]

---

4. See *GP*, sections 10–12 (especially subsections 10a and 12c); 'how' and 'way' translate '*wie*' and '*Weise*,' respectively.

5. For fluency of exposition, I am diverging from the details of Davidson's formulation (for instance, in speaking of states rather than events), but the view presented remains Davidsonian in general character. Note that the "determinacy" discussed here is not incompatible with Quinean indeterminacy, for Quine's point was never that meaning is *totally* indeterminate but only that it is not totally determinate.

According to Davidson, they have that determinacy in terms of (and only in terms of) their respective "places" in an overall rational pattern of talk and behavior. Even on the face of it, this is quite unlike the determinacy that intrinsic properties afford particular things. What Davidson would say about the *way* in which mental states (propositional attitudes) are is less clear. But it must be something like this: an individual indeed has a given attitude just in case ascribing that attitude is part of an optimal "theory" of that individual as rational. The optimality of such a theory is a kind of global equilibrium among many competing constraints; hence, by its very nature, it is subject to occasional global readjustments in response to local changes. As a result, a person can sometimes gain or lose a belief not by a change of mind on that topic but by a revision on some other, which shifts the equilibrium.[6] Clearly, such a way of being is radically different from the actual occurrence (presence at a place and time) of a thing.

When Heidegger says that it is the being of entities that is disclosed, he means both the how and the way of being, for they go together. He does not mean by such disclosedness, however, that the how and way of being or the standard that establishes them is articulately worked out. A region or domain is disclosed, "preontologically," as Heidegger says, insofar as its standard is effectively applied in practice. Thus, Europeans in the Dark Ages may very well have understood one another as having beliefs and desires by tacitly[7] relying on standards of rationality, albeit with no

6. Compare this with Davidson's argument for the "nomological slack" between the mental and the physical: the point is rather that when we use the concepts of belief, desire, and the rest, we must stand prepared, as the evidence accumulates, to adjust our theory in the light of considerations of overall cogency: the constitutive ideal of rationality partly controls each phase in the evolution of what must be an evolving theory. An arbitrary choice of translation scheme would preclude such opportunistic tempering of theory; put differently, a right arbitrary choice of translation manual would be of a manual acceptable in the light of all possible evidence, and this is a choice we cannot make (1980, 222–23).

7. I am using 'tacit' semitechnically in a sense related to but distinct from that of 'implicit.' Both terms indicate something that is meant or done but not explicitly or articulately. They differ, however, in that 'implicit' suggests something which, although not itself explicit or said, is implied by something else that is explicit, whereas 'tacit' suggests nothing explicit but rather silence. Thus, fear of spiders might be implicit in calling (or thinking) them mean and ugly, while it might show tacitly in giving wide berth to woodpiles and dank corners. Standards of decorum and politeness can be applied tacitly, often quite unconsciously, in, for instance, responsive tone and body language.

explicit idea thereof; if so, the realm of the mental was disclosed to them, but only preontologically. Such tacit or in-effect application of standards happens, unspoken and unnoticed, in the everyday adoption and transmission of social practices—what everybody knows "we" do or say under conditions like this. By way of contrast, Dark-Age Europeans could not have begun to understand anything as physical, in Davidson's modern scientific sense, since nothing in their practices reflected the strict-law standard, even tacitly; the being of the physical was not disclosed to them at all.

Heidegger nowhere treats the being of either the physical or the mental in Davidson's senses. Instead, he begins with an account of the being of everyday equipment. Both the differences and the similarities between his discussion and Davidson's are instructive. In the first place, Heidegger, unlike Davidson, does not appeal to explanatory theory as a paradigm of making sense of a domain of entities. Rather, he says, equipment is most properly understood in its appropriate and successful use; for instance, a hammer is best understood as a hammer in the course of smoothly hammering in nails with it. Accordingly, the understanding of equipment need not be mediated by any descriptive vocabulary or, therefore, by the standards for employing such a vocabulary. Hence, finally, this understanding is also in some sense not cognitive but perhaps "pragmatic" or "embodied" in know-how; originary understanding is skillful mastery.

Despite these significant differences, the convergences are at least as important. According to Heidegger, the being of equipment is its *involvement*, and, as with the rationality of mental phenomena, equipmental involvements make sense only holistically. Thus, much as Davidson says, "My general strategy . . . depends, first, on emphasizing the holistic character of the cognitive field," and "the content of a propositional attitude derives from its place in the pattern" (1980, 231, 221), Heidegger says, "To the being of any equipment there always belongs an equipmental whole, in which it can be this equipment that it is" and "In accord with its equipmentality, equipment always is *from* its belonging to other equipment: inkstand, pen, ink, blotter, table, lamp, furniture, window, doors, room" (SZ 68). The *whole* that is invoked here is in each case the *concrete* whole of "actual" propositional attitudes or items of equipment; attitudes and equipment are intelligible as such only as "placed in" or "belonging to" the whole of their concrete circumstances or context.

To characterize a whole, however, it is not enough simply to identify what it comprises; one must also specify the relationships that make of what it comprises a whole. Thus, when Davidson says that the attitudes are placed in a pattern, he means a pattern of rational relationships—that is, a pattern defined in terms of rational *norms*. When Heidegger speaks of equipment belonging to other equipment, he also means a pattern of normative relationships—though not rational, in Davidson's sense. To say that a hammer is a hammer only as belonging to nails, boards, wooden structures, and the like is to say that the equipmental/functional *role* of hammers as such is to drive nails into boards and so on.[8] The normative relationships among equipment that make for a concrete equipmental whole are role relationships (e.g., what a hammer is *for* is driving in nails). Such relationships are called *assignments*, and, as I interpret Heidegger, the roles themselves are *involvements*.[9]

Involvements are the *how* of equipmental being; they answer the question of *what* something is as equipment; a hammer is a *hammer*, for instance, insofar as it plays *that* role, the role of being a hammer. What is the way of being that belongs together with this how? The *way* of equipmental being, its "actuality," lies in the actual *playing* of an equipmental role, something actually *having* that role. Equipment can play or have its role, of course, even while it is not currently being used, so long as it stands available for such use ("ready to hand"). To be available, it is neither necessary nor sufficient that something be workable or effective in a certain role. Thus, home remedies, though ineffective, may be readily available for various ailments, and common chemicals whose healing powers remain unsus-

8. The terms 'norm' and 'role' are not Heidegger's. They are also not prominent in Davidson's vocabulary, though he does not abjure them, as the following passages attest:

The interpretation of verbal behavior thus shows the salient features of the explanation of behavior generally: we cannot profitably take the parts one by one (the words and sentences), for it is only in the context of the system (language) that their role can be specified. (1980, 239)

and

We have the idea of belief only from the role of belief in the interpretation of language, for as a private attitude it is not intelligible except as an adjustment to the public norm provided by language. (1984, 170)

9. The distinction between a nexus of interrelated equipment and a nexus of interdefined involvements—two different wholes—is often overlooked. It is clearly drawn, however, by both Brandom and Okrent—who also both interpret involvements (Okrent's translation is 'functionalities') as roles. See Brandom 1983b, 393, and Okrent 1988.

pected are not therapeutically available today. Something actually plays a role if, according to the customs and practices of a community, it is taken to play that role. *Availability* is the *way* of equipmental being.[10]

Differences notwithstanding, the ontologies of the mental and the equipmental converge in the notion of normative holism. To pursue the presuppositions of this convergence, we must consider more carefully the idea of disclosing as making sense of. 'Makes sense of,' like 'discloses,' has the formal structure of a two-place relation: Y makes sense of Z (or Z makes sense to Y). Each of our examples so far—chess, equipment, the physical, and even the mental—has approached making sense from the direction of Z, that which gets made sense of. To understand making sense, however, we will also, and perhaps especially, have to consider Y, that to which sense is made, that which somehow "does" the sense making. This presents a curious doubling: if we are to understand Y in its capacity as making sense of things, then we must, in effect, *make sense of Y* in that capacity. In other words, Y has to occupy both argument places, once as what we make sense of and again as itself making sense of something else. This structure is not paradoxical any more than helping someone to help someone else, but it requires care if we are to avoid confusion.

Davidson characteristically keeps the issues clear by adopting the formal mode: consider X (an anthropologist or a linguist, say) making sense of Y (some foreigners, say) *as* making sense of Z (their environment, say). What can we (philosophers) say about X's problem, the problem Davidson calls *radical interpretation*?[11] Notice first that it is the general case, of which mental-state ascription and radical translation are but special cases; in effect, "making sense of things" is just a broader characterization of what we earlier called "rationality." Indeed, as Davidson was a pioneer in emphasizing, the special cases are essentially impossible because the holism of interpretation applies to them all simultaneously. That is, not only do the

---

10. 'Availability' translates '*Zuhandenheit*.' In *SZ*, Heidegger says of involvement and availability that each is the *being* of equipment, but they are not the same (*SZ* 69, 71, 84ff.). At *GP* 432, he says that availability is the *way* of equipmental being.

11. Interestingly, Davidson himself uses the 'make sense' locution in both ways: "Making sense of the utterances and behavior of others, even their most aberrant behavior, requires us to find a great deal of reason and truth in them" (1984, 153), and "In our need to make him make sense, we will try for a theory that finds him consistent, a believer of truths, and a lover of the good (all by our own lights, it goes without saying)" (1980, 222).

translations of various terms depend on one another and the ascriptions of various mental states depend on one another, but translations, ascriptions, interpretations of behavior, and so on are all equally interdependent as well. Making-sense-of must make sense as a whole.

We can work our way toward Heidegger by examining further what is presupposed in radical interpretation. Our guide will be the idea of normative holism, beginning in the familiar confines of linguistic interpretation and then generalizing. There are three main points. First, whatever is interpreted must be taken in its *full concretion;* in particular, each item must be taken in its complete concrete context—not just physical circumstances but also conversational, biographical, political, and what have you. Of course, what these circumstances are is itself determined only in the interpretation, but that is just to acknowledge that the interpretation must be holistic. Thus, as everyone knows, speech behavior can be interpreted only "in context," where this means two things: (i) utterances must be interpreted in relation to other utterances, and (ii) they must be interpreted in relation to (nonlinguistic) circumstances of utterance. The point generalizes easily to all interpretable behavior: a batter laying down a sacrifice bunt can be understood only in the context of a runner on base with at most one out; voting for president makes sense only in the context of being a registered voter with a valid ballot during a presidential election; and so on. In sum, if behavior is to be interpreted as making sense of things, it must itself be understood as situated and busy *in the midst of* those things.[12]

Second, whatever is to be interpreted must always already belong to and be construed in terms of a *common institutional framework*. Thus, obviously, if a body of utterances is to be interpreted, they must be taken as uttered "in" a common language and construed in its terms. To say that the language is common is to say that all the utterances are "in" the same language—the same vocabulary and the same grammar, roughly. (If each

---

12. 'Amidst' and 'in the midst of' are my attempt to render Heidegger's use of '*bei*' in the crucial phrase '*Sein bei (innerweltlich begegnendem Seienden)*' (SZ 192) and its many variants. As I interpret it, the point is that dasein is by nature busily engaged in the midst of (or "in the thick of") things—not an indifferent outsider or a passive spectator. This use is correlative with that of '*mit*' in '*Mitsein*' (or '*Sein mit*'), which I take to mean that dasein is by nature communal—in each case, one "among" the others (i.e., not an outsider socially, either). [Haugeland later translates *Mitsein* and *Sein mit* as "co-dasein" and "being-co," respectively.—*Ed.*]

utterance were in a different language, holistic constraints could not get a grip, and interpretation would be impossible.)[13] To say that the language is an institutional framework is to say that it is a nexus of interdefined norms and roles, and, to say that utterances are "in" that framework is to say that they are subject to and made possible by those norms. Again, the point generalizes easily: no behavior could be a sacrifice bunt except in terms of the norms and roles of baseball or a vote except within democratic institutions. As a rule, of course, institutions are not so "institutionalized" as these but work tacitly in the background: the nexus of equipmental roles is a case in point, but most of our other everyday norms are comparably inarticulate and inconspicuous. Notice that the institutional framework is itself holistic, but this should not be confused with the holism of the concrete context. Thus, the norms and roles of baseball (batters, pitchers, fielders, etc.) make sense in relation to one another and as a whole; likewise, the tactical moves and plays in a particular game situation (showing bunt, taking a big leadoff, playing the infield up) make sense in relation to one another and as a

13. Perhaps this position should be associated more specifically with what might be called "vintage Davidson," for more recently (see Davidson 1986) he has backed off the idea that linguistic communication depends on a language (or way of interpreting utterances) that is (i) systematic, (ii) shared by speaker and hearer, and (iii) conventional (or otherwise known in advance). Rather, speaker and hearer need only share a systematic "passing theory" for each utterance—a theory which each generates ad hoc on the basis of a "prior theory" of the other, plus current evidence.

Without argument, let me suggest (in what I take to be a Heideggerian vein) that this view founders on the assumption that people normally *interpret*—that is, produce "interpretations" of—one another's speech. (I deny that radical interpretation begins at home.) Instead, primarily and usually, they "know how to go on" (in the conversation and elsewhere) on the basis of what has gone before (in the conversation and elsewhere). This is analogous to the claim that carpenters do not normally "interpret" the feel of the hammer and the look of the nail but just carry on, fluidly and skillfully. Of course, in conversation as in carpentry, something can go awry, bringing one up short, and *then* interpretation (a passing theory, perhaps) may be needed and helpful.

Two points are here crucial (and hence most in need of argument). First, whatever talkers and carpenters have in advance (their normal skills and know-how), in terms of which they understand what is going on, must be different in kind from the interpretations or passing theories they come up with to handle difficulties, for otherwise, it would itself just be some prior (and presumably unconscious) interpretation or theory. Second, the sort of interpretation or theory that arises in response to routine glitches is essentially derivative and local; that is, it merely effects an adjustment or a "work-around" within the prior skillful repertoire, which remains fundamentally intact.

whole, but these are not the same. The former, the institutional framework as a whole, is, I believe, what Heidegger calls *world*.[14]

Third, interpreted behavior must always be apportioned among *accountable agents*. Imagine a scrambled (or alphabetized) list of all the sentences ever uttered on some distant planet, and consider the problem of making sense of them. We have already seen that they must be situated in their concrete contexts and also allocated to their respective languages. But in addition, they must be apportioned among distinct speakers—the ones *who said* them. Why? Prima facie, because rational coherence is basically intra-individual. Imagine a disagreement in which two people hold incompatible views, each trying to convince the other. If the claims are considered all together, they are a jumble of contradictions, saying first one thing and then the other; however, if they are apportioned to two interlocutors, then not only each position but also the exchange becomes coherently intelligible as point and counterpoint.

Indeed, the very idea of making a claim, inasmuch as that entails taking responsibility for what is said, either to back it up or to back off, requires there to be *someone* whose claim it is, and the obvious generalization extends not only to promises and apologies but equally to bunts and votes. In general, agents—the "who" of actions—must be understood as having *continuing* statuses, most basically in the form of lasting commitments and entitlements.[15] Thus, just as the institution of promising presupposes a single speaker who first promises and then must deliver, so democratic elections presuppose self-identical voters who first register and later vote, not to mention enduring candidates who first establish their credentials, then run for office, and, if elected, serve.

Two deeper questions, however, remain unanswered. First, not all norms are of the sort that entail responsibility—commitment and entitlement—on the part of that to which they apply. Thus, the parts of a complex organism or system can often be understood as having functional roles defined by

14. This interpretation is supported by the distinction Heidegger draws between the "world" as a totality of entities and the world as that wherein dasein "lives" and understands itself and in terms of which entities are freed (the latter is his official sense; for the former, he reserves quote marks) (*SZ* 64f, 85f), and perhaps also by the thesis that significance is the worldliness of the world (*SZ* 86f, 123). It must be conceded, however, that Heidegger's usage is neither entirely clear nor, I think, entirely consistent.

15. Compare Brandom 1983b.

norms of performance. For instance, a heart is "supposed to" pump blood, as much as a carburetor is "supposed to" mix fuel; these are their normal roles, and we may even call them "faulty" if they fail. But they are in no sense committed or obliged (still less, entitled) to fill these roles; hence they cannot be found culpable or blamed as irresponsible if they fail. The structure of the who—of accountable agents—is, by contrast, precisely that of entities who *are* responsible for what they do: they *can* be committed and entitled and hence held to account for how they perform. What we have yet to see, however, is *why* this should be so. What does radical interpretation, making sense of something as itself making sense of something else, have to do specifically with the sort of norms that entail responsibility?

Second, although it is clear enough from the examples how a commitment or entitlement can be regarded as a continuous line or link from one performance to another (a strand of obligation from promise to fulfillment, for instance), it is not yet clear what such strands can have to do with one another. If the registrant and voter must be selfsame (as the enduring entitlement implies), and likewise the claim maker and claim justifier, what further unity can tie these together? Why are not the various strands of accountable agency scattered and unrelated? What, in short, weaves the separate threads of continuous responsibility into the durable coats of personal identity?

Leaving these questions aside for the moment, we have nevertheless already exposed, among the presuppositions of radical interpretation, an essential structure in whatever can be so interpreted: to make sense as making sense of things, behavior must be concretely situated in the midst of those things in terms of a common institutional world and assigned to the agent who did it. This structure is by no means arbitrary (any more than that of context-language-speaker), for it is basically just spelling out what is implicit in normative holism. In articulating it, however, we have made an important transition from Davidson to Heidegger, for this structure is precisely *being-in-the-world*.

According to Heidegger, being-in-the-world is the basic structure, makeup, or constitution of dasein; it is what dasein basically amounts to.[16]

---

16. Heidegger's word is *Grundverfassung*, which Macquarrie and Robinson translate as "basic state," and Hofstadter translates as "basic constitution"; the latter is better. The term 'state' suggests a condition that something could be in or not be in and hence is incidental to the entity itself. Thus, a squadron might be in a state of readiness (or not), a

Such a thesis could, in principle, be informative either about being-in-the-world or about dasein, depending on which was understood already. Here, we have just elaborated an account of being-in-the-world, so the thesis tells us about dasein: in its basic makeup, dasein has the structure who/being-amidst/world, as spelled out in the presuppositions of radical interpretation.

On the face of it, this structure looks like a relation: being-amidst as a relation between self (agent, who) and world. The difficulty with such a view, however, emerges as soon as we ask about the relata. An institutional framework, like a language, is not a self-subsistent entity,[17] which can exist apart from concrete behavior and then be brought, through such behavior, into relation with selves or speakers. Rather, the framework or language is itself determinate only as an essential normative structure tacitly instituted within the whole of concretely situated social behavior. Similarly, agents or selves, understood as loci of accountability, are just a different essential structure instituted within that same behavior. The two structures presuppose and enable one another: behavioral norms require accountable agents if they are to be normative for anyone, and accountable agents require behavioral norms if they are to be accountable for anything. In effect, instead of a relation between two entities, being-in-the-world is a single entity with two interdependent structural aspects: self and world are like two sides of one coin, the actual "metal" of which is the whole of concrete being-amidst.

This reading illuminates an otherwise cryptic passage in Heidegger's introductory discussion of being-in as such:

---

closet might be in a disordered state (or not), a neon atom might be in an excited state (or not). By contrast, as Heidegger emphasizes, it is incoherent to say that dasein might be "in-the-world" or not. But, if we understand being-in-the-world as a "state," this only invites the question: *Why* does dasein *have* to *be* in that state? Why is the alternative incoherent? The problem is in thinking of dasein as one thing (a thinking substance, an ego, a person) and in-the-world-ness as another (a condition that it might-or must-be in). The root of the problem lies in misconceiving dasein: dasein is not something that *has* being-in-the-world, whether necessarily or contingently; rather, dasein *is* being-in-the-world. (My only hesitation in following Hofstadter in translating *Verfassung* as 'constitution' is avoiding conflict with the technical term *Konstitution* and all that is associated with it.)

17. Saying that it is not a self-subsistent entity is far from saying that it is not an entity at all.

But then what else presents itself with this phenomenon than the occurrent commercium *between* an occurrent subject and an occurrent object? Such an interpretation would get closer to the phenomenal content if it said: *dasein is the being* of this "between." Still, orientation to the "between" is misleading. It partakes uncritically in an ontologically indefinite assessment of the entities between which this between as such "is." The between is already conceived as the result of two occurrent entities coming together. (*SZ* 132)

And it is supported also by Heidegger's explicit account of self and world as jointly determining dasein. Self and world belong together in one entity, dasein. Self and world are not two entities, like subject and object, or like I and thou; rather, self and world are the basic determination of dasein itself in the unity of the structure of being-in-the-world (*GP* 422; cf. *GP* 237 and *SZ* 64, 364). Evidently, 'dasein' is not equivalent, not even extensionally, with 'person' or 'individual subject,' both because it (somehow) comprises more than one person and because it comprises more than just people. Yet, unquestionably, 'dasein' is Heidegger's technical term for whatever it is that is essentially distinctive of people, and, in each case, we *are* it. How can this all be?

I shall sketch an interpretation according to which dasein is a "living" (currently being lived) *way of life*. Thus, the Polynesian way of life, surviving (though not unchanged) on many Pacific islands, is Polynesian dasein. Likewise, the "yuppie" way of life, flourishing among the upper-middle classes, is yuppie dasein. Again, there is academic dasein, modern Western dasein, swashbuckling-fighter-pilot dasein, and so on. By contrast, the Aztec and ancient Egyptian ways of life have died out—there is no more Aztec or ancient Egyptian dasein.[18] Like natural languages, ways of life evolve slowly through the years and vary gradually across the landscape; like dialects, lingos, and professional jargon, many ways of life can intermingle and overlap in a single community and even a single individual.[19]

18. In later work, Haugeland augmented this interpretation to give central consideration to the characterization of dasein as the entity that understands being (i.e., a living way of life that embodies an understanding of being). Some of these examples (yuppie dasein, swashbuckling-fighter-pilot dasein, and probably academic dasein) would surely be ruled out under this more restrictive, ontological conception.—*Ed.*

19. This collagelike structure of slowly varying, broader and narrower, crisscrossing unities and subunities is evident not only in dasein as such and languages but also, for

Nevertheless, a living way of life, dasein, is an *entity*—something that there *is*. It is, to be sure, no sort of material thing or property of things; nor is it an abstract entity like a universal or a set; nor, indeed, is a way of life plausibly understood as an event, a process, a pattern, a state, or any other traditional category, ideal or real—any more than a "living" language is. As entities, ways of life do not sit well with the motto "No entity without identity," for their "identity conditions" are anything but well defined. They are definitely mundane, ephemeral, and contingent, yet they are not physical or tangible; like a language, a way of life can be well known, yet it is not obvious how it can be a cause or an effect. In sum, though ways of life in some way *are*, their ontology is surely peculiar. Given all that Heidegger says about the ontology of dasein, such peculiarity seems a point in favor of the interpretation.

If dasein is a living way of life, with being-in-the-world as its basic makeup, what is an *individual person?* What can Heidegger mean when he says we *are* dasein? Remembering the constitutive structure of the who— accountable speakers or agents—we can, I think, take a cue from linguists, who have extrapolated the notion of a local dialect to its logical limit: a living language, as spoken by only one speaker, is an *idiolect.* By analogy, a living way of life, as lived by only one agent or "liver,"[20] would be an idio-way-of-life, or *idio-dasein*—your way of life or mine, for instance.[21] Idio-dasein, like any dasein, has the full structure of being-in-the-world: concrete being-amidst in terms of common institutions to which this one agent is accountable. In fact, of course, an idio-way-of-life is nothing other than the peculiar integration and adjustment of various "public" ways of life as idiosyncratically adopted and lived by one person. To say that we *are* dasein is to say that each of us *is* his or her *own* personal living way of life: we

---

instance, in professions, religious traditions, literary genres, Kuhnian disciplinary matrices, and so on. Needless to say, each of these can be seen as a kind of microcosm of being-in-the-world; indeed, Heidegger explicitly says that sciences (*SZ* 11; cf. 357) and language (*BP* 296) have dasein's sort of being (existence in his technical sense).

20. Barbara Haugeland, psychologist and pâté chef, says, "Where there's a life, there's a liver."

21. Haugeland does not retain this analogy to idiolects or the term 'idio-dasein' in subsequent work. He does retain the preferred term substituted below, 'cases' of dasein. Moreover, he takes Heidegger to use the term 'others' for individual people as entities that are not themselves dasein (they are what Heidegger calls "intraworldly" entities, which dasein is not), although they are constitutive aspects of dasein as its units of accountability.—*Ed.*

are what we do.[22] For convenience and euphony, I prefer to call idio-daseins *cases of* dasein; so, people are cases of dasein—hence, dasein (viz., their[23] dasein).

We have seen that the whole of concrete being-amidst has, on opposite sides as it were, the two interdependent structures, who and world. This tells us, in general terms, that people live and interact accountably, according to common norms, and, in so doing, let equipment be as filling roles. But it does not provide any detail about *how* they do that. How is it that cases of dasein are in the midst of things—busily living their lives—that constitutes the overall structure of being-in-the-world and makes sense of things? Heidegger works out a three-part analysis of being-in as such, an analysis which, at the same time, gives the ontological constitution of disclosedness.[24] The terms of this analysis are *Befindlichkeit, Rede,* and *Verstehen*—which I translate as *findingness, telling,* and *understanding.* In the course of explicating (interpreting) the analysis itself, the point of the translations should also become apparent. Heidegger says that each of these constitutive items must reflect the full structure of who/being–amidst/world.

In asking how dasein is in the midst of things, it will be helpful to resume, as a simplified comparison, our earlier example of chess playing. If we take it in the sense of "living" chess—chess as currently being played—it

---

22. Compare *SZ* 126, 239, and 322 and *GP* 226.

23. This possessive is the one expressed also in Heidegger's *'Jemeinigkeit,'* "in each case mineness" *(SZ* 41f.); it is implicit also in the slogan "We *are* what we do (cited earlier), for what we "do" is, of course, *our* behavior and roles. This "ownership" of our selves and our actions, grounded in accountability, is not the same as, but is the condition for the possibility of, that distinctive self-understanding that Heidegger calls ownedness or authenticity *(Eigentlichkeit).*

24. Compare *SZ* 133 and 180. Note that Heidegger's use of 'in' is seriously ambiguous. At *SZ* 53, he distinguishes three constitutive moments in the structure of being-in-the-world: the "in the world," the "who" (or self; cf. *SZ* 190), and being-in as such. This division is more or less echoed in the topics of the next three chapters and again in the definition of care as the being of dasein *(SZ* 192, 249). But 'in' means fundamentally different things in the first and third items. In the latter, being-in as such, it means engaged and caught up in concrete activities and communities; its modes are the amidst and amongst (of *Sein-bei* and *Mitsein).* But the 'in' of the first item, the "in the world," can mean no such thing, for the world *is* not a concrete situation but rather an institutional framework of norms and roles; here the 'in' is the same as (or a generalization of) the 'in' of 'in English': "Hobbes wrote both in English and in Latin."

has, in its limited way, the full structure of being-in-the-world: accountable players, in the midst of play, in terms of the common chess framework. Thus, our questions about being in the midst of things in "real life" can be introduced and elucidated by simpler parallel questions about being in the midst of play—that is, in the midst of a game.

How, then, is dasein "in the midst of" living its life? Or, to begin with the simplified version, how is chess play in the midst of a game? Well, in the first place, in the midst of a game, play always finds itself already in some definite position—the current position; chess play always takes place in the current position. Living (dasein), likewise, always finds itself already situated; being in the midst of things is being, in each case, already in some definite situation. The expression "finds itself" is Heidegger's.[25] With it he is clearly adverting to the constitutive item in being-amidst that he calls *Befindlichkeit*: that essential character of living dasein that, in each case, it always finds itself already situated. Hence my *"findingness."*[26]

What is it for life or play to find itself already situated in the midst of things, and how does it reflect the full structure of being-in-the-world? It is, first, to find itself confronted with things to be dealt with, ongoing business to be taken care of. Thus, there is the business of your pawn threatening my rook—which I can deal with by capturing your pawn with my knight. This is the way findingness reflects being-amidst as such; Heidegger expresses it by saying that findingness first makes possible a self-directing upon—that is, dealing with. Such confronting, however, makes sense only insofar as things confronted are found already significant, such that they can call for and admit of determinate dealings and need to and can be

---

25. See, for example, *SZ* 135, 188, 340, and 346.

26. The awkward fact that 'findingness' is not an English word is somewhat mitigated by the corresponding fact that *Befindlichkeit* is not a German word. Macquarrie and Robinson's translation, 'state-of-mind,' is really hopeless, in that *Befindlichkeit* is neither a state nor of mind. Kisiel's 'disposition' has the advantage that mood or attunement *(Stimmung)* sounds natural as an ontical mode, but it risks suggesting subjectivity and in any case conflicts with an established philosophical usage. Dreyfus's and Blattner's 'affectivity' has the same advantage as 'disposition' and also accords with Heidegger's remarks about things mattering to dasein and sensory affect, but it sounds too much like Kant's 'receptivity' and thus again suggests being on one side of a subject/object distinction. Guignon's 'situatedness,' which I like the best of these, lacks only the sense of dasein "finding itself" situated, which is relevant to *Befindlichkeit* as disclosure. Finally, for what it is worth, 'findingness' is more or less "literal."

taken care of. Thus, your pawn's angle on my rook is, as a chess position, a threat and, as a threat, important; likewise, as an opportunity, my knight's angle on your pawn. This is the way findingness reflects the world; Heidegger expresses it by saying that findingness grounds the possibility of things mattering. But in concrete confronting, things do not just "call" for attention; rather, they can matter only because dasein is somehow stuck with them as they stand. The only way I can carry on with my game is by dealing with the current position, including your pawn and my rook; I cannot but deal with that position (hence it matters) because it is the position I find myself, so to speak, "plunked down in." For dasein in each case, the current situation is, inevitably, the first situation of the rest of its life. This is how the who is reflected in findingness; Heidegger expresses it by saying that findingness discloses dasein in its thrownness.

Telling (Rede) is the articulation of significance or intelligibility, both in the sense of separating or carving up and in the sense of expressing in words. The carving up is not a matter of focusing attention or arbitrary subdividing but an essentially public or shared way of distinguishing determinate entities in determinate regards. Thus, in playing chess, I deal with your pawn and my rook (two pieces) with regard to the one's threatening the other and as pieces that you likewise deal with. *Because* the intelligibility of the position is articulated in this shared way, I can say to you "Your pawn is threatening my rook," and you could reply, "I'm sorry" (or remain tellingly silent), but equally, I think, *because* we share that language, the position can have that shared intelligibility.[27] Though Heidegger does not make this explicit, we may surmise that concrete being-amidst is reflected in telling what the current position is, the world in telling what a rook or a threat is, and the who in the sharing or communicating.[28] Needless to say, findingness presupposes such telling, and vice versa.

I am inclined to believe, though there is almost no basis for it in the text, that the ur-phenomenon of telling is telling whether behavior does or does

---

27. I am not sure that Heidegger would accept the second clause, but he should, and I suspect he does.

28. 'Telling' is a better English term for this phenomenon than 'talk' or 'discourse' even though it is not really correct as a translation of *Rede* because it is broader and in the direction of Heidegger's meaning. Expressly, I can tell you not only about the position but also how to play, what to do, how I feel, and what someone said; without expression, I can tell your pawn from my rook, that the rook is threatened, and what to do about it.

not accord with the common norms—in effect, telling right from wrong. Such telling would indeed be the originary articulation of significance and would, at the same time, be fundamental to the possibility of correctness (e.g., of assertions). It might also account for Heidegger's architectonic vacillation between falling and telling, for falling is essentially "falling in with" public norms as the determination of right. Finally, this interpretation would connect telling directly with norms, tightly integrating it therefore with the rest of my account.

Understanding, Heidegger says, is projecting in terms of possibilities. But projecting is not predicting the future direction of things, nor is it planning or sketching out a project (even implicitly), and possibilities are not things or states of affairs that might or might not be or become actual.[29] Rather, *possibilities* in Heidegger's sense are the new options and alternatives opened up by norms: roles that things can play and ways that they can play them. Thus, being a pawn and therefore moving as a pawn does (e.g., attacking rooks) are possibilities in the world of chess; being a hammer and therefore being used to drive in nails are possibilities in the world of carpentry. What, then, is "projecting" in terms of possibilities?

Well, how is it that equipment can have the possibilities that it has—that is, have a role? The world, the common institutional framework of roles, is, of course, prerequisite to any entity having a role. But the world itself does not assign any concrete entities to any determinate equipmental roles; nor do intraworldly entities adopt their roles themselves. Rather, it is only in virtue of dasein's concrete being-amidst—selves actively dealing with things and taking care of business—that those things have roles. Dasein deals with things *as* having roles and proper uses, and in virtue of this they *do* have them. You and I and all chess players move rooks only along ranks and files, and we all expect each other to do likewise. We do so move and expect because that is how rooks are supposed to move, but *also*, that is how rooks are supposed to move because that is what we all do and expect. In dasein's practical know-how and sense of propriety, tacitly manifested in concrete taking care of business, dealing with things and one another, those things are effectively "given" roles and understood in terms of them;

---

29. More carefully put, these are not the *basic* phenomena of projection and possibility; in the ontologically derivative case of explaining occurrent (*vorhanden*) entities and events, however, projecting can, perhaps, amount to predicting, and possibility can be the same as not necessarily not actual.

or, in Heidegger's words, dasein *projects* things in terms of possibilities. In English, we can make a pun on 'projecting' and say that, according to Heidegger, understanding is tacit *role casting.*

Dasein's practical casting of the entities it finds itself in the midst of, in terms of publicly articulated roles, just *is* its *making sense of* those entities. Earlier we saw *that*, without seeing *why*, radical interpretation presupposes the sort of norms that entail an accountable who; here we see why. It is only because the who is accountable for how it deals with equipment that dasein's concrete being-amidst can institute the normative framework in terms of which that equipment then becomes intelligible as playing roles. Equipmental roles, unlike the functional roles of organic and mechanical subsystems, are essentially *instituted:* they arise only in conjunction with norms of use—that is, norms to which not the equipment itself but its *users* are accountable.[30] Because—and only because—accountable dasein institutes equipmental roles (tacitly, in socially transmitted skillful mastery) does dasein understand equipment as equipment (in its skillful employment). In sum, it is only because dasein is normatively accountable for how it uses equipment, hence (in that use) institutes intelligible roles, that it can itself be understood as understanding—that is, be radically interpreted.[31]

Dasein's originary understanding is active, tacit in the normal exercise of socially transmitted skillful mastery. It reflects being-amidst as such because it is only in the course of concrete intraworldly dealings that equipment is cast into its worldly roles and thereby made sense of as what it is; Heidegger calls this the *fore-grasp* of understanding. Active understanding reflects the world in that it is worldly norms to which the skillful behavior is accountable and hence worldly roles into which the equipment is cast; the institutional

30. In subsequent work, Haugeland takes such socially accountable institution of roles to be necessary but not sufficient for dasein as understanding being. Dasein also requires the possibility of resolutely taking over responsibility ("owned" existence) for those roles and norms and their mutual intelligibility on the part of its constituent "cases."—*Ed.*

31. By the same token, not every way of having to do with things or being directed toward them is role casting or understanding in this Heideggerian sense. Thus, if a tiger homes in on an antelope or a guided missile homes in on a target, neither one is behaving accountably, in accord with collectively instituted norms and roles, in terms of which it could cast anything *as* an antelope or a target. Because they are not themselves accountable to norms, they cannot "inhabit" an institutional framework in terms of which things could make sense to them. (The tiger/antelope example is Okrent's—see 1988, chapter 5—but my interpretation of it is contrary to his.)

framework is always already the background in terms of which any active understanding is possible. Heidegger calls this the *fore-having*. Active understanding reflects the who in that, in each case, skillful dealings belong to and are guided by some job or endeavor undertaken by an accountable agent—something somebody is doing; Heidegger calls this the *fore-sight*.

When Heidegger introduces his account of understanding as projecting in terms of possibilities, he speaks first and foremost of self-understanding. On the present reading, self-understanding would be casting oneself into roles; part of my self-understanding, for instance, might be my casting myself as a schoolteacher or a chess player. These roles which a case of dasein plays determine not what but *who* it is; even though they are socially instituted and worldly, they differ fundamentally from equipmental roles precisely in that cases of dasein are accountable for how they perform.[32] Thus, if a hammer fails to fill its role properly, it may be defective, but it is not reprehensible; on the other hand, a teacher who missed classes or a chess player who broke the rules would be culpable and blameworthy. To cast oneself in such a role is to *take on* the relevant norms—both in the sense of undertaking to abide by them and in the sense of accepting responsibility for failings.

Dasein's abiding self-understanding—casting itself into roles—is the essential "continuity" that is presupposed by accountability. Promising is possible as an institution only insofar as cases of dasein who make promises can, by virtue of having undertaken that commitment, be expected to keep them; in other words, it depends on cases of dasein *who* cast themselves (understand themselves) as promisers and hold themselves to it. Likewise, mere moving of the pieces of a chess set in accord with the rules, even on purpose, does not automatically amount to chess playing—one might be acting, unaware that it is a game, or indifferent to the outcome. For the move to constitute a chess game, the players must not only move according to the rules but also cast *themselves* as chess players. Thus, dasein's self-understanding is essential to any understanding and hence to disclosing being-in-the-world as such.

Self-casting into roles, however, can never be simple. Even so focused a commitment as keeping a single promise entails anticipating and satisfying prerequisites, recognizing and overcoming obstacles, being able to tell

32. On his later view, cases of dasein are not only socially accountable but also possibly individually responsible for the intelligibility of these roles and their own "occupations" in relation to those equipmental roles.—*Ed.*

when the promise has been kept, and sticking with it until done. Each of these, in multifarious ways, can also require normatively accountable dealing with the world and thus a reidentifiable who. But if they are all to be understood together, as the responsibilities of a promiser, then these separate threads of accountability must be strands in a *single* who. More complicated social roles, such as running for and holding political office, obviously integrate innumerable strands of commitment and entitlement into individual accountable agents. What is more, many of these *same* strands will also be integral to complex roles, such as upstanding citizen, responsible parent, loyal patriot, and so on; thus, the same individual simultaneously plays many roles. In order that anything be understandable as a claim, a checkmate, a bunt, a vote, and so on, it is essential that not only the equipment but also the people be cast in the relevant roles: they must understand themselves as responsible role players.

Insofar as cases of dasein make sense of themselves, we have instances of the formula "*Y* making sense of *Y*," with *Y* in two of the argument places of the radical interpretation formula, "*X* making sense of *Y* making sense of *Z*." But, as we saw earlier, there are two ways in which *Y* can occupy a second argument place in the larger formula. On one reading, *Y* is substituted in the formula for *Z* (things); that is, *Y* makes sense of itself in more or less the way that it makes sense of things—by casting itself in terms of publicly defined worldly roles (and in more or less the same way that everybody else casts it in those roles). This, I think, is what Heidegger means by everyday or "unowned" self-understanding and disclosedness in the mode of publicness. On the other reading, however, *Y* would be substituted in the formula for *X* (Davidson's anthropologist); in that case, *Y* makes sense of itself *as* itself making sense of things—*Y* understands itself not at all as a thing but as a *sense maker.* This possibility, implicit in the story as told so far but not here worked out, is, I believe, what Heidegger means by *owned* self-understanding and disclosedness in the mode of resoluteness.

TWO

Dasein Disclosed

Proposal for a Guggenheim Fellowship

I will write a book interpreting the substantive ("nondestructive") half of Heidegger's *Being and Time*, including the third division (which was, in fact, never written). While by no means "introductory," the work will be written so as to maximize its accessibility to non-Heideggerians, including philosophers whose main background is in so-called analytic philosophy and philosophically sophisticated nonphilosophers. (I have a lot of experience teaching this material at a high level to such audiences.)

My interpretation is distinctive (controversial, "original") in several ways, even aside from the (so far as I know) unprecedented inclusion of the third division. In the first place, I insist that, though what Heidegger calls 'dasein' represents the "human dimension" of his account, the term is not coextensive (never mind synonymous) with 'person.' Rather, dasein is the understanding of being that is embodied in the concrete living of a human way of life. In other words, it is—initially and usually—a "cultural" understanding, whether taken broadly (ancient Greek, medieval Christian), or as specific to a field or discipline (mechanical engineering, chemistry).

This reading is motivated in many ways, of which I mention three. First, it makes excellent sense of Heidegger's pivotal thesis that being-in-the-world—a unitary phenomenon consisting of the world, the "who" (roughly, people), and being-in as such—is dasein's basic makeup. And that, in turn, enables a new and illuminating account of being-in itself as the "heart of the matter" in a way that decomposes and partially displaces the traditional (modern) conception of consciousness. For being-in is the primitive locus of dasein's responsiveness, discrimination, and understanding; yet it is essentially public and out in the open. (This also affords some useful "compare and contrast" points with contemporary philosophy of mind and language—especially Davidson, McDowell, and Brandom.)

Second, taking dasein to be an understanding of being that is initially and mostly cultural makes possible a textually and philosophically rigorous account of Heidegger's famous idea of ownedness (Eigentlichkeit: usually translated "authenticity") and its integral connections with anxiety, death, conscience, and responsibility—his so-called existentialism. For, on the one hand, each of the latter is said to individualize dasein, which would not make any sense if "daseins" were just individuals, and, on the other hand, if dasein is initially something public, then it makes perfect sense to say that individuals can own it—make it their own, in the sense of taking responsibility for it—and thereby individualize it.

Finally, third, the foregoing together open up a new and fruitful approach to what I regard as the paramount exegetical puzzle concerning the published portions of *Being and Time*. The official and abiding aim of the work as a whole is to "reawaken the question of the sense of being"—a project Heidegger also calls "fundamental ontology." But, if that is what he is trying to do, what is all that "existentialism" doing in there? (I must say, it astonishes me how most readings of Heidegger manage to ignore this glaring interpretive issue.) Yet I am (I believe) able to show quite directly how the existentialist themes are not only relevant but actually crucial to the ontology—given my explication of dasein.

In broadest outline—and anticipating a later topic—it works like this. An understanding of being makes possible what Heidegger calls "comportment toward entities as entities," including (but not limited to) making true claims about them. Now, claims about entities are ordinarily justified by observations, experiments, reports from others, inferences, and so on. But, as everybody knows, all of those are subject to error. So, careful investigation requires double-checking, corroboration, and the like. Those, however, make sense only if two other things are in place. First, there must be an antecedent grasp of how multiple results would have to be related if all were correct. And, there must be a commitment among investigators not to accept as all true any combination of results that are mutually incompatible (that is, collectively impossible). (This commitment might be a social or scientific norm.)

A public understanding of being—that is (according to me), unowned dasein—consists of (1) normal ways of finding out what is the case; (2) normal constraints on what is possible; and (3) a general norm not to accept as true anything that would be impossible. This is the minimum prerequisite for "ontical" comportment and truth.

So far, no existentialism. But the threefold structure just described is potentially unstable: the third clause makes a demand that abiding by the first two might not meet. In the face of such a challenge, there are basically two options. The "normal" option is to adjust and tinker until the problem goes away, and that is fine, if it works. The second option—which only some individuals can even contemplate—is to relinquish that whole way of life. To accept this issue as a personal possibility is to take over responsibility for that dasein and, in that sense, make it one's own. Such responsibility still includes, of course, striving to make the way of life work, if at all feasible— while also holding the other option constantly open. But this is the basic structure of "resolute being-toward-death," around which all the existentialist themes revolve.

Heidegger goes on to interpret dasein's being in terms of what he calls "originary time": resoluteness is the originary phenomenon of the future; inheriting the antecedent constraints on possibility is the originary past; and the comportments toward entities that they make intelligible are the present. Resoluteness and originary time take up about half of Heidegger's second division. The other half comprises three arguments "applying" the account of originary time, mainly in ways that show he is entitled to call it that. Though these are important, and I have things to say about them, I want to devote the remainder of my remarks to division III.

It is in this division that the question of the sense of being is to get "reawakened" and (provisionally) addressed. Since, however, there is no actual text, an interpretation has to rely on the "momentum" of the extant divisions, coupled with other things Heidegger said in the same period. Fortunately, there is quite a bit of the latter—the most important of which is "The Basic Problems of Phenomenology" (the lecture course delivered shortly after *Being and Time* was published). Though it too remained less than half finished, what we have does at least formulate the being-question in four "basic problems": the ontological difference, the regions of being, its articulation, and its truth character.

Despite the fact that Heidegger himself did not get around to "solving" these problems, I think I can now see how all four have to go. Here is the barest inkling. First, the sense of being is its intelligibility: it is what an understanding of being "grasps" or "gets." Though there are different such senses (for different fields, e.g.), they all have a common threefold structure. As we saw earlier, any comportment toward entities as entities presupposes a grasp of the distinction between what is and is not possible for them. Possibilities, however, always have to do with concomitant, concrete determinations (properties and relations, e.g.). But to say that some combination is (or is not) possible is nothing other than to say that it could (or could not) be manifested in something dasein "lets be" (acknowledges and acquiesces in). And this trio amounts to a précis of an account of the articulation of being: essence, accidents, actuality.

The earlier anticipation also previewed half of Heidegger's point about the truth character of being. The other half concerns the difference that resoluteness makes. The initial version, grounded entirely in social norms, leaves ordinary ("ontical") truths relative to each existing field or culture. Taking over responsibility for the empirical viability of the whole, however, brings those norms themselves—albeit indirectly—under genuine empirical control. In other words, the rest of the truth character of being is, in effect, an answer to cultural relativism.

The regions of being correspond to ontologically different sorts of entities: equipment, people, numbers, mental phenomena, the entities investigated by physics, and so on. It might seem that these distinctions are easily associated with the different sorts of possibilities and properties the respective entities have. And so they are. But Heidegger maintains that the fundamental differences lie in the respective ways of being ("actuality"), which, in turn, have to do with "letting be." Thus, to acknowledge something as available for a certain role is to let it be in the way that equipment is; to acknowledge something as effective (making a difference) in a dynamical system is to let it be in the way that physical particles and fields are and so on. These differences in ways of letting be are the ultimate basis of regional distinctions.

Finally, the ontological difference itself is grounded in what Heidegger calls "the temporality [Temporalität] of being." Temporality is just originary time but considered more fully in the light of its horizons—which is to say, its finitude. ('Horizon' means boundary or limit.) For each understanding of being, there is one horizon apiece for past, present, and future. Very roughly, they are that some possible/impossible distinctions (and not others) are already in place; that some determinations (and not others) are concomitantly found; and that some ways of letting-be (and not others) turn out to be workable. The "some . . . (and not others)" refrain marks the finitude. The already/concomitantly/turn-out-to-be thread marks the timeishness. This threefold timeish structure of finitude, however, is the distilled essence of the whole account of understandings of being as making comportment toward entities possible. But that is as much as to say that it makes the distinction between being and entities itself possible—and that distinction is precisely the ontological difference. But, with the explication of temporal finitude in its essential relations to dasein and being, the substantive project of *Being and Time* is also brought to completion.

I have the bulk of the division I material already drafted in the form of one long document and portions of several essays. The greater part of the interpretation of division II is also already written up—though not in book-like prose—in recent essays (some unpublished). I have part III roughly organized in my head but not much on paper yet. I do, in fact, expect to complete it all in one fellowship year.

Inasmuch as the interpretation is novel in several conspicuous ways, it might make some ripples in Heidegger circles. Inasmuch as it will be written, to the extent possible, with non-Heideggerians in mind, it might contribute to the ongoing dismantling of the old analytic/continental split. Insofar as it exhibits *Being and Time* as strikingly deep and interesting, it might encourage more noninsular work on Heidegger.

Introduction

Heidegger was born; he was a Nazi; he died.[1]

In the meantime, he published *Being and Time* (1963; English translation, 1962), the most celebrated and possibly the most important philosophical work of the twentieth century. The present essay is an exposition
and interpretation of part I of that work, with special consideration for readers trained mainly in recent Anglo-American traditions. The latter does not
mean that Heidegger will be recast as an "analytic" philosopher in disguise—
far from it. Rather, it indicates only a kind of background and vocabulary
that will be taken for granted.

Two "technical" difficulties confront any such project. First, *Being and
Time* was never actually finished. We know from the introduction that it
was to have had two main parts, each comprising three divisions. Roughly,
part I would have presented Heidegger's own philosophical position, and
then part II would have been a critical reexamination of Kant, Descartes,
and Aristotle in light of those results. But all that ever appeared (under the
title *Being and Time*) were the first two divisions of part I. What is worse,

1. Haugeland customarily opened his courses on Heidegger with this line, implicitly
alluding to Heidegger's opening of his own 1924 Aristotle course with the remark that,
"Regarding the personality of a philosopher, our only interest is that he was born at a
certain time, that he worked, and that he died" (Heidegger 2002/2009, 5/4). Haugeland
also thereby announced both his acknowledgement of Heidegger's disturbing political
involvements beginning in the 1930s and his insistence that Heidegger's politics do not
substantially bear upon the issues he takes up in this book.—*Ed.*

there is reason to suspect that even these may have been rushed into print. Heidegger agreed to release division I only when it became clear that he would need more publications to secure a promotion he sought; he let go of the second division only after the first alone was deemed insufficient. (There may at one time also have been a draft of some or all of division III, but, if so, it seems not to have survived.)

Fortunately, a number of other texts from the same period shed light on what he was thinking. Most important are the (now published) transcripts of his lecture courses, including, especially, the summer 1927 course titled "The Basic Problems of Phenomenology," which is described (in its own first footnote) as "a new elaboration of Division III of Part I of Being and Time." Alas, this course also accomplished less than half of what it set out to do. Nevertheless, along with several others, it tells us a lot about the nature of the overall project and how it was to have been carried out. In addition, there are, especially, the 1929 book, *Kant and the Problem of Metaphysics* (Heidegger 1991) (essentially a revision of part II, division I), and the roughly contemporaneous essays, "What Is Metaphysics?," "On the Essence of Ground," and "On the Essence of Truth."

The aim here is a philosophical account of *Being and Time* as we have it and, on the basis of the momentum developed there, as well as what can be learned from these further sources, a tentative projection of what might have occurred in part I, division III—in effect, an interpretation of the entire "positive" part of *Being and Time*.

The second "technical difficulty" is a consequence of writing in English: the problem of translation. As is well known (not to say notorious), Heidegger pushes his native German to its expressive limits by making subtle use not only of nuance and etymology but also of neologism. Though English is basically a Germanic language, the modern forms have diverged significantly; in particular, our vocabulary now exhibits a large (if somewhat irregular) influence from the French. As a result, many of Heidegger's most striking achievements in German are awkward or even impossible to reproduce in ordinary English.

The problem is only compounded by the fact that the many translators of Heidegger's works have so far failed to settle on any "standard" renditions of his distinctive terms and constructions and have moreover (in my estimation) often made poor choices. Accordingly, I have adopted the following policy: (i) I will, to the best of my ability, rethink all important issues of translation from the ground up; (ii) to the extent consonant with that, I will adopt conventions already extant in the literature (a few of which are my own earlier suggestions); but (iii), when necessary, I will not shy away from new inventions—including some that are, undeniably, unlovely—always explaining them as fully as possible. In other words, the text that follows contains some funny-looking English, but I hope that its strangeness is repaid in precision and clarity.

The Being Question

Heidegger declares the aim of his magnum opus on page one:[1]

> The intention of the following treatise is a concrete working out of the question of the sense of 'being.' (SZ 1)

This purpose must be born in mind throughout, not just because it is easy to lose track of in the course of preparatory analyses but rather and mainly because those analyses themselves are properly intelligible only in light of it. Thus, the famous accounts of everydayness, authenticity, death, temporality, and so on really are essential steps toward working out the "being-question" and liable to be misunderstood apart from it.

That question, however, is not easy to see. At first blush, it looks like a semantic or even logical inquiry: what does the verb 'to be' *mean?* And that invites the patient reply that (aside from its role as an auxiliary) this verb has three main uses in English: to assert actuality ("There is a black dog"); to assert a predicate of a subject ("That dog is black"); and to assert identity ("This black dog is the one that bit you"). But, whatever the merits of such recitations, they do not begin to address the being-question, for they explain neither why those three should turn out to be senses of a single verb nor—and more to the point—what determinate understanding any of them expresses.

---

1. Unless otherwise noted, all page citations to Heidegger's works are to the *Gesamtausgabe* editions, and all of the translations are my own.

That these matters are not trivial can be brought home by noticing how *different* the accounts would have to be for different sorts of entity. Thus, for a *dog* to be—that is, for it to be at all, at a given time—is for it to be alive. It does not come to be until it is born, and it ceases to be when it perishes. A particular ball game, on the other hand, is while it is being played by some players, and it ceases to be only when they (or their successors) give it up. Yet again, a gemstone comes to be when a certain atomic lattice forms under special conditions, and then it persists until that lattice somehow breaks down. Numbers, by further contrast, can *be* even though they have no mass or location, participate in no causal relations, and seem, in some sense, to last forever.

Now, though deliberately motley, this selection is not altogether random. For the point is to exhibit, simultaneously, the scope for ontological variety, along with several dimensions of consistency within that variety. To do so is to make a start on the being-question. In order to spell that out, however, it will be helpful to introduce some special Heideggerian terminology.

1.1 THE ONTOLOGICAL DIFFERENCE

First, we must make a principled distinction between *being* and *entities*—what Heidegger calls the *ontological difference:* "The being of entities 'is' not itself an entity" (*SZ* 6; cf. *GP* 22, 102). This is perhaps the most characteristic and fundamental of all Heideggerian theses. The ability to draw this distinction, he says, is simultaneously what distinguishes people from animals and what makes philosophy possible (*GP* 454–455). To understand the thesis, it is necessary to understand the words in which it is expressed.[2]

Entities are all and only what there is. That is just what the word means: to *be* is to be an entity, and vice versa. So, *everything* that there *is* at all is

---

2. The German word here translated as 'being' *(das Sein)* is a noun formed from the infinitive of the verb 'to be' *(sein);* the word translated as 'entity' *(das Seiendes)* is another noun formed from the present participle of the same verb. Thus they are distinct but closely related. In English, it is not so convenient to form two distinct nouns from the same verb. Accordingly, following Macquarrie and Robinson, I use 'entity' (which comes from the present participle of the corresponding Latin verb) for the second of Heidegger's two nouns. But, given that, I see no reason to follow them in capitalizing 'being.'

an entity—and nothing else is—by definition. Likewise, anything that there ever was or will be, was or will be an entity; everything that there could be or could have been, could be or could have been an entity—and so on. To be is to be an entity, and vice versa, period.

Being, by contrast, "is" *not* an entity. It is not the case that being *is*—at all, ever. This is why there are shudder quotes around the word 'is' in the statement of the thesis: since *entities* are all and only what there *is*, it is strictly inappropriate even to use this verb in speaking of *being.* Yet, since practically all we ever deal with and talk about are entities (or possible entities or former entities and so on), ordinary language is geared almost entirely to this use and therefore affords hardly any resources for talking about being. (Hence the need for awkward devices like those quote marks.)

Even apart from linguistic difficulties, however, the ontological difference is hard to grasp. Does it mean that being "is" *nothing?* Here we must tread carefully. If by 'nothing' we mean no *entity,* then, yes, of course, the point is precisely that being "is" no entity—not even an abstract, ideal, intangible, ethereal, or otherwise strange and elusive one. Being "is" not anything that there is *at all.*

It does not follow, however, that the being-question has no topic or no answer or that there is no need—or no room—for investigation or understanding in this vicinity. It follows only that what we have to investigate and understand "is" no *entity.* Being "is" always the being *of* entities, but it "is" never itself one of them.

An analogy, albeit an imperfect one, may help to convey the structure of the situation. The pertinence of being to entities is something like that of a nation's constitution to its statutes and government. The constitution, in effect, defines what it is for the government to enact a statute and, at the same time, imposes strict conditions on which candidate statutes it could legitimately enact, allowing some as constitutional while ruling out others as unconstitutional. Thus, the constitution both establishes the legislative process by which potential statutes become actual and constrains the allowable results of that process. In so doing, it gives determinate sense to the very notions of legitimate enactment and positive law.

The constitution itself, therefore, cannot be just another such statute or set of statutes—at least, not in the same sense or at the same level. Since it first establishes the process of enactment, it cannot itself have been so enacted, and since it stipulates the constraints on enactable laws, it cannot itself be so constrained. The constitution must be in some sense "prior" to whatever processes and statutes it first gives determinate sense to, and so its own sense and status must be fundamentally different from theirs. Mimicking Heidegger's phrase, one might be tempted to call this the "constitutional difference": the constitution is not itself a (constitutionally enacted) statute.

But the analogy between a national constitution and the being of entities is still not quite right; for a constitution, whatever determinate form it takes, is itself still an *entity*—something that there is. To be sure, it is not an entity of the same sort and status as the processes and statutes constituted in its terms, but it is an entity all the same.

The right way to construct the analogy is to advert instead to the constitution*ality* and enacted*ness*—which is to say, the *being* constitutionally enacted—of those statutes. But then it is not just an analogy anymore. Being constitutionally enacted is not itself an *entity* of any sort but rather the being of the statutes so enacted. It is what makes the difference between there indeed being those statutes at all and there not being those statutes at all. (The statutes themselves, of course, are the relevant entities in this example.)

Thus, when we say that being constitutionally enacted is not itself constitutionally enacted, we are not mimicking the ontological difference but rather formulating a specific version of it.

To emphasize this difference and also to facilitate discussion, Heidegger reserves the term 'ontical' as a contrasting counterpart to 'ontological.' So, just as 'ontological' means "pertaining to *being*," 'ontical' means "pertaining to *entities*."[3] Almost everything we ever think about, work on, hope for, or do is ontical. There is nothing disparaging in this contrast: ontical questions and pursuits, ontical knowledge and understanding, ontical insights and confusions—these are the warp and weft of all our days.

They are just not the business of philosophy. According to Heidegger, the being-question itself is "the fundamental question of philosophy" and "being is the proper and sole theme of philosophy" (*SZ* 27, *GP* 15). Philosophy just is ontology: the science of being (*SZ* 38, *GP* 17).

But what sort of problem can an ontological investigation address? With all that has been said about how extraordinary the being-question is—we

---

3. Thus, the ontological difference might equally well have been called the "ontological/ontical difference."

cannot even use the word 'is' to formulate it[4]—how can it so much as be asked, let alone considered or answered? The way becomes clearer when we realize that, for all its peculiarity, being does not confront us as an un-differentiated monolith. Indeed, making the ontological difference itself explicit is just the first step in bringing the proper and distinctive character of being into view. In the next three sections I outline three further ways in which the being-question—and being itself—have a rich and compelling internal structure.

1.2 THE ARTICULATION OF BEING

The first of these three further structures Heidegger calls the *articulation* of being. Literally, articulation implies a complex of rigid members, at-tached to one another at flexible joints—like the bones in a skeleton, the rods and shafts in an engine, or (more figuratively) the words and phrases in articulate speech.

The point here is that the phenomenon of being must itself be under-stood as comprising several distinct but fundamentally "joined" factors—beginning first with those traditionally marked by the scholastic terms 'es-sence' and 'existence.' Accordingly, Heidegger also refers to the articulation of being as the thesis of scholasticism.[5]

At some level, of course, everybody already knows this: it is implicit in the everyday distinction between asking *what* something is and asking *whether* it is. The philosophical point is rather that, in this distinction, an important ontological insight—one on a par with the ontological difference—first comes to explicit formulation.

Effectively the same basic insight can now also be expressed in the so-called formal mode, which is to say, as an observation about language and logic. In that version, the crucial inseparable factors are not the scholas-tics' essence and existence but rather the more powerful and fundamental devices we now use to express and accommodate them—preeminently including, but certainly not limited to—the formal distinctions among

---

4. Strictly speaking, what we cannot do is to use the word 'is' to talk about being; we can use it to formulate and talk about the being-question, which is an entity (a question).—*Ed.*

5. *GP*, part one, chapter four.

names, predicates, relations, bound variables, quantifiers, and connectives in the first-order calculus.

Perhaps certain other "ontologically significant" distinctions—such as those between quantity and quality or between necessary and contingent—might also "articulate" being, but Heidegger does not mention any.

1.3 WAYS AND REGIONS OF BEING

Yet a third way in which the question of being does not confront a featureless monolith—after the ontological difference and the articulation of being—is the equally familiar distinction among different ways of being and the corresponding partition of entities into different ontological *regions*.[6]

This, too, is familiar. Among its early versions may be Plato's distinction between eternal forms and ephemeral sensibilia. It reappears in the scholastic distinction between the one infinite and many finite entities, Descartes's distinction between thinking and extended substances, and, in effect, of course, our initial quartet of dogs, ball games, gemstones, and numbers. Heidegger's neo-Kantian and phenomenological mentors were accustomed to distinguishing a variety of ontological regions.

The idea shows up in the analytic tradition as well. Thus, C. I. Lewis once remarks (in passing, with no elaboration) that

> the adjective 'real' [here equivalent to 'actual'] is systematically ambiguous and can have a single meaning only in a special sense. The ascription of reality to the content of any particular experience is always elliptical: some qualification—material reality, psychic reality, mathematical reality—is always understood. (1929, 11)

Carnap makes regions of being—what he calls "frameworks of entities" or "worlds"—the central theme of at least one essay (1950). He mentions a number of examples, including the world of things, the language of sense data, the system of numbers, the framework of propositions, and so on. The main claim is that, in order to say whether some entity exists (and presum-

---

6. Although this distinction may still be familiar, it has largely fallen into disrepute in the mainstream of Anglo-American philosophy since Quine (1953). For discussion of this background, see the editor's introduction and also McDaniel (2009) and van Inwagen (2009).—*Ed.*

ably also what it is), one must first accept the relevant framework with its associated language or theory and then abide by its rules. But, unlike the theoretical truth claims that one can make and understand once some system is accepted, that prior acceptance itself is a *practical* decision guided by expediency and fruitfulness. (Sellars, Kuhn, Davidson, and many others develop related distinctions.)

Heidegger likewise occasionally lists various regions (or their corresponding disciplines), but he seldom says much about them. In *Being and Time,* section 3, he mentions history, nature, space, life, language, mathematics, physics, and theology—with a few words about each. His concern, however, is not so much to characterize any of them as merely to note the foundational crises in each as a motivation for raising the being-question in general.

In fact, in the whole *Being and Time* period, there are really only four regions that get examined in any sustained or systematic way. First and foremost, of course, is the region of dasein, which figures in practically every discussion and indeed inspires the title for the present volume. Second is the region of *equipment*—the tools and paraphernalia of workaday life—which is treated especially in sections 15–17 of *Being and Time.* Third (and conspicuously parallel to the account of equipment), sections 25 and 26 briefly sketch the ontological region in which people show up as intraworldly entities. Finally, sections 42–63 of *The Fundamental Concepts of Metaphysics* (1983/1995) comprise a remarkable regional ontology of life (in the biological or ecological sense).

In addition to these specifically regional concepts, Heidegger also often uses another ontological term, 'being-occurrent' ('*Vorhandensein*'), which is not specific to any region but is oblivious of regional differences. Though he never stops to explain what he means by it, the point is clear enough. To understand an entity as occurrent is to understand it as real—that is, as an independent *thing* that bears properties in the traditional philosophical sense. But the mark of reality in that sense is *independence:* a thing is *at all* and also is *what* it is *all by itself.* So, its determinacy is proper to it and it alone—in the form of *properties.* (Relational properties are proper to their relata severally.)[7]

---

7. In his annotated working copy, Haugeland wrote the following in the margin at this point: "mention language (subject/predicate)."—*Ed.*

Now, there is no denying that there *are* real, occurrent things, indeed occurrent things of ontologically different sorts.[8] What is questionable is rather whether everything is occurrent: whether to be at all is just to bear properties and stand in relations. The affirmative answer is succinctly captured in Quine's elegant and influential slogan: "To be is to be the value of a bound variable" (Quine 1953, ch. 1). Heidegger's equally emphatic negative answers, by contrast, take several forms (corresponding to various regions) and rather more exposition.

I.4 THE TRUTH CHARACTER OF BEING

The association of being and truth is long-standing. It is tempting (and traditional) to regard the relation between them as essentially *semantic:* being manifests itself in entities, truth manifests itself in claims *about* those entities. Indeed, we introduced the being-question itself in terms of the word 'is' as it shows up in ordinary propositions about dogs, elections, and numbers. So this "aboutness" would seem to be the heart of the matter.

What does truth have to do with being? An initial clue is this. In the relation between entities and ordinary ontical claims about them, the entities are always in the driver's seat. [Entities are such that they determine what is and is not true—that is, what is true *of them.* The determinacy of entities is that there are truths about them—truths that are determined *by* them.][9] The claims are *beholden to* the entities in the sense that they are supposed to accord with them (and not vice versa). Entities in general precede and are independent of whatever claims may be put forward about them. But that general precedence and independence is not an ontical determination of, say, this entity or that. Rather, it belongs to all entities *as entities:* it is an *ontological* determination of entities as such—a determination of their *being.*

---

8. Thus, though it will not matter [in this initial discussion of the being-question (ed.)], there can be strikingly different "ontologies" that nevertheless concur in understanding being as being-occurrent. Idealism and theism are no less susceptible to the tacit conception of entities as independent bearers of properties than is the crudest materialism.

9. Haugeland's working copy seems to indicate the insertion of the bracketed text at this point but does not indicate clearly whether it was to replace or supplement the remainder of the paragraph.—*Ed.*

To bring out the same precedence and independence in another way: if the aboutness of a claim breaks down or is somehow faulty, the fault is always in the claim, never in the entity. Now, in a broad sense, this sort of fault is *falsehood*—a failure in the thesis to be *"true to"* whichever entity or entities it is supposed to be about. (Telling the truth is "telling it like it is.") Hence, the earlier *ontological* precedence and independence of entities relative to claims are conditions of the possibility of *ontical* truths and falsehoods *about* them at all. And this is at least part of what Heidegger means by the "truth character of being": the being of entities is such that there can be truths and falsehoods about them.

But there is, I think, another and deeper part. Prerequisite to any true (or false) claims about entities is some *understanding* of their being—an understanding that can itself be more or less "faulty." Yet, unlike entities and ontical claims, being "is" not antecedent to and independent of our understandings of it. Being "is" *only in* how it is understood.[10] But then how can such understandings fail or be faulty—how can they ever be *mis*understandings? By what standard could they so much as be judged shallow or confused or misguided? To what are understandings of being *beholden* at all?

I argue that an essential aim and (unfinished) achievement of *Being and Time* is to show how—without circularity or vacuity—understandings of being are beholden to *entities:* the very same entities to which ontical claims are beholden. Exhibiting that ontological beholdenness will complete the explication of the truth character of being.

1.5 THE BASIC PROBLEMS OF PHENOMENOLOGY

The first two divisions of part I of *Being and Time* (which are all we have) were published in April 1927. The following month, Heidegger began a lecture course titled "The Basic Problems of Phenomenology," which he himself described as "a new elaboration of the third division of part I of *Being and Time*."[11] In these lectures, he identifies and gives initial treatments of

---

10. This distinction—between entities' independence of dasein and the dependence of the being of entities upon dasein's understanding of being—is a central thesis of *Being and Time.—Ed.*

11. That description is in a footnote on page 1 of the published text—presumably inserted at the time of publication (1975).

four such "problems": the ontological difference, the articulation of being, the regional modifications of being, and the truth character of being. These, accordingly, are the *basic* problems that confront the question of the sense of being.

1.6 EXAMPLES

By way of illustrating the ontological distinctions and terminology introduced in this chapter, I conclude by sketching three artificially "simplified" examples of ontological regions—emphasizing both how they are analogous and how they differ. (The examples are not Heidegger's, and I do not suggest that he would endorse any of them.)

Chess Phenomena.   The phenomena that can show up in chess games—pieces, moves, positions, threats, and so on—are entities in a distinctive (if rather modest) region of being exclusive to chess. Our modes of access to these phenomena—what might be called "chess perception" and "chess action"—include recognizing pieces and where they are on the board, seeing threats and opportunities, appreciating strengths and weakness, and, of course, making moves.

No one ignorant of chess is capable of such access; such a person is unable even to *see* the pieces and their positions, let alone make moves. To be sure, if a game is being played with little figurines, someone ignorant of chess can see and manipulate those. But I think it can be *proven* that the figurines are not identical to the pieces. Thus, one and the same chess game might be started with one set of figurines and later finished with another. The *pieces*, however, must retain their identities over that transition. For, if white moved a rook before the transition, then white cannot later castle with *that* rook, and it would be fatuous to protest that it is a different rook because white is using a different *figurine*. Therefore, the rook itself cannot be identical to either figurine.[12]

If that is right, then there are chess pieces, positions, moves, and so on only in the midst of individual ongoing chess games—and numerically the

12. The same point can be made even more vividly in the special situation in which both chess players are playing blindfolded, for, in that case there need be no "physical" pieces at all.

same piece, position, or move cannot belong to more than one game. But, in saying this, we effectively determine the ontology of chess phenomena. Their *way-of-being* or *that-being* is happening or playing a role in the course of a particular chess game—that is, a game played according to the rules of chess. And the *what-being* of those phenomena is the role they play, the difference they make, in such games, according to those same rules. *What* a rook *is*, for instance, its "essence," is nothing other than be-ing a piece in a chess game that moves as a rook does (along ranks and files and in castling), and such a piece *"actually exists"* just as long as it fills that role in some ongoing game. Finally, the *thus*-being of a chess piece would include those determinations that it happens to have on some occasion but need not have had—determinations that are allowed but not required by the rules—such as what square it happens to be on or what opposing pieces it happens to threaten.

What is *possible* in chess is, needless to say, just what the rules enable and allow. Accordingly, the *sense* of the being of chess phenomena—that in terms of which they themselves, as well as their accessibility, possibility, and that-, what-, and thus-being, are *intelligible*—is governedness by the rules of chess.

Physical Phenomena.   By *physical* phenomena I here mean just those investigated and characterized by mathematical physics (so, not "physical" in everyday senses such as physical labor or physical beauty). Much as the sense of the being of chess phenomena is governedness by the rules of chess, the sense of the being of physical phenomena is governedness by the laws of physics, and to be physically possible is to be compatible with those laws. But physical laws are quite different from the rules of any game. In the first place, they are empirical—which is to say they must be discovered or ascertained rather than made up and imposed by us. Second, they are unlimited in spatial and temporal scope in a single universe rather than confined to many finite, self-contained games. Third, they take the form of mathematical formulae, specifying necessary relationships among quanti-tative magnitudes as functions of relative place and time.

Accordingly, the mode of access to physical phenomena is measurement of these magnitudes in conjunction with one another at determinate spa-tiotemporal locations or calculation of them from others already known. The what-being of the phenomena so accessible is their character as speci-fied and governed by the laws. For instance, the what-being of electric charge—*what it is*—is nothing other than what the laws of electromagnetism say about how instances of it must or may relate to other instances of physical magnitudes in space-time. A more complex physical phenomenon, such as a molecule, a hurricane, or a star, is then just a spatiotemporal configuration of such magnitudes, the stability and/or development of which is constrained by those same laws. The thus-being of physical phenomena is the values that particular magnitudes happen to have but need not have had—values that the laws permit but do not require. And so, finally, the way-of-being—that it is—of any physical phenomenon is just these magnitudes having nonzero values at particular points or spans of space-time.

Intentional Phenomena. For the purposes of this example—and *only* those purposes—I will use 'intentional' (and related terms) in the senses explicated by Dennett (1971) via what he calls the *intentional stance*. (Heidegger would never have treated intentionality in this way, but, since the idea is familiar and accessible, it can be useful as an illustration.)

According to Dennett, intentional phenomena (beliefs, desires, perceptions, actions, inferences, and so on) are justly attributable to "systems" in a certain sort of interpretive stance—namely, an interpretation that finds the system to be largely rational. The relevant notion of rationality is what is sometimes called "belief-desire" or "instrumental" rationality. This imposes two constraints on acceptable interpretations: (i) the system should be construed as consistently adopting beliefs and desires only in ways that keep them appropriate to its circumstances (roughly, true and salutary); and (ii) its behavior should be such as could rationally be expected to maximize the satisfaction of its desires, given its beliefs. Inasmuch as those circumstances and that behavior are both observable, such interpretation itself can be empirically grounded—hence, a legitimate mode of access to the imputed phenomena. Finally, since the constraints imposed by rationality delimit acceptable interpretations, they also determine the pertinent notion of possibility.

The what-being of intentional phenomena is their respective potential roles in these systematic rationalizations and accordingly has the two dimensions recognized in decision theory: propositional content (that which is believed or desired) and attitude (believing it or desiring it, for instance). Their that-being or way-of-being can be nothing other than being "had" or "held" by some intentional system justly so interpretable, and their thus-being would be those incidental relationships in which they happen to fall, such as figuring in some particular inference on some occasion. Last but not least, the sense of the being of the intentional (on this view)—the analog of rule- or law-governedness—is rationality or "reason-governedness."

The question of the sense of being for some region or other is the topic of what is called a *regional ontology*. As the foregoing sketches suggest, though they differ from one another in various ways, these ontologies have much in common. Accordingly, there is a prior and more fundamental issue about the character and possibility of any ontologies—any understanding of being—at all. To raise that issue is to ask the being-question: the question of the sense of being *tout court*. This question is the topic of what Heidegger calls *fundamental ontology*—and also the official topic of *Being and Time*. Its priority over all regional questions is called the *ontological* priority of the being-question. (As we will soon see there is also an *ontical* priority of that question.)

2

Philosophical Method

How does one *do* philosophy? Heidegger says that ontology is the "science" of being. But it is not a science like any other: there are no experiments to perform, no surveys to conduct, no bones or artifacts to unearth. How, then, are results obtained and validated?

These are questions of *method*—something philosophers have always grappled with. Descartes, for instance, sought unshakable foundations for knowledge via his method of hyperbolic doubt and the clear and distinct ideas that could survive it. Kant introduced the method of transcendental critique, which changed the focus from substantive knowledge itself to the conditions and limits of its possibility. Russell and Moore developed the method of conceptual analysis, which changed the focus again, this time to what words like 'know' really mean. And so on.

Heidegger, needless to say, also changes the focus—in his case, to the *sense of being.* The thematic thread continues, however, inasmuch as understanding the being of entities is prerequisite to any genuine knowledge of them. Indeed, the continuity with Kant is even closer since Heidegger regarded the transcendental doctrine of elements (especially up through the principles) as amounting to an explicit regional ontology of physical nature. Thus, he could say the following (near the end of his 1927/1928 lecture course on Kant):

> If we radicalize the Kantian problem of ontological knowledge, in the sense that we do not limit this problem to the ontological foundation of the positive sciences, and if we do not take this problem as a problem of judgment

but as the radical and fundamental question about the possibility of under-standing being at all, then we shall arrive at the philosophically fundamen-tal problematic of *Being and Time*. (*PIK* 426)

It should be noted, however, that this remarkable assimilation extends only to the *topic* of investigation, not to its method. The official method of *Being and Time* is not transcendental critique but *phenomenology*.

2.1 PHENOMENOLOGY: PHENOMENON AND LOGOS

Heidegger adopted both the term 'phenomenology' and the basic method-ological conception of it from Husserl. Though he acknowledges Husserl's priority—both by name and by quoting his well-known maxim, "To the things themselves!"—Heidegger's own account of the method turns out to be importantly different.

We are introduced to this alternative understanding via the origins of the word itself. But the etymologies are not intended to carry any probative force, whether against other uses of the term or in favor of Heidegger's own. Rather, they are primarily an expository device (which happens also to show that Heidegger's version is not gratuitous).

On the face of it, the word 'phenomenology' is formed on the model of names for sciences—'geology,' 'biology,' 'sociology,' even 'ontology'—suggesting it should mean "the science of phenomena." But Heidegger wants something more illuminating and inclusive. [Because the goal is to reawaken the question of the sense of being, he wants something that works not merely for *ontical* but also for *ontological* questions. That would be][1] more like an account of *evidence*—equally relevant to philosophy (ontology), em-pirical sciences, mathematics, and all other sorts of rigorous investigation. (To ground one's results always on genuine evidence is just what Husserl's maxim expresses.) So everything turns on what it means to be "evident" in the appropriate sense and how that can be brought about.

The underlying idea that Heidegger wants to exhibit and exploit can be elicited by going even further back into the Greek roots. The basic word

---

1. The complete sentence in brackets was indicated as a marginal addition to this para-graph, with no definite location specified. The final three words were added to facilitate the inclusion of the marginal addition.—*Ed.*

stem for the Greek noun 'phainomenon' is 'pha-' as in 'phaos' or 'phos,' which means "light." But it is not light in the contemporary scientific sense of rays or photons but rather "clear daylight": the light or brightness in which things are clearly visible. From this comes the verb 'phaino,' meaning literally "to bring to light" and thus also "to exhibit," "show," or "make manifest"—in the plain light of day. Then two grammatical transformations complete the derivation. The first converts the verb into the Greek counterpart of our reflexive, and the second forms a noun denoting the subject/object of that reflexive verb. These transformations give the noun 'phainomenon,' with the literal sense of "that which brings itself to light, shows itself in itself, or is manifest in and of itself."

But 'phenomenon,' like many words, has come, over the years, to have a number of distinct (though related) senses—in Greek as well as German and English. Thus, in the lingo of empirical science, "the phenomena" typically include not just what is *immediately* manifest (in and of itself) but also whatever can be *made* manifest via careful observation, detection, or measurement. But, while that, plausibly, is just an extension of the original sense, other common expressions seem actually to violate it. Thus, so-called occult phenomena are occult precisely in that they tend *not* to show themselves, and if mirages are "desert phenomena," then what purportedly shows itself is not there at all.

Yet even these expressions directly presuppose the basic, etymological sense. Thus, the very idea of occult phenomena requires "manifestations"—at séances, for instance. So they must "show themselves" after all, though only indirectly and when coaxed. In the meantime, the manifestations as such still have to be manifest in and of themselves. Likewise, though the mirage "lake" is not really there (even as hidden or occult), it still has to seem to be there and, moreover, in plain view. But that means that whatever is really going on must somehow be *mimicking* a lake that is showing itself in and of itself.

When Heidegger turns to 'logos,' the other component of the term 'phenomenology,' he does not appeal to its etymology but rather to its ordinary Greek sense *and*, more particularly, to Aristotle's treatment of 'logos' as a special case of that. The standard, primary meaning of 'logos' is "word" or "talk." Heidegger says that what talking comes down to is *making* what you are talking about clear or manifest (to someone else, for instance) and cites Aristotle's explication of this as 'apophainesthai,' especially in the form of 'apophansis,' assertion. But 'phainesthai' is just the Greek reflexive" of '*phaino*,' mentioned earlier, and '*apo-*' is a prefix meaning "from." So, ety-mologically, '*apophainesthai*' means "to show itself from itself."

Heidegger interprets this to mean, at the most basic level, that in mak-ing an assertion a speaker *lets* what is being talked about show itself from itself by pointing it out—putting it on exhibit, so to speak. If, for instance, I discreetly mention that your shoelace is untied, I draw the shoelace to your attention so that you can see, "from" the shoelace itself, that it is un-tied. By pointing out the untied shoelace (something I could also do with-out words), I *let* it be seen—let it *show* itself from itself. Of course, there are many other (and less straightforward) uses of assertion—not to men-tion other forms of speech. This is just an especially basic use (and, more-over, just the one needed for the etymology of 'phenomenology').

2.2 PHENOMENOLOGY AS METHOD

It *is* striking how nicely the two stories fit together. The *logos lets* the phe-nomenon show itself from itself (by pointing it out). The phenomenon is that which shows itself in and of itself. So, the logos of the phenomenon—phenomenology—*lets* that which shows itself in and of itself show itself from itself (by pointing it out). And *that* is the method.

But why, if something already shows itself in and of itself, does anybody have to *let* it show itself from itself? I mentioned earlier the case in which, although something shows itself plain as day, it has been overlooked—not noticed. Or, in a slightly more interesting variant, the phenomenon might have been noticed but mistaken—perhaps through carelessness or as a re-sult of some inadvertent assumption. Then pointing it out could encourage a more conscientious notice or even a concerted examination so as to let it show itself *from itself.* (This might involve looking in a better light or with attention to some particular aspect.)

An especially vivid and powerful way of letting phenomena show themselves—in philosophy and elsewhere—is explicit or formal demon-stration (proof). The premises are granted or already established, and the argument then lets the conclusion show itself as thereby also granted or established. (To demonstrate just is to *show* by exhibiting or pointing out.)

A more difficult situation arises when things do show themselves but only in a disguised or distorted way. Perceptual illusions may be the most familiar example, but much more important are "illusions" engendered by conceptual or doctrinal prejudice. All too often, we simply fail to see what is in some sense "right before our eyes" simply because we "already know" it *cannot* be there—even if it is. But (sometimes) we can be *brought* to see it by having it pointed out—perhaps slowly and in conjunction with other things we have missed.

The suggestion that philosophy should be grounded in what shows itself—what is self-evident or manifest in itself—is hardly unprecedented. What, after all, is a clear and distinct idea if not an idea in which something *shows itself* clearly and distinctly—that is, in and of itself? What is a counterexample to a conceptual analysis if not an example that *shows itself* in and of itself as satisfying the concept but not the analysis, or vice versa? Even transcendental critique, epistemological reduction, and formal modeling must appeal eventually to what is "manifest on the face of it."

Yet these very assimilations reveal that we have yet to bring out what is distinctively Heideggerian. To do that, we need to approach the question of method from another angle. What basic *problem* or *danger* is it meant to resolve or guard against? What *danger* or *threat* is the philosopher in question most worried about? If we can identify this, then we might be able to see why one determinate method or another seems called for.

So, for instance, what haunted Descartes was the danger of being duped or deceived—of "falling for" the mere appearances of things and thus failing to grasp them as they really are. That worry was fueled, no doubt, by his commitment and pioneering contributions to the new science, an essential tenet of which is that things *are not* really as they first seem but quite different (as the lump of wax example is supposed to illustrate). Therefore, he needs a method that can get past such deceptions and lead to the underlying truth instead. For *this* purpose, hyperbolic doubt and clear and distinct ideas could seem admirably suited.

Kant, on the other hand, was not worried about deception at all. His main concern was the ease with which we can seem to talk (and even theorize) sensibly about things we cannot really understand. Thus, *transcendental* illusion is not an illusion of knowledge but an illusion of intelligibility. Therefore, the aim of transcendental critique is to delineate the conditions and limits of all human cognition of objects and thereby identify the bounds beyond which it cannot intelligibly go.

Moore and Russell, by further contrast, were exercised not so much by the danger of gross unintelligibility as that of local confusion—in other words, not the risk of making no sense at all but rather of not making *clear* sense in specific contexts or connections (and therefore falling for bad arguments). But, if that is the wolf at the door, then, of course, conceptual analysis—not just of words but also of logical forms—is the ideal defensive strategy.

2.3 PHENOMENOLOGY AS ONTOLOGY

Heidegger's project is to reawaken the question of the sense of being. Thus, taking him at his word, the problem is that the question has fallen asleep. But what could that mean? To push the image a little further, we might say that, although the question is still "alive," it lies dormant, remains inert, languishes in oblivion. Less figuratively: though there *is* still a real—perhaps even an urgent—question, nobody pays attention to it anymore or even realizes that such a question could arise.

Why not? It is not that the being-question does not matter. No, it is because it *seems* already to have been answered—indeed, easily and long ago—because the answer is trivial and obvious. What is this answer, so clear to anyone who gives it a second thought and ratified by sound common sense? We all know, of course: to be is to be an occurrent thing. Descartes, Kant, Husserl, Russell, Moore, Quine, and many others are all equally guilty—but, at the same time, all equally *victims*—of that ubiquitous, complacent, invisible, sometimes even smug taking-for-granted.

Heidegger's demon—the lurking danger in philosophy's way—as he sees it, is not deception, not unintelligibility, not confusion, but precisely this unimpeachable, question-smothering, scarcely even noticed *sound common sense*—the opiate of ontology.

But the reason common sense is such a threat to philosophy is not just that it is ubiquitous, complacent, and smug and not even just that it is also profoundly misguided. Rather, it is that the particular misunderstanding promoted by common sense and the tendency to impose it exclusively are both built into the structure of dasein itself—the very structure that makes any understanding of being possible at all. That is what makes it so *dangerous* and, by the same token, what makes phenomenology so *hard*.

Heidegger begins his discussion of method (*SZ* §7) by distinguishing three senses of the word 'phenomenon.' The first, called the *formal* conception, is what we have already seen: the phenomenon is that which shows itself in and of itself. Now, 'formal,' in Heidegger, always means lacking determinate content. So, 'phenomenon' in the formal sense is completely neutral as to *what* shows itself in and of itself. The other two senses are not in this way neutral.

In the *ordinary* conception, phenomena are always *entities*. This is the sense in which Kant used the word: the objects of experience *qua* what can appear in and of themselves to empirical intuition are phenomena. Heidegger has no objection to this use of the term, though he himself wants to focus on another.

In the *phenomenological* conception, the phenomena are not entities themselves but rather their *being*. The being of entities, however, does not ordinarily show itself *thematically* at all but rather remains implicit in those entities as entities. Thus, it is something like the Kantian forms of intuition, space, and time. They do not ordinarily show themselves *thematically*, either, but remain implicit in the spatiotemporal relations among empirical objects. But, just as space and time, as formal intuitions, can be *made* thematic, so, too, can the being of entities, and, as such an explicit theme, it can show itself as a phenomenon in the phenomenological sense.

Dasein is an entity, so it is a phenomenon in the ordinary sense. But existence—the sort-of-being of dasein and the topic of the existential analytic—is a phenomenon in the phenomenological sense. What is more, it is this way-of-being above all that is subject to the risk of getting buried and forgotten under cover of commonsense obviousness. Hence, the existential analytic above all must let its "object" show itself *in and of itself.* Only as phenomenology is that analytic so much as possible.

2.4 HERMENEUTIC PHENOMENOLOGY

We began with the question, how does one *do* philosophy? So far, we have considered phenomenology, the official answer that Heidegger provides in his own section on philosophical method (SZ §7). But most of that discussion addresses *what* the phenomenologist does, not *how*. Letting being and dasein "show themselves in and of themselves" may indeed be just the ticket for fundamental ontology. But all we have heard about how to do that is: "by pointing them out." Yet the question of "how to do it" would seem central to an account of *method*.

Heidegger emphasizes in section 7 (including in its title) that he is presenting only a *preliminary* conception of phenomenology, but he never gets around to explaining any fuller conception. (*The Basic Problems of*

Phenomenology also promised an extensive discussion of method that was never delivered.) There are, however, two important hints of what remained to be said, both directed at the "how to" question. (I say "hints" because, though both are clearly fundamental in the methodology of *Being and Time,* neither is actually explained there; the only sustained discussions are in his lecture courses.)

The first "hint" occurs in a few lines near the end of the "method" section:

> [T]he methodological sense of phenomenological description is *interpretation [Auslegung]*. The *logos* of the phenomenology of dasein has the character of *hermeneuein.* . . . The phenomenology of dasein is *hermeneutics* in the original signification of the word, in accord with which it designates this business of interpretation. (SZ 37)

The original signification of the Greek verb '*hermeneuein*' is 'to translate,' 'to interpret,' 'to announce,' 'to put into words,' 'to give utterance to.' So it includes both more and less than our own word 'interpret.'

Broadly speaking, to interpret is to make sense of something: to discern and articulate its meaning or significance. But this formulation, like the word itself, can intend either of two quite different endeavors.

In one familiar sense, we speak of "interpreting" revealing facts or telltale signs, such as experimental data, medical symptoms, or clues to a crime—facts which are therefore "significant" or "meaningful" in the context of the investigation they contribute to. But such interpretation always has the form of a *causal* inference: one figures out what must have happened or be happening, given its known effects. Thus, the clues or data have no significance *except* insofar as they bear on these inferences; apart from that, they are quite meaningless.

Another kind of interpretation, however, does not infer from effect to cause at all but rather aims to express in a *different, more accessible way* the meaning or significance of something that *already had it* prior to any investigation. So, the canonical example is interpretation of a text, especially one written in a foreign language and/or context (such as the *Bible*). Such a text does not suddenly become meaningful simply because it bears on some current investigation; rather, it already meant something when- and wherever it was first written and read. And the task of interpretation is to figure out and reexpress, as nearly as possible, whatever that meaning was.

Hermeneutics is interpretation only in this second sense: reexpressing more accessibly what something *already* means *in the context of some way of life.*[2] But that does not mean it is limited to texts. On the contrary, there is a clear and familiar sense in which rituals and ritual objects, social institutions and statuses, nonverbal works of art, historical events, and even body language are meaningful in the lives of a people—and *therefore* amenable to hermeneutic interpretation. (Indeed, texts themselves are cultural-historical phenomena and, as such, can be hermeneutically interpreted in ways that go beyond construing the words on the page.) With these latter in view, we can see why other connotations in the Greek—like 'announce' and 'give utterance to'—might become important.

Human life—or, more precisely, dasein—is the original form and source of all meaningful phenomena of the sort that admit of hermeneutic interpretation. Hence, prima facie, it is not surprising that the method of the existential analytic should be hermeneutic. Crucially, however, Heidegger's project is not anthropology, archaeology, or "culture studies." There is more than one way in which the meaningful structures in a way of life can be obscure, and not all of them—or even the most recalcitrant—have to do with their being foreign or remote.

Thus, in our own daily lives, meaningful structures can happen to be hidden merely by remaining tacit or inexplicit, hence unnoticed. In that event, the task of phenomenological hermeneutics is simply to bring them into view *by pointing them out.*

Far more interesting and important, however, is Heidegger's account of a kind of hiddenness that is not *accidental*—an obscuring distortion of dasein and being that is integral to the very structures that make understanding possible in the first place. Common sense is both essential to dasein and essentially misguided. To put the point another way: dasein *inevitably* misunderstands both itself and being from the start. But this suggests an unnerving methodological "short circuit." How could those obscuring distortions ever be exposed and rectified except in dasein's *understanding*—the very same understanding that allegedly presupposes them?

Everyday understanding, however, and whatever its inevitable initial limitations, is never *wholly* unresponsive to observations and connections.

---

2. So, for instance, "interpretation" in the sense of assigning semantic values to the elements of a formalism is not hermeneutic; nor is "decoding" the information carried by natural signals, such as neural firings or interactive insect behavior. On the other hand, what Davidson calls "radical interpretation" is, indeed, a pinched sort of hermeneutics. But—among other differences—Davidson only *talks about* interpretation (a philosophical topic), whereas Heidegger also *engages in it* (a philosophical method).

Thus, by careful, cumulative stages, it can be *brought* to see—or bring itself to see—phenomena and possibilities to which it was and could not but have been antecedently blind. In other words, though inevitable at the outset, the misunderstandings are not inescapable. At bottom, this is the essence of all methods, scientific as well as philosophical, that carry understanding beyond the confines of common sense.

It is characteristic of hermeneutic investigations that they are *holistic:* the various parts of the interpretation are interdependent, subject to the maximizing constraint of finding that what is being interpreted makes consistent sense overall. Thus, one begins tentatively with whatever seems clearest on the surface, looks for patterns that integrate and extend those appearances, notices what seems newly clear on that basis, all the while critically revisiting earlier ideas and so on. This explains the familiar image of hermeneutics moving "back and forth" or "in circles" as it painstakingly homes in on a coherent way of reexpressing the whole meaning of whatever it is trying to render intelligible.

We see this in the architectonic of *Being and Time* even at the grossest level. It begins with a *preparatory* analysis of dasein in its "everydayness"; then revisits and elaborates the structures so exhibited in terms of the possibility of "ownedness"; revisits and extends again in the light of "timeishness" [*Zeitlichkeit*] as the sense of dasein's being; and would—if finished—have gone another round via "temporality" [*Temporalität*] as the sense of being *at all*—thereby addressing at last the being-question.

2.5 FORMAL INDICATION

The other hint of a methodological "how to" in *Being and Time* is the occasional—but never explained—invocation of so-called *formal indication.*[3] As noted earlier, Heidegger uses the word 'formal' to stipulate a lack of concrete or determinative content,[4] and to indicate is to point at or point out. Hence, just from the expression itself, a formal indication would be an indicating or pointing at that does not characterize or descriptively specify whatever it is that is pointed at.

3. There is an especially helpful discussion in the 1929/1930 course. See *Fundamental Concepts of Metaphysics,* §70.
4. See pp. 69–70.

So, the simplest mundane example would be mutely pointing at something with one's index finger. When successful, that suffices to identify the indicated item without characterizing it at all. Of course, one can also use indexical *words*—like "that over there"—and still remain completely formal. In fact, however, *complete* formality is not really the point. Rather, the aim is to maintain a "studied neutrality" as to what the intended phenomenon is and what it is like. Thus, noncommittal specifications, serving merely to direct attention (like "that big, fuzzy-looking thing") are not ruled out either—as they had better not be if formal indication is to be a *philosophical* method. For philosophy, which does not have a lot to *point at* is almost entirely verbal.

Heidegger in fact says (in the 1929/1930 lectures cited earlier, 1983, pp. 425, 430) that *all* philosophical concepts are formal-indicative, and, to underscore the point, he lists a number of examples: existence, mineness, world, finitude, individuation, history, the 'as,' the moment, freedom, ownedness, resoluteness, death, the 'not.' Each of these concepts is also prominent in *Being and Time*, but only two—existence and mineness—are explicitly picked out as formal-indicative.

The reason that all philosophical concepts are formal-indicative can be seen from either of two sides. First, ordinary language itself is essentially an everyday public phenomenon and, as such, invariably embodies and takes for granted a commonsense understanding of being. In particular, it takes for granted that to be is to be occurrent. Indeed, the dependence is reciprocal: the understanding of being as being occurrent is itself essentially a reflection of the logical grammar of ordinary language.

But none of the philosophical concepts on Heidegger's list is compatible with this ubiquitous, unnoticed assumption that to be at all is to be occurrent. (That assumption itself is one of those nonaccidental obscuring distortions mentioned in the last section.) The problem, however, is not just that commonsense concepts are, for whatever reason, inadequate for philosophy. No, the real and—if I may put it this way—*sinister* difficulty is that ordinary language and common sense are relentlessly *homogenizing.* They absorb into themselves and redigest all contrary conceptual innovations, spitting back out homonymous domesticated simulacra—as if nothing had changed.[5]

5. Haugeland's manuscript did not proceed far enough into *Being and Time* to take up explicitly section 35 on *Gerede* ("idle talk"), but this discussion is strongly suggestive of one aspect of what Haugeland would have said about the ontological significance of *Gerede.*—Ed.

Therefore, all viable philosophical concepts must remain *directly* grounded in the phenomena themselves—as opposed to those comfortable public accommodations. And that, seen from this first side, is *why* they must be formally indicative.

But, the very same reason, seen from another side, is even more striking. Grasping philosophical concepts—concepts like world, finitude, individuation, and the rest—is no mere cognitive achievement. You do not actually *understand* them except insofar as they are making a real difference in how you live. In other words, you cannot genuinely come to have those concepts without also changing as a person.

This is not a semantic point about the use of words but a substantive point about what understanding such phenomena amounts to. To take the sparest example: one would not understand the phenomenon of contradiction if one did not also *reject* all manifest instances of it as necessarily false. *Actually responding* in that way—"in real life"—is not a distinct result or consequence of the understanding but rather integral to it as such. *Understanding* contradictions as such *essentially includes* repudiating them.

Heidegger is maintaining, for all *philosophical* concepts, something like that "integralness" of each individual's understanding with his or her own concrete living. Thus, *understanding* freedom, resoluteness, finitude, and the like includes—or is even tantamount to—living in a certain way. That is why characterizations of them, attempts to capture them in words, must always and essentially fall short.

Therefore—and this is the second side of the reason given earlier—philosophical concepts can be expressed only as formal indications. Their content is not a what but a how: namely, how to live, how to *be* dasein. Thus, to come to understand them is to *change* how one lives and, so, who one is:

> These concepts are indicative—which is to say: their import is not to mean and say in a direct way what is referred to, but rather just to give an indication of, a pointer to, the fact that whoever understands this conceptual nexus is called upon to bring about a transformation of his self into dasein. (*GM* 430)

3

Dasein

The three central topics of *Being and Time* are being, dasein, and time. Yet dasein, the only one not mentioned in the title, takes up most of the book—at least in the divisions we have. It is important to understand why that should be.

Heidegger initially introduces and highlights dasein as the entity that asks the being-question:

> [W]orking out the being-question entails making an entity—the inquirer— perspicuous in its being. Asking this question is itself essentially deter- mined, *qua* way-of-*being* of an entity, by what is asked about—namely, being. That entity, which we ourselves in each case are, and which includes inquiring among the possibilities of its being, we call dasein. Posing the question of the sense of being explicitly and perspicuously re- quires a prior and suitable explication of an entity (dasein) with regard to its being. (SZ 7)

In other words, we must investigate dasein first *because* dasein is the entity that inquires into the sense of being—and not just incidentally but as an inquiry that is integral to its own way-of-being.

Understanding being is itself a being-determination of dasein. (SZ 12)

That is, having an understanding of being—indeed, an understanding of both its own being and of the being of other entities—belongs to dasein's being as such. And that is as much as to say that dasein is *essentially* (or "by definition") the entity that understands being.

3.1 DASEIN AND HUMAN BEING

The noun 'Dasein' is an ordinary German word that can be translated as 'life' or 'existence,' as they are used in phrases like "a life of luxury," "a squalid existence," "the meaning of life," "the struggle for existence," and so on. But it can also be used for existence in the traditional philosophical sense, as when Kant refutes the "ontological argument" for the *Dasein* of God.[1] As a verb, *'dasein'* literally means "to be there" (*da* = there, *sein* = to be), typically in the sense of being present at or attending (some event, say), but it can also just mean "to exist."

Heidegger, however, has appropriated this word for his own special purposes, giving it a distinctive philosophical sense that is related to, but not the same as, any of its ordinary meanings. He mostly uses the noun, but the verbal sense of "being there" is sometimes important in his associations and wordplay. (Though in German a noun is always capitalized, I will treat 'dasein' as a naturalized English word and neither capitalize nor italicize it.)

In its distinctive Heideggerian sense, as we have just seen, dasein is the entity that understands being and that we ourselves in each case are. Thus, dasein is an *entity* (not a way-of-being), and we—people—*are* that entity. Now, the latter amounts to an equation, and it is immediately tempting to take "us" (people) as the known quantity and dasein as the unknown to be determined thereby. But, while that might be helpful initially, Heidegger's purposes ultimately run the other way. The lengthy analytic of dasein will offer—among other things—a radically new understanding of people as such.

Thus, the term 'dasein' follows in a long tradition of philosophical expressions for what is distinctive of humanity. Aristotle held that people are linguistic and political animals; Christian scholastics maintained that immortal souls are what make us people; Descartes found our fundamental distinction in the capacity to think; Kant found our distinctiveness in our capacity for finite knowledge and freedom; Hegel found it in historically developing spirit; Dilthey emphasized historical communal living; Husserl posited a transcendental "I" ("ego"), and so on. No two of these are equivalent, and dasein is not the same as any of them.

---

1. Kant, *Critique of Pure Reason*, A 592 = B 620.

One dimension of variation among those alternatives is how they are individuated. So, for instance, immortal souls, thinking things, free rational agents, and transcendental egos—whatever their other differences—are alike in being apportioned one per person. Each individual person is or has one of them, all to him- or herself. Developing spirit and communal life, by contrast, are suprapersonal: there is not a separate one for each person, but, on the contrary, many individuals—indeed, generations—all participate together in the same one. Finally, linguistic and political animals might be understood either way, depending on whether the emphasis falls on 'animal' or on 'language' and 'polity.'

How, then, is it with dasein? Is there a distinct dasein for each person, or do many people participate together in one and the same dasein—or is it somehow some of each? Though most readers take the first answer (one dasein per person) for granted, I think the matter is not so straightforward either textually or philosophically. I will argue that the term 'dasein' is meant to encompass *both* sides of this (prima facie) duality in a way that highlights their essential interdependence.[2]

A first clue to this reading may be the peculiar interplay of singular and plural in the aforementioned formula: dasein is the entity that we ourselves in each case are. 'Dasein' and 'entity' are singular; 'we ourselves' is plural; and 'in each case are' is somehow supposed to identify them. The phrase 'in each case' translates the German particle '*je*,' which typically indicates some kind of distribution or apportionment, as in: "eight ounces of milk *for each* child" or ". . . per child" or just ". . . *apiece*." But that, by itself, does not settle the question of whether there is a distinct, separate dasein for each of us, or whether instead we each respectively "share in" some dasein (or daseins) that is (or are) common to a number of us—or both.

A clearer and subtler view emerges when we consider two remarkable examples that Heidegger offers of the *being* of dasein.

---

2. This conception of 'dasein' as encompassing both sides of the individual/collective duality marks one of the key changes in Haugeland's view since his early paper "Heidegger on Being a Person" (this volume); the early view emphasized the collective and worldly aspects of dasein as a "subpattern of the anyone," while assigning a less prominent role to dasein's individuation "in each case."

3.2 EXISTENCE: DASEIN, SCIENCE, AND LANGUAGE

'*Existenz*,' like '*Dasein*,' is a perfectly ordinary word that Heidegger appropriates for his own philosophical purposes. In fact, in everyday parlance, the two are nearly synonymous. But, in Heidegger's usage, although they are intimately related, they are not at all equivalent—not even close. *Dasein*, as we have seen, is an *entity*—something that there is. *Existence*, on the other hand, is the *way of being* of that entity—hence not anything that there is at all. Thus, the difference between them is (one version of) the ontological difference. More precisely, existence is the *that*-being or *way-of-being* of dasein. In this regard, it echoes the scholastic term 'existentia,' which also named a way-of-being *(actualitas)*. But the way-of-being of dasein is quite different from *existentia = actualitas*. In Heidegger's sense, *only* entities in the region of dasein exist. This can be disconcerting since it means that, strictly speaking, *nothing else exists* at all. But the strictness is merely terminological. Entities in other regions of being do not "exist," but they still *are* in various other ways—namely, the ways-of-being pertinent to their respective regions.

What does it mean to exist? To ask this is to ask the being-question itself for the distinctive region of dasein: what is the sense of *dasein's* being? We will not be in a position to answer fully for some while, but we can get a preliminary grasp by turning now to Heidegger's two examples (keeping in mind that each is somewhat specialized and neither is ever really developed):[3]

> As ways in which man behaves, sciences have the sort-of-being of this entity (man). We call this entity '*dasein*.' (*SZ* 11; cf. *SZ* 357 and 392)

> Languages themselves are never anything occurrent like things. Language is not identical with the collection of words recorded in a dictionary; rather, insofar as it is, language is just as dasein is—that is, language exists, it is historically. (*GP* 296; cf. *SZ* 166)

So sciences and languages *exist*—in the strict sense reserved for entities in the region of dasein. Therefore, they *are* entities in that region. Now, as

---

3. It should also be kept in mind, though it will not matter in the present context, that the two examples are not on a par. Language is integral to dasein, whereas science is only a possible and "advanced" manifestation of it.

our exposition progresses, these assimilations will illuminate science and language, but, at the present stage, when we have a firmer grip on them than on dasein, the illumination can shine in the other direction.

Sciences and languages are entities—there *are* some of them. What does it take for such entities to *be* (that is, to be *at all,* as opposed to not being)? In other words, how do we understand their *way* of being (their *"that-being"*)? Neither sciences nor languages last forever; they come and go historically. So we can get a handle on their way-of-being by considering the difference between those that there still are and those that there once were but have since ceased to be.

There now is a science of chemistry, for instance. By contrast, there used to be a science of alchemy, but there is not anymore. Why not? What changed? The basic answer is pretty obvious: people stopped doing it. Alchemy, like all sciences, was a practice or discipline. When people stopped practicing (and teaching) it, the practice itself ceased to exist. And much the same can be said of languages: Italian, for instance, still exists, whereas Etruscan no longer does. The difference, obviously, is that, while many people speak Italian these days, nobody speaks Etruscan anymore.

To express this difference, we often say that Italian is a *living* language, whereas Etruscan is a *dead* one.[4] And, in essentially the same sense, we could easily say that chemistry is a living science, whereas alchemy has "died out." So, to a first approximation, the way-of-being of sciences and languages—namely, existence—is "living" or being "alive" in the sense of currently being practiced or spoken.

But the qualifier "to a first approximation" is crucial. Not just any complex, socially sustained behavior patterns will do, and for at least two reasons. (It is no accident that sciences and languages are the ones that Heidegger singles out.)[5]

In the first place, as we saw at the beginning, dasein is *by definition* the entity that has an understanding of being. Now, if sciences and languages are to qualify, we clearly cannot take this "understanding" in a narrowly psychological sense. But it is not hard to see how living prac-

---

4. In one of the passages cited but not quoted earlier, Heidegger pointedly asks: "What way of being does language have, if it can be 'dead'?" (*SZ* 166).

5. This is a change in Haugeland's view since "Heidegger on Being a Person." There he cited "chemistry, philately, Christmas, and Cincinnati" (p. 9 in this volume) as examples of dasein, whereas only chemistry now remains exemplary from that group.—*Ed.*

tices, like chemistry or Italian, might implicitly incorporate or embody[6] understandings of being—understandings which their practitioners subliminally acquire in learning the practice. (Indeed, more than a little of traditional Western ontology is plausibly implicit in ordinary Western language.)

On the other hand—and this is the point—not every extant, socially propagated practice embodies such an understanding. For instance, an *accent* with which some language is spoken might persist for a while in some province and then "die out." But it is hard to see how an accent, just as such, could embody any determinate understanding of being.[7] And, if that is right, then accents (and whatever else is like them in this way) are not dasein, nor is their way-of-being existence in the technical sense.

The second qualification is an elaboration of the first. Being *alive*, in the sense relevant for existence, cannot just mean "going through the motions"—rehearsing variations on the same old patterns by rote or ritual. Mere permutation and recombination of stock moves is quite as "deadly" to an embodied ontology as dropping the corresponding practice altogether. The kind of "vitality" that is implied in a *living* language or science, one that (still) embodies an understanding of being, essentially involves an element of *venture* or *risk*, hence a kind of openness and going forward. Existing is essentially a *risky* existing *forward*. (This fundamental idea of "risky forwardness" is taken up in detail later.)[8]

With these two clarifications in place, we can now wrap up the point about sciences and languages and resume our introductory characterization of dasein. Needless to say, dasein is more than just science and language. These are just relatively modest and transparent versions of the phenomenon, well suited therefore as illustrations. Moreover, neither has been treated with anything like the philosophical thoroughness it deserves. And that is because the motive at this stage has been merely to use them as clues to the character of dasein and existence as such. In order to capture that general lesson in something like a slogan, I will say that dasein is a *way*

6. I am, of course, using the terms "embody" and "incorporate" figuratively.

7. This will be clearer when we have a more developed account of understandings of being.

8. The previously unpublished talk on "Temporality" (in part three of this volume) begins to lay out aspects of this issue, but Haugeland did not live to write the chapters of the book that were to address division II of *Being and Time.—Ed.*

of living that embodies an understanding of being.[9] And existence, the way-of-being of such a *way* of living, is its (still) *being-lived* in the sense just sketched.

3.3 DASEIN AND PEOPLE

With that preview in place, we can now return to the question of what it means to say that we ourselves *in each case are* dasein. The answer has two parts. First, following out Heidegger's examples, the formula would have to go like this. Chemists themselves in each case *are* chemistry (the discipline), and Italian speakers in each case *are* Italian (the language). So "in each case are" has to mean "are the respective practitioners or speakers of"—that is, the practitioners or speakers without which chemistry or Italian would not exist at all. The point is that sciences and languages exist *only in* their being practiced or spoken by "us"—individual people. Likewise, dasein as such exists *only in* being "lived" by us as our "way of life."[10] That is the first part of what it means to say that we ourselves in each case *are* dasein. For expository convenience, I will take advantage of the English phrase 'in each case' to introduce the new expression *case of dasein* as a general term for us as individual people insofar as our respective individual ways of living embody such understandings.[11]

The second part of the answer is symmetrical with the first. We ourselves would not be *people* if we did not live a way of life that embodies some understanding of being. Understanding being (and all that it entails) is what distinguishes us in the known universe—the very distinction that words like 'rational,' 'free,' and 'responsible' were meant to capture: the distinctiveness of *dasein.* So the second sense in which we ourselves in each case *are* dasein is that, qua *people* at all, we each *live* dasein.

It is crucial to keep in mind that these understandings of being are "embodied" primarily in how we live. It is these (embodied) ways of living that are distinctive of dasein qua dasein. Hence, even though the term is initially

---

9. Among other interpretive advantages, the phrase "living way of life" sits well with the colloquial connotations of the German word 'Dasein,' reviewed earlier.

10. As the *charcutière* insists: "Where there's life, there's a liver."

11. Haugeland's manuscript included this sentence as a separate paragraph, but in parentheses, one paragraph further down. We take the parentheses to indicate his indecision where to place this remark and have chosen to move it and remove the parentheses.—*Ed.*

explicated with the observation that "we are ourselves" dasein, the concept of dasein as such is not thereby tied down to humanity. (Whether there could be nonhuman dasein or humans without dasein will not be considered here.)

3.4 SELF-UNDERSTANDING AND THE EXISTENTIAL ANALYTIC

According to Heidegger, philosophy just *is* ontology: the science of being. From the point of view of ontology, however, dasein is not just one more entity. It is, by definition, the entity that *does* ontology. The point is not, of course, that, in each case, it does ontology scientifically—that is, explicitly and theoretically. It only means that, qua existing dasein, it has at least some understanding of being and that it comports toward entities *as entities* on the basis of that understanding. Understanding being is a determination of dasein's own being. Thus, Heidegger says that dasein itself "*is* ontologically"—or, at least, "*pre*ontologically" (SZ 12).

The qualification 'pre-' means two things. First, negatively, it acknowledges that dasein's understandings of being need not be (and, indeed, usually are not) explicit or "scientific" in the earlier sense. But second, and more positively, it also acknowledges that explicit, theoretical ontology—which is to say, *philosophy qua science of being*—must begin from and develop out of whatever implicit, pretheoretical understandings dasein already embodies.

Among the phenomena that dasein always embodies some understanding of (in its way of living) is itself—and therefore also its own sort of being: existence. Since these both loom so large in the account, Heidegger gives them special names. Dasein's *ontical* understanding of itself as an entity and especially of its own self as a particular case of dasein is titled *existentiell*[12] understanding. This is what we ordinarily mean by "*self*-understanding"—the way we each understand ourselves in our lives, careers, relationships, historical situations, and the like.

Existential self-understanding, by contrast, is dasein's *ontological* understanding of dasein as such. In other words, it is dasein's understanding of

---

12. *'Existentiell'* is a made-up word, evidently designed with the double purpose of being clearly related to *'existential,'* yet also clearly not the same.

its own being: *existence.* The explicit, systematic pursuit of existential understanding is called the "existential analytic" of dasein. Though it was never intended as the main point, that analytic in fact makes up the bulk of *Being and Time.*

Finally, there is one more sort of concept to introduce and situate. In traditional ontology—most notably in Aristotle and Kant—certain concepts are singled out as fundamental in the sense that understanding and deploying them is *prerequisite* to understanding and deploying more routine concepts. Such prerequisite concepts are standardly called 'categories.' So, for instance, one could hardly grasp the familiar idea of "twelve cold ones on ice" without effective prior mastery of the *categories* of quantity, quality, and relation.

But a table of categories can never be ontologically neutral (or "innocent"). Both Aristotle's and Kant's, for instance, silently (unwittingly) *take it for granted* that to be is to be an *occurrent thing.* They have no alternative to consider or counterpose.

Heidegger, by contrast, has several alternatives to compare, develop, and deploy. Perhaps the best known is his regional ontology of *equipment* in division I, chapter 3 of *Being and Time*, and there is an equally remarkable regional ontology of *people* in the following chapter.[13] By far the most important, however, is the so-called existential analytic, which amounts to a regional ontology of dasein itself and which in fact occupies most of the book as we have it.

The fundamental ontological concepts pertinent to phenomena in this region—the concepts analogous to traditional categories in the ontology of occurrent entities—are called *existentialia* (singular = '*existentiale*'). Heidegger could just as well have said that the existentialia *are* categories, albeit a special sort of category specific to entities that exist; the effect would have been the same.

---

13. This interpretation of the subject matter of chapter 4 of division I is a correlate of Haugeland's distinctive interpretation of dasein. Instead of treating this chapter as an application of the ontology of dasein to our everyday encounters with one another in the world, Haugeland is treating chapter 4 as a regional ontology of individual people as intraworldy entities, which is distinct from his overall account of dasein as an entity that is not intraworldly. He thereby readily explains why Heidegger used the term "others" rather than "dasein" to denote other people we encounter; his own coinage, "cases of dasein" is nevertheless intended as a more perspicuous replacement for "others" as he understands Heidegger to use that term.—*Ed.*

3.5 HAVING ITS BEING AS ITS TO BE

Perhaps the most important *existentiale*, because it lies at the heart of how dasein relates to the being-question, is also the most difficult to express. Here are four of Heidegger's own introductory efforts, all drawn from the same page:

> [Dasein is] distinctive in that, in its being, that being is *at stake* [or *at issue*] for it.[14] (SZ 12)

To say that, in its existing, dasein's existing is at stake or at issue for it means at least that, *in* living its life in each case, *how* it lives that life is both up to it and fundamentally important to it. It can *choose,* and the choice *matters.* But that is not all it means.

Life decisions, of course, can range from the trivial (which socks to wear) to the consequential (which career to pursue or lifestyle to adopt). These, however, are not really the sort of issue that Heidegger has in mind. Farther down the page, he writes the following:

> And because this entity's essence cannot be defined by citing any "factual what"—its essence lying rather in the fact that, in each case, it has its being as its to be [*seiniges zu sein*]—we have selected the term 'dasein,' as a pure being-expression, to designate it. (SZ 12)

The first thing to notice is that this 'to be' is not Hamlet's—not even grammatically. In the prince's plaintive question, the particle 'to' is part of the infinitive. But, in the German '*zu sein*,' the verb '*sein*' is itself the infinitive, and the 'zu' is doing something quite different. In particular, it indicates that what follows is *imposed* or *incumbent on* the subject— as in "The defendant is *to* stand silently" or "The children are *to* clean their rooms daily." In other words, it stipulates a kind of burden or responsibility.

So the claim is that the *essence* of dasein lies in the fact that, in each case, it has its being as its *burden* or *responsibility.* What that means is clarified as the passage continues:

---

14. The phrase "is at stake" translates the German idiom "*geht um,*" which signifies that what fills the blank is what is "at issue," "at stake," "of interest," or "really important" in something or what it is "all about."

> Dasein always understands itself from [*aus*] its existence, from a possibility of its self, to be [*zu sein*] it itself, or not it itself. (*SZ* 12)

This says further that the burden is an either/or—that there are two ways for dasein to respond to it: *either* by being it itself *or* by not being it itself. But how could a case of dasein not be "it itself"? The next sentence explains:

> Existence is decided, whether by taking [the matter] up or by omission, only by the particular case of dasein. (*SZ* 12)

Deciding its existence—its life—by *omission* (by *not* taking the matter up) is how a case of dasein responds to this responsibility (the responsibility that is its essence) by *not* being it itself. That response, needless to say, really amounts to *ir*responsibility—in other words, to a kind of shirking.

Though they are not yet explicit in this preliminary passage, two further points are worth mentioning by way of anticipation. First, the responsible/irresponsible distinction, expressed here as the issue that is at stake in dasein's "*to* be," is the same as the owned/unowned distinction that will loom so large in later discussions. Second, what is ultimately at stake in this issue is dasein's understanding of being. It cannot be emphasized too often: that is what the whole book is about.

3.6 FUNDAMENTAL ONTOLOGY

The being-question is an ontological question; it is the defining topic of ontology. And, as we also know, having that question as a question for it is an ontological determination of dasein. It is an *existentiale:* definitive of the being of dasein (existence) as such. On the other hand, *how* dasein in any given case understands being and *how* it responds to the burden of that question, are *existentiell* (hence *ontical*) determinations. In other words, they are a matter of the concrete lives of the respective individuals.

But these lives are invariably and necessarily lived in the world, interacting with intraworldly entities *as entities*.[15] As Heidegger puts it (another

---

15. Haugeland has not yet introduced Heidegger's technical term 'intraworldly' *(innerweltlich),* understandably, due to the concept's dependence on the concept of 'world,' which he explicates in chapters 4 and 5 in this volume (with some foreshadowing in the

preview of things to come): "being in a world" belongs essentially to dasein (SZ 13). Thus, understanding dasein essentially *includes* an understanding of that world and the entities that show up in it. And that means, in turn, that understanding the being of dasein presupposes an understanding of the being of those entities. So, even when an ontology—a regional ontology of some science, say—addresses the being of entities other than dasein, its preontological foundations must lie in the understanding of *dasein's* being:

> Therefore, *fundamental ontology,* from which all others can first arise, must be sought in the *existential analytic of dasein.* (SZ 13)

And that is why the existential analytic takes up the bulk of *Being and Time.*

As we have just seen, this pursuit can be undertaken only in the concrete, worldly ways of living of individual cases of dasein. (Equivalently, that is the only way any *philosophical* inquiry is possible.) Symmetrically, however, these worldly ways of living characteristically involve comportments toward entities *as entities.* (This, ultimately, is what distinguishes dasein's behavior from that of animals.) But that same [qualification of dasein's comportment toward entities, namely][16] "*as entities,*" also *presupposes* at least some understanding of being. So, implicitly, the question about the intelligibility of being as such is always already built into everyday, ontical living. And this is what Heidegger calls the "*ontical* priority of the being-question."

3.7 EXISTENCE, MINENESS, AND OWNEDNESS

Being and Time—part one, division I, chapter 1—begins with a reiteration of the (grammatically peculiar) formula that we are ourselves in each case dasein.[17] This is followed immediately by the two formal indications just mentioned (the only two that figure prominently as such in the whole book): the being of dasein is *in each case mine,* and dasein's "*essence*"— insofar as we can speak that way at all—*lies in its existence.* They are listed

---

current paragraph). All entities other than dasein are intraworldly in the sense that they are disclosed only in their being and thus are intelligible only as entities within the interrelated roles and functions articulated by dasein as a living way of life.—*Ed.*

16. The bracketed phrase has been interpolated for clarification.—*Ed.*

17. Recall the beginning of chapter 4 of division I.

together, with somewhat varying formulations, four more times, including on the first page of the next chapter and on the first page of division II.[18]

In-each-case-mineness [*Jemeinigkeit*] is alternatively expressed by saying that (in each case) *I myself* am dasein. To put it awkwardly but perhaps vividly: mineness = "I-myself-ness." Whether it knows it (or to whatever degree), each case of dasein is its own life—it "has" its life as its *own* (as *"mine"*). But keep in mind that this is a point about *dasein*—*not* about people ("cases of" dasein). It is characteristic *of dasein* that each "case" of it is respectively "mine."[19]

That dasein's "essence" lies in its existence is alternatively expressed by saying that, in its being, dasein's ability-to-be is *at issue* or *at stake* for it—which implies, in turn, that (in one way or another) it always comports itself understandingly toward that ability-to-be. But it also implies, more dramatically, that dasein's ability-to-be can never be fixed or "finalized": it is *always still* "at stake" for as long as dasein is at all.

That is why the word 'essence' is in shudder quotes, for an essence is nothing if not an antecedent fixity. Traditionally, the essence of something determines *what* it is. We have seen that dasein is never a "what" but always, in each case, a "who."[20] Now the point of that becomes clearer. The second formal indication indicates that *who* dasein is, *in each case*, lies in *its* existence. But that existing is just its living its life. So, the two indications together imply not only that the who-it-is of dasein is respectively "mine" but also that this, too, is in some measure "up to it." Therefore, it can never be "antecedently fixed"—not fully, anyway[21]—*who* somebody is

---

18. See *SZ* 41ff., 53, 116ff., 231, 313; cf. 114, 179. The word 'I' is mentioned in passing as a "noncommital formal indicator" at *SZ* 116.

19. Haugeland's manuscript inserts two lines of 'xxxxxx' before the next paragraph, perhaps suggesting that he planned to add additional material at this point. There is neither an evident gap in the flow of the two paragraphs, however, nor any indication of whether any addition would have further explicated "in each case mineness" or taken up one or more additional topics.—*Ed.*

20. Haugeland has not yet discussed this issue, which is taken up in chapter 6 in this volume.—*Ed.*

21. Surely only the most thoroughgoing determinists or fatalists think that a person's life is fully fixed antecedently. The point Haugeland is making here, however, becomes clearer if we consider the contrast between cases of dasein and entities that are not dasein. A cat's life is also not fully fixed antecedently, but its essential nature as a cat is so fixed. A case of dasein has been partially fixed antecedently by the "occupations" that one

because it is something that dasein in each case, in some measure, *chooses*—and for which that person is therefore, to that extent, responsible. But these are quite antithetical to any "what-like" essence.

Heidegger also calls dasein's abilities-to-be its *possibilities*—possible ways that it *can* be. But this must be read carefully because the word 'possibility' can be understood in more than one way. In one sense, possibilities are things that might be or become actual. Thus, if snow is possible tonight, and it does snow, then that possibility has been actualized. In another sense, possibilities are alternatives or options. If there are two possible routes to your destination, and you take one, you have not actualized that route but opted for it. In yet a third sense, possibilities are uncertainties: if the milk might be sour, and you then determine that is, you have neither actualized or nor opted for that possible sourness but merely confirmed it.

None of these, however, is the sense in which *dasein is* its possibilities. Rather, *dasein's* possibilities are *capacities* or *capabilities.* Thus if, after years of study and practice, you are now able to play the violin, play football, or play the stock market at some level, then so playing is now one of your *possibilities* in the sense that Heidegger means when he says that dasein is its possibilities—dasein *is* what it *can* do.

Now we are in a position to address a question that has been hanging over this whole discussion. The previous section concluded with the claim that philosophical—that is, formal-indicative—concepts are intelligible only insofar as individuals are called upon to bring about a transformation in themselves. The present section began with two explicit formal indications: that the being of dasein is *in each case mine* and that *its "essence" lies in its existence* (which is to say, its ability-to-be is at issue for it).

How does understanding these concepts call for a transformation in the individual? Heidegger says the following:

---

has and is taking up, but that does not in the same way determine its essential nature, which is instead to exist (see pp. 127–128 in this volume on Heidegger's distinction between an equipmental role—*Bewandtnis*—and a person's occupations—"what it does, uses, expects, avoids" [*SZ* 119]). The point of Haugeland's qualification ("not fully fixed") is thus to leave room for what Heidegger calls the "facticity" of dasein's existence, its always having to take a stand on its own past even though how it takes up that past in existing is never settled in advance. Thanks to William Blattner and Steven Crowell for constructive comments on this point in Haugeland's text.—*Ed.*

That entity for which, in its being, that being is at issue comports itself toward its being as its ownmost possibility. Dasein is, in each case, its possibility. . . . And because, in each case, dasein essentially is its possibility, it *can,* in its being, "choose" and win itself, or it can lose itself—that is, never win itself, but only "seem" to. But it can have lost itself, and not yet won itself, only insofar as, in its essence, it is possibly *owned*—that is, its own. The two modes of being, *ownedness* and *unownedness* (these expressions are chosen terminologically in the strict senses of the words), are both grounded in the fact that dasein at all is determined by in-each-case-mineness. (SZ 42ff.)

This is, to be sure, a dense passage. Yet, even without quite saying so, it makes perfectly clear that, in understanding its existence and mineness, dasein is *called upon,* in each case, to "own" itself.

Now, the character of that call (conscience) and what it calls for (ownedness) can be fully treated only much later in our exposition. But, since it comes up here and there along the way, a few remarks about the latter may be useful.

I have translated '*eigentlich*' with 'owned' rather than the usual 'authentic' for three reasons. First, Heidegger goes out of his way to say that he means the word in its *strict* sense, and the word is directly formed from the adjective '*eigen,*' which means *own* (as in "a room of one's own"). Second, while '*eigentlich*' standardly means *actual, real,* or true (cf. "authentic"), Heidegger also goes out of his way to repudiate that reading: "the *Uneigentlichkeit* of dasein does not signify any 'lesser' being or 'lower' degree of being" (SZ 43), such as nonactual, unreal, or untrue.

But finally, and most important, 'authentic' just does not make sense in this context, for what it means is "having the origin it purports to have," hence genuine, bona fide, or "the real thing"—as opposed to fake, counterfeit, or fraudulent. *Uneigentlich* dasein, however, is certainly "the genuine article"—indeed, it is dasein in its default and most common condition. What differentiates *eigentlich* dasein is rather that it has "owned up to" and "taken over" (as opposed to having evaded or shirked) the kind of *responsibility* for itself and who it is that we just saw is called for in understanding the two formal indications. That is why I have adopted the translations 'owned' and 'unowned.'

4

Being-in-the-World

Dasein can be characterized in several different fundamental ways. It is introduced as the entity that asks the being-question and that, moreover, always already understands being somehow or other. This is really the main point about dasein. It explains *why* dasein is a central topic in a book devoted to "reawakening" that question.

But dasein is also singled out as the entity that we ourselves in each case are. This provides an initial insight into the topic of our discussion—an insight further enriched by two formal indications (of which, more in a moment).

Yet *by far* the most elaborate and detailed exposition of dasein is in terms of what Heidegger calls "being-in-the-world": dasein's *basic structural makeup* or what dasein basically *amounts to*. A preliminary account of it will occupy this and the next three chapters.

4.1 DASEIN'S BASIC MAKEUP

Being-in-the-world is introduced as dasein's *Grundverfassung* or *Seinsverfassung* (SZ 52f), but there is an issue about how to understand the words. The verb *'verfassen'* means to compose—as in composing a letter, poem, or sonata. So, the gerund *'Verfassung'* can denote either such composing or the resulting composition. So, but for one crucial difficulty, the obvious rendition of *'Grundverfassung'* would be "basic composition." The difficulty is that, unlike *'verfassen,'* 'compose' literally means "put together," and Heidegger is adamant that being-in-the-world is *not* put together—it is no sort of compound or composite but rather an essentially *unitary* phenomenon. Accordingly, I will translate '*Grundverfassung*' as "basic makeup" and sometimes gloss that as what dasein "basically consists of" or "basically amounts to."[1] Being-in-the-world is the most "ground-level" structural characterization of dasein.

Though being-in-the-world is essentially unitary, it is also rich and multifaceted and can therefore be considered in different regards or with different emphases. Heidegger himself immediately identifies three such regards or aspects and organizes his entire discussion around them. They are as follows: (i) the "world" of being-in-the-world; (ii) the "who" of being-in-the-world; and (iii) the "being-in as such" of being-in-the world. Yet, important as this structural articulation is, it is even more important to keep always in mind the *prior unity* that it articulates:

> Self and world belong together in the single entity, dasein. Self and world are not two entities, like subject and object, or like I and thou, either, but rather, self and world are the basic determination of dasein itself in the unity of the structure of being-in-the-world. (*GP* 422)

On the essential point, that is about as clear as it could be.

Even so, it does no more than assert the point, with no guidance at all on how to understand it. Accordingly, since so much turns on it and since it runs so counter to our usual habits of thought, I want to say a little more by way of explanation. The three aspects of being-in-the-world are, of course, intimately related, and so it can seem—even from the very terms used to identify them—as if the broad shape of that "relatedness" is already clear. In particular, it is very difficult not to start off with something like the following picture: the "who" is roughly a person (or some people); the world is

---

1. The noun '*Verfassung*' has come to have several other meanings as well, including the condition or state that something is in (for instance, a building or an athlete) or the constitution (of a nation or government). But the former would be quite misleading in this context because a condition or state of something is, in general, contingent and temporary. And the latter should be avoided here if for no other reason than that 'constitution' already has a quite different established use in philosophy (for which the standard German is '*Konstitution*'). More deeply, both alternatives miss the essential point that being-in-the-world is not something that dasein "has" but rather what dasein basically is.

roughly things; and being in as such is then roughly the relation between them.

But this seductively familiar picture is roughly inside out. Everything turns on how we understand the expression "relation between." The "natural," almost inevitable, understanding of it goes like this: first, there are two items that might or might not be related to one another (in some way that happens to be of interest). If it turns out that they are so related, then there is also a relation—a third, possibly abstract, item with the original two items as its relata.

That is basically how Descartes saw things. First, of course, there could, in principle, perfectly well be a mind without there being any world or a world without there being any mind. Therefore, neither depends on the other either for its actuality or for its essence. That is why Descartes had to establish not only *first*, the actuality and essence of each relatum but also *subsequently*, the actuality and essence of the relation between them.

What would it mean to turn such a picture right side out? The essential move is to *start* with "the between." The point is not to imagine a relation without relata (like the smile without the cat) but rather to conceive a structure in which the relata *presuppose* the relation—not just in their character but also in their being at all.

So, consider the difference between the following two relational structures: an arrow pointing to an apple and an insurance company selling and servicing insurance policies. The arrow and apple could each certainly be, and be what it is, even if the one were not pointing at the other—or, indeed, even if the other were not there at all. Each is, in itself, quite independent of the other and hence of any relation between them.

By contrast, there can be no such thing as an insurance business that does not sell and service insurance policies, nor an insurance policy that is not sold and serviced by an insurance firm. So, unlike the arrow and the apple, the insurance firm and its policies each presuppose not only the other but also (and more fundamentally) the specific *relation* between them—the selling and servicing.

Though both analogies are at best partial, we can say that Descartes understood the relation between the mind and the world as more like that between the arrow and the apple, whereas Heidegger understands the relation between the "who" and the world of being-in-the-world as more like that between an insurance company and insurance policies. In the latter structure, the respective "relata" (the company and its policies) both *presuppose* the concrete, ongoing interactions (that is, the business of selling and servicing). Carrying on the business is, so to speak, "prior," and the "relata" emerge only as poles or moments of that interactive structure. This is what I mean by turning the relational picture "right side out."

Likewise, in the basic structural makeup of being-in-the-world, being-in as such is "prior" to the who and the world in something like the aforementioned sense. Like the insurance company and its policies, the "who" and the world make sense only as poles or moments of the totality of interactions "between" them—which is to say, of being-in as such.

In thinking of relations and relata, we find it almost impossible to break free of this assumption that the relata are independent ("substantial") items and that the relation between them is just an abstraction, wholly dependent on those relata for its being. I will therefore venture one more analogy in an attempt to bring a fundamental alternative into view.

Since this point is simultaneously so fundamental and yet also so elusive, I will venture a further illustration—this one more schematic but perhaps therefore also more vivid. A typical understanding of binary relations might be modeled by a weight lifter's barbell. The weights at either end of the bar are the relata, and the bar itself is the relation between them. The point is that, in this picture, the weights themselves do not depend in any way on the bar (still less on each other). One could perfectly well have unrelated weights.

What would it take to turn this more schematic version of the standard picture "right side out"? Consider the contrast between a weight lifter's bar (with weights on either end) and a silver dollar (with heads on one side and tails on the other). It makes perfect sense to imagine one weight without the other or either or both weights without the bar. Furthermore, the weights are removable and interchangeable at will. They are independent of each other and of the relation between them, the bar.

By contrast—the other side of the analogy—it makes no sense at all to imagine a silver dollar with no silver or a heads (obverse) with no tails (reverse). The heads and tails of a silver dollar are wholly *dependent* on the silver between them, the metal of which the coin itself is made. No metal, no coin—*hence*, no heads or tails, either. To be sure, there are further conditions on being a legal coin. Yet, there is an obvious sense in which the silver is the heart of the matter: given the requisite conditions, whither goeth the silver, so goeth the coin (for as long as it is at all). This image can be pressed only so far, but the point at stake is absolutely fundamental.

Now the point is that the structure of being-in-the-world is more like that of a coin than like that of a barbell. In that structure, being-in as such (like the metal) is the heart of the matter; the "who" and the world are like the heads and the tails, without which that metal could not amount to a coin. So we can also say, flirting with cliché, that the "who" and the world are two sides of one coin—the coin that is being-in-the-world, the basic structural makeup of dasein.

I have said that dasein is a living way of life that embodies an understanding of being. So, such a way of life is what being-in-the-world is the basic structural makeup of. Roughly, being-in as such is the *living* of that way of life, the world is the *where-in* of that living, and the "who" is the *by-whom* of that living. I say "roughly" because Heidegger provides a distinctive characterization of each of these three moments—a characterization that does not exactly coincide with what the words would ordinarily lead one to expect.

4.2 EVERYDAY BEING-IN

Prepositions are among the most flexible and yet idiosyncratic of words. What is more, their idiosyncrasies do not always match up across languages. Heidegger makes careful, technical use of quite a few of them—to the extent that there will sometimes be issues of translation. There is, to be sure, no question of how to translate 'in,' but there is a very real question of how to understand it.

The most common sense of 'in' is spatial, as when we say someone is *in* the city, *in* the building, or *in* the bathtub—that is, located inside some spatial boundaries. Clearly, the 'in' of 'being-in-the-world' cannot be understood in this spatial-location sense. The point is not, of course, that the "who" might be located *outside* the world but that this 'in' is not a matter of location at all.

We may say of someone that she is *in* the army, *in* college, *in* the working class, *in* a movie, *in* trouble with the law. None of these senses is spatial; moreover, no two of them are quite the same. Yet they are alike in specifying a kind of status or standing relationship. While such statuses are definitely *worldly* (in the relevant sense of 'world'), they cannot be what is most fundamental. Being-in-the-world is *living*: it is essentially *not static* but rather active, engaged, involved. The 'in' of 'being-in' is ultimately and most basically the 'in' of *engaging*-in, *participating*-in, actively *involving*-oneself-in. Such active, engaged living-in is what *being*-in is all about.

Though being-in-the-world is necessarily and always a *unitary* phenomenon—with three aspects—the central being-in aspect is clearly "first among equals." (The coin metaphor reflects both the unity and the priority.) The analysis of being-in as such is the heart of the existential analytic. It is significantly more complicated and detailed than the analyses of either the world or the who. Indeed, the chapters on the latter come earlier in the order of exposition and are, to some extent, merely preparatory for the crucial chapter on being-in.

In another clear sense, however, all three chapters are merely preparatory. Heidegger undertakes the existential analytic in two phases. Thus, the initial examination of being-in-the-world as a whole is followed by another, more focused treatment—concentrating especially on matters that will turn out to be relevant to the being-question (which is the ultimate topic of the whole project).

The first phase is, so to speak, generic. It addresses dasein in what Heidegger calls its "ordinary everydayness," the way dasein is "initially and usually" (e.g., SZ 16, 43). In other words, we start with ordinary, everyday life—buying groceries, changing a lightbulb, chatting with friends, watching TV—nothing distinctive of any particular profession or pursuit. The rationale for beginning in this way is to avoid getting misled at the outset by phenomena or emphases that are characteristic only of highly specialized ways of living.

It should also be noted that, although dasein is initially and usually unowned, everydayness as such is technically neutral between ownedness and unownedness. (Even owned dasein has to walk the dog.) The basic structures that will be exhibited in the analytic of everydayness are characteristic of dasein *tout court,* not just unowned dasein. Owned being-in-the-world can be understood only as a specific modification of those more general structures as manifested in everydayness.

Though Heidegger does not explicitly say how the analytic might be led astray if it began with some specialty, I think at least part of it is not hard to surmise. Philosophy from Plato forth has often been particularly impressed by mathematics and theoretical science. But these specialized ways of being-in-the-world are (among other things) distinctively directed toward obtaining and establishing objective knowledge. Accordingly, the so-called problem of knowledge—what it is and how it is possible—has assumed a disproportionate and potentially distorting centrality in philosophical investigations of dasein and its world.

4.3 KNOWLEDGE AS A FOUNDED MODE

Knowledge is a *mode* of being-in-the-world. Moreover, according to Heidegger, it is a *founded* mode—which means that it presupposes and depends on other modes that are more fundamental. Any attempt to understand knowledge and its possibility without regard to this foundedness is bound to go awry.

For example, if one *begins* by considering a knower and some thing that it knows, then one is "innocently," almost imperceptibly, launched on a "barbell" picture of knowledge itself as a relation between them. The respective terms of that relation, the knower and the thing known, are then almost inevitably conceived as the subject and object of the knowing (and the "who" and "world" of dasein become effectively invisible).

Given this beginning, it will seem clear that the knowing must itself belong to the knower—the subject that knows—not to the object or (still less) to some medium hovering between them. (If René comes to know an object, that is a change in René, not the object.) But knowledge is not an externally observable property of any knower, so it must be somehow "inside" ("subjective"). The object, on the other hand, is still "outside," and that raises the question of how the knowledge can ever "get out from" whatever it is inside of—how it can make contact with or "transcend to"—its object. It is all very well to protest that the "inner sphere of immanence" is not to be taken as any sort of enclosure or container. But, when one asks for the *positive* meaning of that "innerness," then, in Heidegger's phrase, silence reigns.

Needless to say, there is more to epistemology and its troubles than that. But it may be enough to show how *different* things can look from another angle. If we *begin* with everyday being-in-the-world, not with some special "problem of knowledge," then our ordinary dealings with worldly things are relatively unproblematic: we handle them, use them, change them around, throw them away, and so on. But there is simply no puzzle at all about how our *hands* can "get outside to" or "make contact with" all the worldly stuff we deal with. Whatever 'outside' means, our hands are already "out there," too—and *so are we*.

Heidegger explicitly says that dasein itself is "always already 'outside' in the midst of entities" (*SZ* 62). This is just what being-in-the-world means in the sense of 'in' explained a few pages back. To start with *that* understanding, however, might seem to beg the essential question. If the whole problem is how knowledge can be related to the world in the first place, then taking it for granted that dasein basically *is* being-in-the-world seems to *help itself* to the desired conclusion by slyly building it into the terminology. The retort is as obvious as it is devastating:

> [W]hat authority has decided whether and in what sense there should be any problem of knowledge at all, other than the phenomenon of knowing itself and the sort of being of the knower? (*SZ* 61)

In other words, the charge of question begging can cut either way: neither the problem nor its resolution can be antecedently prescribed by stipulative definition. Rather, the phenomena must be addressed as they initially present themselves—that is, by letting them show themselves in and of themselves.

The issue of factual knowledge arises in daily life when there is an interruption in routine, skillful taking care of business—what Dreyfus (1991, ch. 4) calls "absorbed coping." In the face of a problem, one steps back and brings additional skills into play. For instance, it can become useful to stop and examine what is happening more deliberately, perhaps also consulting with others. Such consultation involves still further everyday capabilities, including putting things into words—questions, suggestions, observations, and the like. These verbal formulations articulate the situation and do so, moreover, in a way that can be retained, repeated, and passed along. And not only that: individual verbal claims can also be challenged and then either vindicated or withdrawn.

Talking, too, is originally and fundamentally public, one of the essentially interactive ways of living that go to make up being-in as such. But, at the same time, it makes possible a derivative mode in which verbal formulations are retained but not actually expressed. These silent verbalizations—in particular, those of vindicated claims—are the basic, primitive form of articulate knowledge as a founded mode of being-in-the world:[2]

> [P]erceiving something known is not going out to seize some booty and return it to the "cabinet" of consciousness; rather—even in perceiving, retaining, and preserving—knowing dasein remains, as dasein, outside. (*SZ* 62)

---

2. Haugeland here is implicitly building a connection between Heidegger and Sellars's (1997) *Empiricism and the Philosophy of Mind,* which explicitly models thought as inner speech.—*Ed.*

5

The World of Everyday Dasein

With this chapter we begin the analysis of being-in-the-world—dasein's basic makeup—and, more specifically, the world "side" of that makeup. At the same time, we begin the first phase of the existential analytic of dasein, the phase devoted to everydayness. The everyday world is that wherein everyday life is lived, and much of the account will be taken up with the intraworldly entities in the midst of which it is lived. But the ultimate goal is an understanding of the "worldishness" *(Weltlichkeit)* of this world.

5.1 FOUR SENSES OF 'WORLD'

At the outset, Heidegger distinguishes four different senses of the word 'world.' Of these, only one (the third) is the sense of 'world' in the compound expression 'being-in-the-world'—the sense in which the world is a constitutive aspect of dasein. But all four will ultimately prove important in the reawakening of the question of the sense of being.

These senses of 'world' fall into two pairs, each consisting of an ontical sense and an ontological counterpart. In the first sense, the ontical member of the first pair, a world is the totality of all the entities that have some particular sort of being. So, a familiar world, in this sense, is the physical universe: the totality of physical entities (including their interactions) as investigated by physics. A quite different world (though still in this first sense of the term) is a totality of living things: a world investigated by biology and ecology. Yet again, there is the world of mathematical objects (the "universe of mathematical

99

discourse"). Finally—and perhaps pushing the limits—complete individual chess games (*not* the "world" in which chess games are played, with players, competitions, etc.) might be seen as the "microworlds" within which chess moves, pieces, and the like can show up and be understood.

It is worth noting that, although each of these worlds is by definition a totality, what 'totality' *means* varies from one to the next. Thus, the totality of the physical universe is understood in terms of the unity of space-time as a dynamic mereological sum of all matter and material forces.[1] The totality and unity of a biological world, by contrast, is intelligible primarily in terms of ecological interactions, forming a relatively self-contained whole of interdependent needs, resources, and "strategies." Different yet again, the totality of mathematical entities is something like a maximal set of consistent structures amenable to purely formal definition and proof. Finally, the kind of totality appropriate to chess "worlds" would be the completeness of individual games.

As the examples illustrate, each world in the first ontical sense corresponds to a particular region of being (though there may be more than one such world corresponding to the same region). Accordingly, a world in the *second* sense (the ontological counterpart of the first sense) is just such a region: the physical, the biological, the mathematical, the "chess-ish," and so on.[2] (These all happen to be associated with fairly definite "disciplines"; but that's not essential—they just make convenient examples.)

---

1. Modern physics suggests that the unity of space-time is more complexly entangled with physical dynamics than the notion of a mereological sum of matter and material forces suggests, but that only reinforces Haugeland's more basic theme of the multiple senses in which there is a world as an intelligible "totality" of entities.—*Ed.*

2. The difference between these first two senses of 'world,' the ontical sense, which refers to the totality of entities that have some particular sort of being, and the ontological sense, which refers to the region of being of those entities, is one version of the ontological difference between entities and their being. Heidegger's example to illustrate this difference highlights an important theme that will soon figure prominently in Haugeland's interpretation, namely that Heidegger understands the being of entities modally, in terms of their intelligible possibilities.—*Ed.*

For instance, when one talks of the 'world' of a mathematician [in this second sense], 'world' signifies the realm of possible objects of mathematics. (*SZ* 65)

By contrast, 'world' in the first sense refers only to the totality of actual entities with that particular sort of being. In the mathematical case, the actual entities are coextensive with the totality of possible entities, but the difference still holds: the region concerns what constitutes their possibilities, whereas the totality is the mathematically possible entities themselves.

'World' in the *third* sense, another ontical sense, is the term as it appears in the expression 'being-in-the-world.' This is the sense in which we speak of the "wide world of sports," "the world of high finance," a "woman of the world," someone living in "his own little world," and how preachers mean it when they denounce "the ways of the world." Its extension includes but is not limited to the world (or worlds) of everyday life. It is not limited to the latter because, after all, there are distinctive "life-worlds" appropriate to the respective disciplines as well and also other specialized ways of life. Thus, there is clearly a "world of physics" that is not the totality of physical entities at all but rather the professional world in which physicists, qua physicists, live and work. (Think of physics itself as a living way of life.) The entities that show up in this world are not quarks and quasars but rather research projects, experimental apparatus, funding agencies, journal articles, and so on—plus, of course, students and colleagues.

Fourth, and finally, there is a second *ontological* sense appropriate not to the totalities of entities that can show up in the respective regions but rather to these various worlds in which dasein is lived. Heidegger introduces a special technical term for this new ontological sense. He calls it *worldishness* [*Weltlichkeit*]—that is, the worldishness *of* all those lived-in worlds in sense three. Now, dasein, with those worlds as moments of its basic makeup, is an *entity*. That is why the third sense of 'world' is *ontical*. But the existential analytic is an *ontological* analysis of the *being* of that entity; so, in the end, we must explicate not just lived-in worlds themselves but also and especially their worldishness.

5.2 EQUIPMENT, AVAILABILITY, AND ROLES

Lived-in worlds are as diverse as dasein itself. For the purposes of his preparatory analytic, Heidegger focuses on simple special cases: the familiar worlds of domestic life and craft labor. A "world" in this sense is a *milieu*: a setting or an environment within which people live, work, and play.

The analysis begins with an account of the ordinary entities that show up[3] *within* such worlds—the intraworldly entities that, initially and usually,

---

3. I should acknowledge that I am taking a liberty here in using 'show up' to render the verb '*begegnen*.' Generally, it means to "meet," "encounter," or "come across" (especially if by chance), as in "bumping into" a friend at the bus stop or "stumbling across" a lost

we employ, cope with, produce, and consume in the course of daily living. The basic reason for starting this way is obvious: lived-in worlds, too, are totalities of entities. And, as we have just seen, what 'totality' *means* depends on the sort of entity getting totted up.

Heidegger calls the intraworldly entities that show up initially and usually in everyday living *equipment*.[4] Equipment includes items or "stuff" such as tools, utensils, outdoor gear, machinery, buildings, apparatuses, supplies, ingredients, raw materials, work spaces, vehicles, roads, toys, and so on—in other words, all the diverse paraphernalia of everyday work and play.

Equipment cannot be equated with things or objects in the traditional philosophical sense of actual *realia*. In other words, items or "pieces" of equipment are not *occurrent* entities. One way to see the difference is to compare *how* they show up: our primary modes of access to them. The traditional, primary mode of access to objective things has always been perception. The thing stands on its own, over against us there, and we observe it disinterestedly from here—look at it, feel it, and so on—to find out what it is like. Or perhaps we "probe" it or subject it to "controlled conditions" and then observe. Either way, the aim is to ascertain what can truly be said of it on the basis of empirical evidence.

How different it is with a spatula, a hammer, or a tennis racquet. To be sure, these, too, can be observed and measured, but what matters, in the way that is most appropriate to them, is not what can be "objectively" found out and said but how well they work for the business at hand. And, for that, the thing to do is pick it up and try it out. Our *primary* mode of access to equipment is not observation but hands-on use, and the principal aim is not finding out about it but getting some job done.

---

book behind the couch. As Heidegger mostly uses it, however, entities are the *subject* of the verb, and dasein, if mentioned at all, is its indirect object. So, "strictly," one would have to read him as saying that entities encounter (bump into, stumble across) dasein—which is so bizarre that most translators quietly interchange the grammatical subject and object. But, since making the entities the subject of the verb is clearly an important choice (consonant with the conception of phenomenology as letting them "show themselves"), I think a more faithful compromise is to choose a different English verb—one that can intelligibly take the entities as its grammatical subject.

4. Actually, there are two radically different sorts of entity that show up initially and usually in the everyday world. The other sort is people. Following Heidegger, I will treat them in separate chapters, but bear in mind that, apart from the other, each chapter is "one sided."

Heidegger calls these engaged, hands-on modes of access *dealings* (*Umgang:* "going about" one's business). Driving a nail into a board with a hammer is dealing with all three at once—and, accordingly, a mode of access to each of them. To contrast dealings with perceptual finding out ("observation") is not, of course, to suggest that they are blind or ignorant. One could hardly drive a nail, never mind a car, if one could not see or did not know how. The point is rather that the *kinds* of sight and knowledge are qualitatively different.

The name Heidegger gives to the nonobservational awareness involved in and prerequisite to skillful performance is *circumspection* or around-*sight (Umsicht).*[5] Though focal and concentrated where necessary, around-sight is mostly a preoccupied, nonfocal rapport with the current situation—what is going on and how it is going overall. The keyboard, for example, ought to be the last thing on a typist's mind. A truck driver should attend to the traffic and the route (more or less, depending on conditions) but hardly ever to the steering wheel or the pedals.

It is not just that paying attention to equipment is not needed when things are going smoothly and well; it is that it *gets in the way.* Unless there is some unusual problem or other special issue, focusing on the keyboard or steering wheel will actually *interfere* with efficient typing or safe driving. Even the intent ballplayer (who had better at some point concentrate on the ball to be caught) is not interested in any objective properties of the ball but only in what it will take to move or stop it in some way. Thus, it is normal and appropriate for equipment to *withdraw* or *disappear* from explicit notice precisely when it is serving most properly as equipment. This tendency to withdraw is a *positive* characteristic of equipment as such.

Skillful dealings are concrete ways of being-in-the-world (living) and, more specifically, ways of *being-amidst (Sein bei),* where the intended connotation is "being *in the midst of*"—engaged in, busy with—intraworldly activities and the entities they involve. Being-amidst is a *mode* of being-in (as in "*being-in*-the world"): namely, the ubiquitous mode of "taking care of business" with equipment and the projects in which it is used or dealt with. You invite me for coffee, and I say: "Give me a few minutes—I'm *in the midst of* washing up the dishes." Life is like that.

Dealings themselves are entities, too. There *are* dealings—this driving of this nail, for instance. Perhaps one will say they are more like processes

---

5. Note that, despite the term, around-sight is not exclusively visual.

or events than like things, but, insofar as they "actually happen," they are *entities* all the same. Hence we can ask about their *being*, and Heidegger duly gives it a name: the being of all ways of being-amidst is *carefulness (Besorgen)*. But this certainly does not mean that, in an ontical sense, dealings are never *careless* (incautious, negligent, sloppy) or *carefree* (unencumbered or irresponsible). Rather, it means that these are deficient modes of careful being-amidst.

A *deficient mode* (a notion that we will need again soon) is a condition that is intelligible only as a *lack* or *failure* of some other mode that is conceptually prior. Thus, illness is a deficient mode of health, darkness is a deficient mode of light, being totally surrounded by no more beer is a deficient mode of still having all the beer a person could want, and so on. (Note that, despite the common etymology, not every deficient mode is a defect.) So the point is that carelessness and carefreeness are intelligible only as departures from a more basic care*ful*ness, which is conceptually prior.

The strategy now is to explicate equipment, first ontically and then ontologically, via consideration of its essential involvement in these dealings. The opening move is to point out that, characteristically and nonaccidentally, equipment is intelligibly and appropriately used only *ensemble*—that is, together with other equipment. In the usual case, for instance, using a hammer does not make sense without also using a nail, and vice versa. Indeed, on the whole, lumber, pencils, squares, saws, chisels, benches, and so on are likely also to be involved, and, by the same token, uses of any of them in complete isolation would not make much sense, either. Details will vary, but the underlying structure of "essential togetherness" remains.

Heidegger sums it up with a lovely slogan: "Strictly speaking, there never 'is' an equipment" (*SZ* 68). This exploits the fact that '*Zeug*' (like our own 'equipment,' 'stuff,' and 'paraphernalia') works like a mass noun; hence, it does not admit a plural or an indefinite article. The point, of course, is not grammatical but ontological. It is a claim about the *being* of equipment—namely, that equipment as such is not *intelligibly possible* in isolation from other equipment. There cannot be just one.

So it is what would now be called a "holism" thesis, structurally analogous[6] to those familiar with the philosophy of language. There could not be

---

6. In the light of Heidegger's remarks (quoted earlier) that languages (and sciences) have the being of dasein, the present comparison may be more than just an analogy.

just one word or just one sentence. On occasion, there might be isolated single-word or single-sentence utterances. But even these, like all language use, presuppose for their intelligibility many other utterances and conversations that have already taken place. A language is essentially an established repertoire of *interdependent* verbal possibilities. Words and grammatical forms *can be at all* only as belonging to such a repertoire.

Likewise, equipment is possible at all only as participating in a "repertoire" of various interdependent appropriate uses of it, along with other equipment. But, equally clearly, that "participation" cannot mean being in use every single minute. There can still *be* a hammer (lying on the bench, say) while the carpenter is busy sawing or even home for dinner. Rather, the hammer must be ready and available for appropriate use, with other equipment, when it is needed. And it is just that *availability (Zuhandenheit)* that Heidegger identifies as the *being*—more specifically, the *that*-being—of equipment.

One sentence after the aforementioned slogan, Heidegger adds: "Equipment is essentially 'something in-order-to'" (*SZ* 68). In other words, there is always something that equipment is *for;* screwdrivers are for driving screws, frying pans for frying food. All equipment is "for" something, and this, too, is essential to understanding its being. Heidegger explains the point more fully in terms of what he calls *assigning* and *assignments.*[7] What equipment is assigned to is a role[8] in some task or endeavor.

Now, some such roles are temporary and ad hoc, as when one uses a heavy wrench or even a rock to drive in tent stakes or uses a hammer to hold down the paperwork on a windy day. But equipment proper always has a *standard* role (or small range of roles) *proper to it*—that is, for which it is *specifically* appropriate. Hammering in nails, for instance, is specifically appropriate to hammers, and driving screws to screwdrivers. These are their proper roles, and having these proper roles is what makes them

---

7. *Verweisungen.* The verb *'verweisen'* basically means to send something off somewhere, as in remitting a payment, referring someone to an article (or an expert), or even expelling a miscreant from school. If *equipment* is "sent off," this must mean to do its "job" (whatever it is *for*). That is why I adopt Macquarrie and Robinson's translation "assign" (but *not* their alternative 'refer,' which is quite misleading).

8. Heidegger's word is *'Bewandtnis,'* which is ordinarily used only in a few idiomatic expressions and does not admit of any straightforward translation. My choice of 'role' is based both on those idioms and on how Heidegger uses the term in context.

hammers and screwdrivers, respectively. So, assigned proper roles are the *what-being* of equipment.

5.3 AVAILABILITY AND OCCURRENTNESS

Since the contrast between being-available and being-occurrent is so important, yet so unfamiliar (philosophically), it is worth dwelling on for a moment. The essential point but also the hardest to get used to is that it is an *ontological* distinction—that is, a distinction between different sorts of *being.* We have already noted the contrast between around-sightful dealings and disinterested observation as modes of access to the respective entities.

A more conspicuously ontological contrast is that between holistic *inter-*dependence and metaphysical *in*dependence. Descartes says the following:

> By *substance,* we can understand nothing other than a thing which exists
> in such a way that it needs no other thing in order to exist. (1983, 23)

Thus, by *definition,* a substantial thing is absolutely independent of anything else. Now, strictly, that definition applies only to God because everything else depends upon Her. But there is a secondary sense for those things that depend only on God and nothing else—such as the physical universe and immortal souls. And, below these, there is a descending hierarchy of still more dependent entities, such that relative independence is a kind of ontological status marker.

Cartesian details aside, this conception of thinghood in terms of independence is characteristic of all traditional metaphysics. One way in which it manifests itself is in the fundamentally allied notion of a *property.* In both the legal and the ontological senses, a property is what *belongs to* something and to it alone. So, for instance, the shape and mass of a particular quartz crystal are properties which it has *all by itself* quite apart from anything else in the universe. (Relational properties are just the same except that they belong to particular pluralities of things.[9])

Equipment does not have *properties* (relational or otherwise). This is not to say that it is indeterminate or isolated but rather that its determinations

---

9. Remember the "barbell" picture of relations in the last chapter.

are of a different character. Instead of properties, equipment has, as we have seen, *appropriatenesses* and assigned *proper roles*. These, too, identify a sort of "belonging" but in a remarkably opposite sense. To be appropriate is to be appropriate *for* (in, with, amidst, etc.) something. But that is precisely a way of *belonging to something else*—some project or "business" (and so also to other equipment). Appropriatenesses and roles simply do not make sense one by one or in isolation.

But this *"lack"* of independence is not a mark of abysmal "ontological status" relative, say, to *real* things. Rather, it is an essentially *positive* character of an ontologically distinct *sort* of entity altogether—a sort for which *inter*dependence is a "mark of being," and *in*dependence would amount to *not* being at all.

And now we see why the respective modes of access are also so different. The properties of independent things are, by definition, all manifest right there "in" those things themselves—all you need is some way to discern or measure them to find out what they are. The appropriate roles of equipment, on the other hand, are exactly *not* "in" the individual items but rather in the interdependent ("holistic") *nexus* of equipment, materials, and feasible projects. Accordingly, the primary mode of access to those items—*as what they are*—can be nothing other than such use itself ("hands-on dealings"). Finally, therefore, what is learned or "found out" about equipment, in this most immediate and specifically relevant sort of access, is not so much "facts" about it as how and when to use it, how well it serves, and so on.

5.4 UNAVAILABILITY AND COMING INTO VIEW

If equipment, qua equipment, tends to withdraw and disappear, then how does it ever come to thematic notice? How can it become the *theme* of explicit consideration or discussion? As a further, separate question, more urgently, how can we (even in principle) bring the everyday *world* into view? Heidegger finds several answers to these questions, each interesting for other reasons as well.

The first and perhaps most basic answer emerges from the phenomenology of *interruption:* a breach or breakdown in the smooth progress of work. Something needed is not as it should be—it is defective, broken, missing, inaccessible, unsuitable, obstructive, or whatever—and normal progress is diverted or even brought to a halt. The typical upshot is that attention comes to a particular focus, concentrated on the disruptive problem and what to do about it.

Thus (to modify an earlier example) if you are driving down the road and the steering wheel suddenly comes off in your hands or the gas pedal gets stuck, then the wheel or the pedal will no longer withdraw from view or go unnoticed—quite the contrary—and emergency problem-solving efforts will immediately come to the fore.

By way of illustration, Heidegger mentions three broad varieties of breakdown and gives their consequences names. In the first example, something that was supposed to be usable turns out not to be because of something wrong or defective *about* it. In that case, he says the defective item itself becomes *conspicuous*. Second, something might be unusable not because of anything wrong with it but because something else is missing—nails without a hammer or a bow without arrows, for instance. Then the unusable equipment (the nails or bow) is said to be *obtrusive*. Finally, work might be held up not because anything is defective or missing but because some other stuff is in the way, blocking progress. In such a case—say, you cannot get back to work because somebody has covered your bench with a bunch of bricks—then what is in the way (the pile of bricks) is termed *obstinate*.

More interesting than these specifics, however, is what is common to them all. In the first place, we get a new technical term: equipment that is unusable (for whatever reason) is said to be *unavailable*. Now, given that availability is *the way of being* of equipment, *un*availability might seem tantamount to *not being* at all or not being equipment anyway. But that is a misunderstanding. Unavailability is not the same as utter *non*availability. Rather, it is a *deficient mode* of availability. In other words, it is a way of being that is intelligible only as a deviation from availability (in the full and proper sense), which is conceptually prior.

But, phenomenologically, what is important about unavailable equipment is that, in "sticking out like a sore thumb," it always does so *in context*. That is, the essential *interdependence* of equipment is also highlighted and brought into view. For instance, the lost hammer is *missing* (rather than just absent) precisely *because* the nails, lumber, and so on are useless without it. But this first "lighting up" of the interdependent context *as such* is an initial manifestation of the everyday *world*. Thus, the phenomena of interruption and unavailability are integral to the phenomenology of dasein's basic makeup: being-in-the-world.

But that is not all. In addition to and along with unavailability, equipmental breakdown also lets mere occurrentness come into view as an extreme case. This means at least that, in bringing absorbed dealings to a halt, it lets entities show up in a way that is not immediately tied to their roles and assignments. The nails and wood can be seen as "just sitting there"—taking up space, as it were. Such entities open up the prospect of decontextualized "observation," and thence even pure disinterested objectivity.

It seems to me, however, that what Heidegger says about availability and occurrentness here is ambivalent and possibly confused. On the one hand, in introducing availability, he protests against the all-too-easy assumption that the entities that initially show up in careful dealings are "mere things" or even things that are also, somehow, "invested with value" (SZ 67ff.). And, in summarizing, a few pages later, he reiterates that:

> The sort of being of these entities is availability. That should not, however, be understood as a mere characteristic that they are taken to have, as if such "aspects" were read into the "entities" that initially show up—as if some world-stuff, initially occurrent in itself, were in this way "subjectively colored." . . . *Availability is the ontological-categorial determination of an entity as it is "in itself."* To be sure, "there is" anything available only on the basis of the occurrent. Would it follow, however—admitting that thesis for a moment—that availability is ontologically founded in occurrentness? (SZ 71)

These certainly seem to say that availability and occurrentness are distinct ontological categories and, in particular, that available entities are not to be understood as occurrent entities "in themselves" but with some distinctive character "added on" by dasein.

Yet, in the very next section, he says that, in conspicuousness, an unavailable piece of equipment shows itself as an equipmental thing that has also been occurrent all along; that, in obtrusiveness, it reveals itself as merely occurrent; and that, in obstinacy, the occurrentness of the available announces itself as the being of that which still lies before us (SZ 73ff.). In apparent conflict with the preceding, these seem to say that available entities are also always occurrent entities and that the disruptions that lead to unavailability (a deficient mode of availability) reveal this.

What I cannot see is how, if being-available and being-occurrent are two distinct *ways of being,* they could ever both belong to the same entity. How can a single entity *be* in two different ways? To be sure, any available hammer—any hammer that *there is*—is somehow "made of" various oc-current physical atoms, suitably arranged. The question is what that shows—and, in particular, whether it shows that the hammer and the arrangement of atoms are numerically identical. This is a version of what has come to be known as a question of *token identity*,[10] and it may be that Heidegger just did not have the resources to think it through clearly. This may also be a case in which the digital structure of language and grammar insinuates itself into ontology (as occurrentness).[11]

Be that as it may, there are two main lessons to take from the discussion of equipmental breakdown and unavailability. Both have to do with how something can possibly come into view, given the absorption of everyday being-amidst and the tendency of equipment to withdraw. The first is the manifestation, in breakdown, of the holistic interdependence of equipment, raw materials, projects, and so on. This interdependence, made visible via its disruption, is our initial glimpse of the everyday world as such and its sort of totality (wholeness). And the second, as we have just seen, is the emergence of "mere" occurrentness as a distinct, intelligible way of being—defined at the most general level by its lack of interdependence.

5.5 BRINGING THE WORLD INTO VIEW: SIGNS

Heidegger's second approach to bringing the world into view is through a discussion of signs. Presumably this is not really needed, given the account just finished, by way of unavailability. But signs are an important phenom-enon in themselves, and this preliminary account will be exploited later. Also, it allows Heidegger to clarify just what he means by "assignment."

Signs are a kind of equipment. Therefore, like all equipment, their char-acter is determined by assignments to specific roles within an overall assignment-nexus—that is, by what they are "for." The distinctive sort of role that is characteristic of signs in general is *indicating*: what a sign is *for* is to indicate something. Thus, to indicate is a kind of assignment, but not

10. Recall that, in chapter 1, I argued against the token identity of chess pieces and the wooden or plastic "markers" that make up a chess set.

11. Haugeland highlighted the issue of the insinuation of the digitalness of language into ontology in the margin as a point for him not to forget but without any definite indi-cation of where it needed to be incorporated into what was said on that page.—*Ed.*

all assignments are of this kind. A hammer, for instance, or a frying pan also has an assigned role, but those roles are not to indicate (indicating is not what hammers and frying pans are for).

This distinction is important because the word 'Verweisung' (assignment—see §5.2 and note 7, this chapter) often means a directing or referring of someone to something—for instance, to a specialist or a resource. Indicating can be understood as a kind of referring in roughly this sense, namely as referring or directing one to whatever is indicated. Thus, Heidegger can say that signs have Verweisungen in more than one sense: as equipment in general, they have assignments (to what they are for), but as *sign*-equipment in particular, they also have "references" (to what they indicate). In emphasizing the distinction, he makes clear that, by 'Verweisung' in general, he means assignment, *not* reference (SZ 77ff.).

To illustrate the structure of signs and their specific character as equipment for indicating, Heidegger considers a simple example: the turn signals on a car. What is immediately noteworthy about such signs is that, unlike most equipment, they are "conspicuous" precisely when and in functioning as they are supposed to. Not for nothing are turn signals brightly colored flashing lights. Signs, in order to function effectively as signs, must draw and direct attention—which is to say, they cannot have a positive tendency to withdraw and disappear altogether.

To what are signs supposed to draw and direct attention? Not to themselves, obviously, but, in the first instance, to whatever they indicate. But what, ultimately, is that? Heidegger points out that, although in one sense the turn signals are used by the driver of the car, their *primary* users are really nearby pedestrians and drivers of other vehicles. These are the people to whom the signals indicate something, the people whose attention is drawn and directed. Prima facie, what their attention is drawn to is the imminent turn of the signaling car and thus its future path. But this is of no interest unless it makes a difference to the positions and paths of those pedestrians and other vehicles themselves. So, what these others must do, in responding appropriately to the signal, is attend to and adjust their *own* situations in the light of the future path of the turning car.

Therefore, Heidegger argues, what the sign or signal ultimately indicates and must indicate in order to serve its purpose is the larger situations and business of those to whom it indicates. Thus, the pedestrians and other drivers need attend not merely or even mainly to the turning car itself but rather to their own options for getting or staying out of its way—and, from among these, to those that will avoid other mishaps and least disrupt whatever they themselves are up to. In other words, what a sign ultimately indicates is the current around-world and manner of being-in of those to whom it is a sign. More specifically, it "orients" that being-in with regard to its surroundings, and, in so doing, it brings the interrelated availability of whatever else is around into an explicit overview. And that is why signs are another way of bringing the everyday world into view.

In sum, signs are equipment and so, like all equipment, have assigned roles—what they are for. But signs are distinctive in that what they are for is indicating, ultimately for indicating a new orientation within an around-world that itself comes into an explicit overview. Thus, like the phenomenon of equipmental breakdown (when something needed is unavailable), the phenomenon of signs provides a way in which an interrelated whole of equipment and thus the around-world within which equipment is intelligible can come into view.

5.6 SETTING EQUIPMENT FREE AND LETTING IT BE

Heidegger says that dasein's world sets equipment free, releases it, lets it be, lets it show up, and lets it have roles.[12] What is more, he says similar things of other entities, including people and the occurrent objects discovered by natural science.[13]

These are, it will be agreed, peculiar locutions. In order to see what they mean, we must try to understand what provokes them, what issue they are responding to. In a treatise about the sense of being, even the idea of an *entity* is not to be taken for granted. What the word 'entity' *means* is itself the question—yet it is remarkably difficult even to notice what all we assume in our ordinary understanding of it.

Just for instance: it is virtually impossible not to take it for granted that there *have been* entities "since the creation" (or the big bang or whatever). But in that case, talk of dasein's world "*letting* them be" would seem gratuitous at best—and "letting them have been" only sounds worse. These are strong,

---

12. The German verbs are *freigeben, entlassen, sein lassen, begegnenlassen,* and *bewendenlassen.* These terms are introduced in §18 and recur fairly often, especially in §§24, 26, and 69.

13. See, for example, *SZ* 118 and 363.

confident reactions that almost anyone would have. Whatever we eventually decide about them, it must be acknowledged that they reflect "intuitions" (that is, assumptions) *about being.* Heidegger is undertaking, among other things, to "loosen up" such assumptions and pull them out where we can take a look at them. That does not mean that they are to be repudiated—though it may for the first time raise that prospect and make it a genuine option.

In the present section, I will consider only the special case of equipment. Keeping in mind that dasein's world (or sometimes just dasein) is the grammatical subject of the odd verbs, we can now read Heidegger's initial explanation of what they mean:

> Ontically, to let-have-a-role means this: within some factical carefulness, to let something available *be* thus and so, *as* it thenceforth is, and *in order that* it be so. In principle, we take this ontical sense of "letting be" ontologically. And that's how we interpret the sense of the antecedent setting-free of what is initially available intraworldly. To let "be" antecedently does not mean to bring something first into its being and produce it, but rather to discover in its availability what is, in each case, already an "entity," and so to let it show up as the entity with this being. (SZ 84f)

One of the points of this passage is that, *ontically,* equipment is first discovered via letting it have a role (in some worldly project), thereby letting it not only *be* but *already* have been available. (In particular, it is not first discovered as occurrent and only later assigned to something.)

The deeper aim, however, is ontological: to understand how—in terms of its availability and roles—we can make the *being* of equipment intelligible. In other words, how can *those* concepts function as *ontological* concepts—that-*being* and what-*being*—at all? This is the question on which those odd locutions are supposed to shed helpful light.

Heidegger does not pause to explain how they can do that, but I think we can make some progress by looking more closely at the words themselves. (Here we can just stick to English; it is close enough.) For the pivotal expression 'let be,' we can distinguish four basic senses:

Accepting or *putting up with:* This is what we mean by "let it be" when we advise someone not to resist something such as an affront, injustice, or failure—but just accept it.

Allowing: To let be can mean to permit—in the sense of not preventing—as when the Robinsons let their children be a little rowdier on Saturdays.

Enabling: Or it can mean to permit in the more positive sense of making possible—as when a new highway lets a city be approached from the south or a dam lets the spring floodwaters be held for the summer crops.

Effecting: Finally, to let something be can mean to bring it about or make it so, as when God said, "Let there be light" (and there was light)—but equally, I think, when a geometer says, "Let C be the midpoint of line AB" or the ballplayers say, "Let this sidewalk be the goal line" or the appropriate official says, "Let the games begin."

Now, with regard to equipment, the idea of *effecting* comes immediately to the fore. When someone drives in tent stakes with a rock, she is *letting* that rock *be* a hammer in the sense of making it the case by using it as one. And that seems easily generalized: a living way of life, qua living in the world, lets all kinds of equipment be—in the sense both of being equipment at all and of being what it is—by assigning it to standard roles.

Mere effecting, however, would be mere fiat, as if roles could be assigned in any way whatsoever. If assignments were random and unconstrained, however, they would also be gratuitous and vacuous. But, of course, they *are* constrained: our camper *could not* drive in her stakes with a handful of wet sand—it simply would not work—and she just has to accept that. And this point, too, obviously extends to standard roles: by and large, dasein has no option but to accept and "put up with" what will and will not get the job done in general.

But what does that mean? Do parched fields and trees "accept and put up with" wind and drought? If so, then we have not yet identified anything distinctive in dasein letting something be. The difference is this: by assigning equipment to roles in a role-totality, dasein also first opens up the very possibility of equipmental *breakdown* (being defective or inappropriate, for instance). It is in enabling this new and distinctive kind of *fault* or *failure* that dasein gives itself something that it (and *only* it) can and must accept and put up with.

Thus we see, at least in outline, that letting equipment be has a surprisingly intricate structure. In particular, three of the four listed senses of the verb 'let be' are involved in an interdependent way. Dasein lets equipment be in the *effecting* sense by assigning it to its roles in the first place. Yet it cannot "effect" equipment with carte blanche, but only in also *accepting* and *putting up with* what will and will not work. Finally and most tellingly, however, this putting-up-with presupposes the distinctive sort of break-down or failure that is itself *enabled* and *made possible* only by the original assignment to roles.

It will turn out that letting-be is an even deeper and more general onto-logical phenomenon than this initial exhibition can yet suggest. But the basic threefold structure just sketched will remain throughout.

5.7 EQUIPMENT AND THE FOR-THE-SAKE-OF-WHICH

In his treatment of availability and roles, Heidegger does not use either the modern language of normativity or the ancient language of teleology—though either could easily seem apropos and even implicit. Presumably the reason is to steer clear of tacit assumptions built into traditional (and contem-porary) accounts. While normativity as such is more or less ignored, teleol-ogy is directly taken up—albeit without using the term and only to make a particular point.

In this discussion, standard teleological vocabulary ('purpose,' 'aim,' 'goal,' 'reason,' and the like) is completely avoided—no doubt because of its psychological or "intentional" implications. Instead, we get more neutral, down-to-earth terms made up of prepositions and relative pronouns: the "for-which," the "to-which," the "amidst-which," and so on. Equipment as such is available *for* fulfilling its respective role, *to* accomplish something, *in the midst of* some larger task or project. Accordingly, fulfilling that role is its *for-which*, what is to be accomplished with it is its *to-which*, and the task or project is its *amidst-which*. Thus, without mentioning any intentions or purposes, it can be said that the role of a hammer (what it is typically for) is pounding nails, to get them driven in, amidst some board-fastening task.

Tasks and projects themselves, however, are no more intelligible in isola-tion than equipment is; they, too, are always *for* something. So, for example, fastening those boards may be for holding up a roof, which is for enclosing a house, which is for protection from the weather. Each role is intelligible as the role that it is only in relation to such contexts of possible use.

But that looks like a formula for a teleological regress, which inevitably raises the question, where does it all stop? (What, for instance, is protec-tion from the weather *for?*) The canonical "stopper" for such a regress is something that "matters for its own sake" and so is not "for" anything else at all. And, indeed, what Heidegger says can easily sound like just such an answer:

> [T]his [protection from the weather] "is" for the sake of dasein's accommodations or lodgings—that is, for the sake of a possibility of its being. (SZ 84)

By itself, this might be read as saying that possibilities of dasein's being, such as a place to live, are the ultimate for-whiches that matter for their own sakes—and hence stop the regress. But the continuation of the passage makes it clear that Heidegger is not interested in stopping any regresses. Rather, he moves up a level from particular for-whiches and specific roles to the *totality* in which they each participate and which is prior and prerequisite to them all:

> *Whatever* role any available item may have, it has in each case been predelineated from out of the role-totality. In a workshop, for example, the role-totality that constitutes the available in its availability, is "earlier" than any individual equipment—and likewise, that of a farm, with all its implements and real estate. (SZ 84)

And it is this *totality itself*—not some regress within it—that "goes back" to the for-the-sake-of-which:

> The role-totality itself, however, goes back finally to a to-which amidst which there are no longer *any* roles and which is itself not an entity with the sort of being of what is available within a world. Rather, this to-which is an entity the being of which is defined as being-in-the-world—that is, an entity to whose being-makeup worldishness itself belongs. (SZ 84)

The entity whose being is determined as being-in-the-world is, of course, dasein. But, as the passage explicitly says, nothing ever has a role "in the midst of" this entity for the obvious reason that it is not a task or project. Nor would it make any more sense for the role-*totality* itself to *have a role* in the midst of anything. Therefore, when dasein is characterized as the "to-which" of that totality, the term 'to-which' cannot have its usual sense of that which is to be accomplished by something's fulfilling its role in the midst of some task or project. Thus, Heidegger goes on:

> This primary to-which is not any to-that as a possible amidst-which of some role. The primary "to-which" is a for-the-sake-of-which. The "for-the-sake-of," however, always has to do with the being of *dasein,* for which, in its being, that being is essentially *at issue.* (SZ 84)

Accordingly, though the *overall* purposiveness or goal directedness of tools and tasks as such—the role-*totality*—does "go back" to dasein's for-the-sake-of-which, this does not stop any regresses within that totality at all. Rather, it grounds the *whole* structure in something quite different: namely, something that has to do with dasein's *existence*, as that which is essentially at issue for it. This something, here called dasein's "for-the-sake-of-which," will soon be further specified as its *ability-to-be* [*Seinkönnen*].

5.8 THE WORLD AND ITS WORLDISHNESS

The phenomenon of the world comes to light at the intersection of two lines of thought that have been developing for more than a chapter. On the one hand, the world is an integral aspect of dasein's basic structural makeup, being-in-the-world. Hence, dasein's essential *self*-understanding is inextricably *worldly*. On the other hand, the world is in some (not yet specified) sense the *totality of intraworldly* entities—a totality within which alone they can be the entities they are. Not until we see how these two lines come together can we understand the everyday world.

The dense, crucial paragraph [that brings these two lines together] makes heavy use of the prepositional constructions that we have just encountered, plus two important new ones: 'from out of' [*aus . . . her*] and 'out onto' [*auf . . . hin*]:

> The antecedent letting-have-roles of . . . [equipment] amidst . . . [endeavors] is grounded in an understanding of such things as letting-have-a-role, the amidst-which of the role, and the of-which of the role. All that, and what-ever is else underlies it—such as the to-this, as that amidst-which it has the role, [or] the for-the-sake-of-which, back onto-which every to-which ulti-mately goes—must be antecedently disclosed in a certain intelligibility. And what is that in-which dasein, as being-in-the-world, preontologically understands itself? In its understanding of the above relational nexus, das-ein has assigned itself from an ability-to-be, for the sake of which it itself is, to an in-order-to. (And this is so, whether its ability-to-be is explicitly or implicitly grasped, owned or unowned.) That in-order-to [to which it as-signs itself] prescribes a to-this as a possible amidst-which of a letting-have-a-role—which, by its structure, lets there be a role of something. In each case, dasein always already assigns itself from out of a for-the-sake-of-which to the amidst-which of a role. In other words: in each case and insofar as it is, dasein always already lets entities show up as available. That wherein

dasein antecedently understands itself in the mode of self-assignment is that out-onto-which it antecedently lets entities show up. The where-in of this self-assigning understanding, as the out-onto-which of that letting entities show up with the sort of being of roles, is the phenomenon of the world. And the structure of that out-onto-which dasein assigns itself is what makes up the worldishness of the world. (SZ 86)

The world is the "in-which" or "where-in" of being-in-the-world. What that means depends on what 'being-in' means. I have said that being-in-the-world is *living*: engaging-in, participating-in, actively involving-oneself-in. The world is that in-which we are active, engaged *participants*—thus, my earlier examples: the world of the theater, the world in which physicists live and work, and so on. What is it to live or actively involve oneself in such a world? With this, we are ready at long last for the "punch line," the official raison d'être of this entire discussion. We are engaged in a preliminary existential analytic of dasein, with the more immediate aim of exhibiting the world aspect of being-in-the-world. The analytic is only preliminary because it has so far considered only everyday dasein—that is, unowned dasein (and also dasein that is not specialized, such as scientific dasein). What is worse, even this preliminary account is far from complete, especially inasmuch as it has not yet taken into account dasein's communal aspect. Even so, we are in a position to bring the everyday world clearly enough into view that we can characterize it ontologically—that is, in its worldishness—which has been the point of the entire chapter.

For there *in fact* to be equipment with specific roles, there must *in fact* be a role-totality within which those specific roles make sense. Thus, a role-totality is an *ontically* enabling condition for there being equipment with any of the roles that it comprises. This is the way in which a role-totality lets equipment be. But there must also be some *ontological* condition of the possibility of any such roles, role-totalities, and ontical letting-be at all—that is, a condition of *their* making sense. Heidegger refers to this condition as that *out-onto-which* [*Woraufhin*] equipment is freed or let be—a designation which, at this point, we can understand only by seeing how he uses it.

The entity that lets entities be is *dasein*—that is, a living way of life that embodies an understanding both of its own being and of the being of other entities. Since dasein's basic makeup is being-in-the-world, its embodied understanding of its own being includes an understanding of being-in-the-world and, hence, of the world as a moment or an aspect thereof. It is this understanding of the world that we are now trying to make explicit—at least with regard to everyday being-in-the-world.

The world in this sense is the in-which of dasein's being-in and thus the in-which of its self-understanding as being-in-the-world. But what is that? Heidegger says, dasein understands itself in each case by *assigning* itself, from out of an ability-to-be for the sake of which it is, to an in-order-to— that is, to something that it is to do or get done. Never mind that he has not yet explained dasein's ability-to-be or its for-the-sake-of-which. It is the self-*assignment* to something that it is to do that does all the work here—namely, by prescribing tasks or projects amidst which equipment can show up as available for its own assignments or roles. In other words, in assigning *itself,* dasein *lets equipment* show up—and so *make sense—* as equipment. Accordingly, the *world,* as the in-which of dasein's *self*-understanding, is also the out-onto-which of its letting equipment be, hence a condition of the intelligibility of equipment at all. This double characterization as in-which and out-onto-which is the understanding of the world that we have officially been striving for.

But it still does not give much of a feel for what Heidegger is talking about. It is important to appreciate, for instance, that the everyday world is a concrete whole that is richly dynamic and meaningfully structured. Thus it includes not just the *kinds* of tasks and projects that there are or might have been but also all the various *particular* tasks and projects that there *in fact* are, in all their nitty-gritty interrelationships, complexities, and gory details, and also all the tools, materials, by-products, and whatever else has a role or is available for a role in any of those tasks and projects. Moreover, even at a given moment, it is not just these in an instantaneous "time-slice" but rather includes all their relevant histories and prospects. Tasks and projects, by their very nature, always have a pertinent past and future, and these belong essentially to what they are.

Nor, finally, is the world of everyday living just some inert and senseless surroundings but rather a vital and dynamic milieu fraught with tension and tedium, fury and calm, promise and menace. Think of the local "world of sports," even in some isolated town. The playing of the games, of course, is the living being-in—*not* the world. But the league, the team standings, last year's humiliation, the tied score, the position on the field, the number of minutes left on the clock, the threat of rain—these all belong to the meaningful and life-filled in-which of that playing, that is, to the *world.*

Now we can ask about the worldishness of such a world. Heidegger points out that the everyday world is structured throughout by *relationships* among things—ways in which one thing is *important* to another, relationships that *matter* to everyday living in that world. These can be as simple as the role of nails in hammering boards together or as complex as an industrial infrastructure. All such relationships are subsumed together under the general term *signifying*, and the interconnected totality or nexus of them all is called *significance*. Therefore, significance is the overall structure of the everyday world qua world that dasein lives in. That the world is so structured is its worldishness.

The Who of Everyday Dasein

Dasein is a living way of life that embodies an understanding of being, including its own being. Its basic structural makeup is being-in-the-world—or, more fully articulated, who/being-in/world. Having considered the everyday world as one "side of the coin" (in its everydayness), we now turn to the other: the *who* of everyday dasein.

6.1 HOW NOT TO APPROACH THE WHO

The very word 'who' signals that our topic is people: those who live the way of life that dasein is. But it is not just another word for 'person,' as the architectonic already makes clear. As the counterpart of the world in the structure of being-in-the-world, the who (like the world) is a "level up" from all intraworldly entities—including individual people.

The main aim of the present chapter is to characterize this higher-level phenomenon ontologically—which is to say, existentially. As before, however, we approach "from below" via the relevant entities. In other words, in the order of exposition, people will play something like the part that equipment did in the world chapter. Yet, the parallel should not be overestimated. People differ from both equipment and substantial things at least as dramatically as those two do from each other.

The core idea of a substantial thing is *independence:* not needing anything else (save, perhaps, a creator) either to be at all or to be what it is. In particular, neither whether it is nor what it is "in itself" depends on any *actual* relations to any other entities. ('Being-occurrent' is a kind of umbrella term for ontologies of this sort.)

Among the leading lessons of the previous chapter, however, was that equipment cannot be understood in this way. Equipment is essentially *inter*dependent. What it is—its respective *role*—depends inextricably on role relations with other equipment and with users. If there were no such relations, there could be no such roles and hence no such equipment. (There could be no nails without hammers, no pens without ink, and so on.) As we have seen, this amounts to a sort of *holism* (a term that Heidegger did not have—though he surely had the idea).

People are interdependent, too, of course, and not only with each other but also with their equipment, projects, institutions, and the like. There could be no vendors without customers, and vice versa, not to mention products to sell and means of payment. Cases of dasein are unintelligible except as competently ensconced in a familiar world that is "holistic" not only practically but also *socially*.

Therefore, Descartes was already off on the wrong foot—indeed, twice over—when he said, definitively: "I am a thinking thing." For, by 'thing' he certainly meant 'independent substance'—the very antithesis of ontological holism. And, by 'thought' he certainly meant explicit cognition as opposed to inarticulate, skillful know-how.

Yet there remains something else in Descartes's seminal thesis that is at once profound and fundamentally elided in practical-cum-social holism: the *"I am . . ."* Descartes speaks in the *first person* and also only for his own benefit, like a diarist. That these were clear and important to him is manifest in various ways, including not least his choosing the literary form of a "meditation." The voice is that of the *I-myself* and so *(ostensibly)* is the ear, in a kind of private monologue.

This innovation is sometimes said to have ushered in a new philosophical era of "subjectivity," "innerness," and "privacy"—the era of "philosophy of mind"—developments with which Heidegger is not sympathetic. Being-in-the-world is precisely *not* "inner" in the sense of being "in" one's own self or soul but rather being *"out"* in the world.

Even here, however, the word 'out' is in quotation marks because what's *really* in question is the traditional inner/outer distinction as such. For the point is certainly *not* that modern philosophy got the inner/outer (or subjective/objective or private/public) distinction right but just got the I-myself on the wrong side of it.

Rather, the point of being-in-the world as the basic structure of dasein is that those distinctions do not carve the phenomena at the joints. The I-myself does not belong on *either* side of an inner/outer or a subjective/objective distinction. Dasein's basic makeup is just not articulated along that sort of dimension.

At the beginning of his analytic of dasein, Heidegger gave two formal indications of its topic: first, that the essence of dasein lies in its existence, and second, that dasein is in each case mine.[1] In a discussion of the *"who,"* it is easy to suppose that the latter of these indications—in-each-case-mineness—is the more relevant. What is more, in highlighting Descartes's I-myself, that is effectively what we have been doing.

But it is not obvious that this approach exhibits the "who" of everyday *being-in-the-world:*

> It could be that I myself, in each case, am precisely *not* the who of everyday dasein. (SZ 115)

The point is not, of course, that mineness or the "I-myself" might be *irrelevant* to the question of the "who" but only that the connection is subtle and not what one might first suppose.[2]

Even so, there remains an ostensible methodological argument that the investigation ought to begin with the "I-myself." For is it not sound procedure to start with what is most evident? And is not the givenness of the "I" to itself more evident than anything else—more so, for instance, than that of the "external world" or "other minds"? Well, maybe sometimes and to some extent, but either way it is beside the point. The self-givenness of the "I," whatever its credentials, is not the same as a mode of access to either being-in-the-world as dasein's basic makeup—or, therefore, the who as one of its constitutive moments.

But there are further grounds for caution. Those credentials themselves are far from unimpeachable and for a fundamental reason. What is given in immanent self-reflection is conditioned from the outset by concepts and assumptions drawn from "sound common sense." Indeed, the very idea of introspective self-knowledge and the incorrigibility that is sometimes

---

1. SZ 41ff.; that these are formal indications is made explicit at SZ 114 and 117.

2. The next four paragraphs have been interpolated from a section of the manuscript titled "Outtakes from Section 6.4). For more extensive explanation, see note 5 in this chapter.—Ed.

supposed to attend it is thoroughly commonsensical—which is why they are so easy to explain to undergraduates.

But common sense is not an infallible guide to philosophy and, above all, not in regard to questions of fundamentals. In particular, the question of the sense of being, including especially the being of dasein, is utterly alien to everyday understanding—which is why it is so hard to explain to anybody.

An understanding of dasein's being is embodied in the very way of life that dasein is, and that implies that those who live that way all share in that public understanding, at least initially and usually. But that does not mean that it is not a *mis*understanding. Quite the contrary: as will emerge, the default public understandings of dasein and of the "I-myself" always are misunderstandings in certain specific and nonaccidental ways.

Accordingly, Heidegger proposes (rather abruptly) that we temporarily reorient our discussion, giving more emphasis to the *other* initial indication: that the essence of dasein lies in its existence. And, in the same spirit, he stipulates that the "I" ("I-myself," "ego") should itself be understood—for the moment, anyway—only as a noncommittal formal indicator (SZ 116). This is tantamount to suggesting, as he explicitly points out, that we undertake to understand the "who" of everyday dasein *existentially*—that is, in terms of *how* the living way of life is lived. It also suggests—what he was not in a position to observe—that, for the moment, we adopt an orientation more like that of social holism.

6.2 CO-DASEIN: THE WAY-OF-BEING OF OTHERS

As in my discussion of the world, I will approach the phenomenon of the who via several preparatory topics and considerations. The salient difference, of course, is that this time I will begin with people rather than equipment (or things).

Heidegger's official term for individual people is 'others.' That may seem to imply "other than me," but he is quick to insist that it means everybody, *oneself included* (SZ 118, 126). The term 'other' is coextensive with the term 'person.' Thus, taking the terminology at face value, one is oneself just another other. But that only means that each of us is "just another" person, living in the world along with everybody else.

Now, these individual people—others, like you and me—are intraworldly entities. We are in no sense separate from or "outside of" the world, somehow "looking in." Rather, we show up to ourselves and one an-other as entities *within* the world, to be dealt with and understood in what-ever ways are appropriate for the sort of entities we are. Indeed, dasein it-self sets people free and lets them be, just as it does available equipment and occurrent things (SZ 118n, 120ff., 123). For, manifestly, our everyday lives involve intelligible dealings not only with equipment (and things) but also and crucially with each other.

Ontologically, of course, others are an entirely different *sort* of entity from either equipment or things. Their way-of-being is neither availability nor oc-currentness but rather what Heidegger calls *co-dasein* (*Mitdasein: SZ* 118, 120, 125, 140; *GP* 396). Alas, this term, too, is potentially misleading, for it could easily suggest some special mode or variant of dasein. But co-dasein can be nothing like that since dasein itself is an entity (albeit a distinctive one), whereas co-dasein is a way-of-being, hence not any entity at all.

What, then, does it mean to say that the way-of-being of people is co-dasein? Clearly, it must mean at least this: to be a person at all is to be a copar-ticipant in a way of life that embodies an understanding of being—in other words, a fellow member of the community whose way of life that is. Hei-degger himself, however, does not put it that way. In fact, he does not intro-duce a separate term for community at all. Instead, he says that the world of dasein is a *co-world* and that being-in is *being-co* others (Mitwelt and Mit-sein, respectively, SZ 118). These, moreover, are unmistakable counterparts of terms we already know from the preceding chapter. The world as co-world corresponds exactly to the world as around-world (Umwelt), and being-in as being-co others corresponds to being-in as being-amidst *(Sein bei)* equipment and projects—as the workshop example amply illustrates in both cases.

So it is not that community is left out or even downplayed; it is just not separately named. And that is because it is intelligible only as an integral factor in the everyday world as a whole. Everyday dasein's community *just is* its world, considered with a certain emphasis. Or, to put it another way, the terms 'about-world' and 'co-world' do not name distinct parts of the world, still less distinct worlds, but rather the world itself from different points of view.

There are, in fact, quite a number of such "parallels" corresponding to these two aspects of dasein's worldedness. For we have not only the around-world/co-world and being-amidst/being-co pairs but also the conspicuous analogy between equipment and others as intraworldly entities and there-fore, too, that between availability and co-dasein as their respective ways of being. And, as counterparts to around-sight *(Umsicht)*—our subliminal awareness of how a project is going, we have also *considerateness (Rücksicht)* and *indulgence (Nachsicht)*—as our subliminal awareness of how personal interactions and relationships are going.

More interesting, however, is car*ing*ness *(Fürsorge)* with regard to others as the counterpart of care*ful*ness *(Besorgen)* regarding equipment. Both are modes of care *(Sorge*—of which more later), and both have their various deficient modes (negligence, indifference, perfunctoriness, and the like). But caringness is structurally richer than carefulness in that it exhibits a spectrum of positive (nondeficient) modes between two opposite extremes.

Positive caring is playing a sincere, unselfish, contributory role in how others are doing in their lives, and it is this contributory element that exhibits the spectrum of possibilities. One extreme is the familiar "jumping in and taking over," which youngsters and invalids so often resent (though also often appreciate).

The interesting case, however, is the opposite extreme, which Heidegger describes as "leaping forth and liberating" *(SZ* 122v).[3] This is precisely *not* taking over responsibility for how someone else lives but rather leading the others toward the ability to take that responsibility for themselves—for their own lives. In other words, it is leading someone toward the possibility of ownedness. Certainly, this is not anything you can make anybody do— that would mock the point—but something more like setting an example and perhaps articulating it. (That is the reason for odd expressions such as "leaping forth" and "leading.")

But once this character of leading and liberating by example (whether articulate or not) comes into view, it becomes clear that the individuals involved need not actually be acquainted—they need not even live in the same century. Thus, Antigone, Socrates, Jesus, Galileo, Lincoln, Gandhi, King—these and countless others—can, by their example, leap forth and liberate anyone with eyes to see. Not only famous heroes, however, not only revered pioneers, leaders, or martyrs but also any individual who understands and owns responsibility can *show* another how that is possible across any distance of space or time.

---

3. Notice that, although the words are similar, this "leaping forth and liberating" has nothing whatever to do with setting entities "free" and letting them be, as discussed earlier. The latter—a "release" from unnoticedness and unintelligibility—pertains to *all* phenomena, whereas the former—roughly a release from unownedness and irresponsibility— makes sense only in regard to individual people.

6.3 OCCUPATIONS: THE WHO-BEING OF OTHERS

When we ask about an unfamiliar item of equipment or natural object, we generally want to know *what* it is—some specification of its *kind* (what it is for or what it is like). When, by contrast, we ask about an unfamiliar person, we usually want to know who the person is—some identification of that particular *individual*. Thus, the distinction between the pronouns 'what' and 'who' is not just whether the topic is a "thing" or a person but also whether it is a kind or an individual. The fact that these two distinctions coincide reflects something important about people: it matters which one is which. The ontological term 'co-dasein'—glossed as participating in a communal way of life that embodies an understanding of being—has been assigned to the way-of-being of people (others). But how are we to understand the "what-being"—or, as we had better put it, the *who*-being—of these entities? Heidegger says the following:

> Among what is carefully dealt with in an around-worldly way [*im umweltlich Besorgten*], others show up as what they are: they *are* what they are occupied in [*was sie betreiben:* what they engage in, do, or make their business]. (SZ 126)[4]

In other words, what—or, rather, *who*—people are is a matter of their *occupations*, taken broadly. Thus, it includes not only what they do "for a living" but also—and often especially—their home lives, social lives, and civic lives, their avocations and hobbies, even their habits, inclinations, and dreams. These are the basic ways in which people qua *people* are similar to and/or different from one another, hence individually determinate.

It is worth noting that this point is quite routine and familiar. Suppose you indicate someone across the room and ask me who she is. I might reply, "Oh, that's Alice Johnson. She's my son's new math teacher at Washington High—but I hear that her real love is the cello, and she's trying to organize an ensemble." Such answers, more or less elaborated, are entirely

---

4. Haugeland normally translates Heidegger's technical term *Besorgen* as "carefulness," but that translation sacrifices its traces as a verb and thus complicates the translation of *Besorgten* in the passage quoted. Having translated *Umwelt* as "around-world" to emphasize the preposition "um" and keep the term distinct from any connotations of an organismal environment, the adjective *umweltlich* requires the awkward "in an around-worldly way."—*Ed.*

commonplace, and they illustrate perfectly what is meant by saying that who people are is what they do: their occupations.

Now, just as the co-dasein of others is ontologically analogous to the availability of equipment, so these occupations are analogous to equipmental roles. Indeed, the analogy is so apt in some quarters as to invite the corporate abomination "human resources." Yet, analogies go only so far. To understand occupations as such, we need to explicate them in their own terms and as essentially distinct from equipmental roles.

There are lots of differences, of course. Occupations are typically more flexible and adaptable than roles; they usually must be learned and then require some intelligence and judgment in their exercise; moreover, in the meantime, each person has a great many occupations, whereas equipment tends to be fairly specialized.

But I think the fundamental difference is something else. Unlike any equipment, people can choose their occupations. To be sure, there are always pressures and constraints, but this basic *capacity* for choice is intrinsic to being a person at all.

Given what has been said earlier about identity and occupations, this point can be put in a more striking way. Within the obvious practical limits, it is always up to each individual person *who to be*. We have each chosen who we are (if only by default), and we can each always choose again. By contrast, it is never up to any item of equipment what to be. (This is the root of the distinctive individuality intended in the question "Who . . . ?" as opposed to the generality implied in the question "What . . . ?")

6.4 CONFORMISM AND THE EVERYDAY SELF[5]

The official topic of the present chapter is: the "who" of everyday dasein—the counterpart of the everyday world in everyday being-in-the-world. But,

---

5. Haugeland's manuscript includes two different versions of section 6.4, each titled "The Everyday Self and the Anyone," plus a selection of "Outtakes from Section 6.4" and a section 6.5, titled "The Who of Dasein," which repeats almost verbatim much of the longer version of section 6.4. The composite version below accepts that Haugeland intended to place the discussion of the "anyone" as the who of dasein in a separate section 6.5 and divides the various passages accordingly (as noted earlier, one of the "outtakes from section 6.4" was moved to section 6.1 as more thematically relevant to that discussion of whether there should be methodological priority to the "I myself").—*Ed.*

for the very reason [that the parallel is between the everyday *world* and the "who" of everyday dasein], this "who" *is not and cannot be* the "who-being" of others that we have just been discussing.

To confuse the *occupations* (who-being) of individual people with the *"who"* of everyday dasein would be like confusing the *roles* of individual items of equipment with the everyday *world*. In either case, it would amount to a confusion of structural "levels": being-in-the-world (who/being-in/world), as the basic makeup of dasein, is "a level up" from all intraworldly entities—people and equipment alike. Thus, the concept of the "who" is both a "level up" and on the "opposite side of the coin" from any intraworldly entities—including, in particular, intraworldly others.

Yet, [while avoiding this confusion between structural levels,] it is at least as important to see that the structural parallels between people and equipment are not complete. In the last two sections, we worked through a sort of "compare and contrast" exercise between equipment and people as intraworldly entities. The analogies are impressive as far as they go, but there is fundamentally more to people than any such exercise can exhibit. We have three further telling clues to the character of what is omitted.

For one thing, as we have just seen, people do not merely "show up" in the world as whoever they happen to be. People can choose their own occupations and thereby choose who they *themselves* are. But that means, in each case, choosing who *I myself* am. There is nothing remotely comparable to this self-choosing—or therefore, that "I myself"—in the realm of equipment. Second, the very term 'others' is conspicuously odd. For, even though it subsumes everybody—one is oneself "just another other"—one is precisely not an "other" *to oneself*. Rather, in each case, dasein is *I myself* to itself. Finally, of course, there remains the formal indication that dasein is in each case *mine*.

This phenomenon of the I-myself—the self that is respectively mine—is what Heidegger temporarily set aside in the first section of this chapter. Now, having completed the account of people as intraworldly entities, we are finally ready to take up the issue of mineness and selfhood but only to the extent that it bears on the official topic of the whole discussion: the "who" of *everyday* dasein.

One familiar way of introducing this new consideration is to observe that people have different "perspectives" on themselves and each other. Borrowing a grammatical distinction, it is often said that individuals have a "first-person" perspective on themselves but only a "second-" or "third-person" perspective on each other. Adopting these terms for a moment, we can say that, having characterized the everyday way in which ordinary people show up in a "third-person perspective" to one another, we are now going to address the everyday way in which those same ordinary people show up in a "first-person perspective" to themselves.

Prima facie, such a shift might seem odd or even hopeless. Is it not, after all, one of the canonical features of the "first person," the I-myself, that "access" to it is private and privileged? Certainly. But our concern is not to breach the "confidentiality" of any particular I-myself. Rather, it is to characterize the everyday I-myself as such, to understand mineness and self-hood *existentially*—in terms of *how* a way of life is lived. (How this plays out in particular cases is another subject.)

Heidegger begins genetically—that is, with a phenomenological account of how the everyday I-myself comes to have the character it has. In everydayness, people do not just work, play, and transact business with one another. They also attend to and worry about each other's behavior and especially their own and others' relative status and success. Differences among people, of whatever sort, are disturbing to being-co-one-another. So there is a ubiquitous, subliminal effort to tamp them down—an effort that may, of course be resisted by whoever happens to be "ahead" at the moment.

But Heidegger makes this point in a way that allows him to extend it with some slick wordplay. The term he uses for 'difference' is 'Abstand' (which more literally means 'distance'). Its derivative adjective, 'abständig,' however, does not mean 'distant' or 'different' (as one might suppose) but rather 'decadent,' 'stale,' or 'insipid'—as in forests that are overmature or old beer that has "gone off." Yet what we find in the text is not that adjective itself but its (still more derivative) abstract nominalization, 'Abständigkeit'— which is not a "dictionary word" at all.

'Abständigkeit,' whatever it means, is an existentiale (*SZ* 127); so, wordplay notwithstanding, we have to take it seriously. How can we unify, in a single concept, the etymological sense of distance or differentness, the explicitly noted fact that we are all concerned (in a way that is disturbing) about how we compare with others and the colloquial connotations of decadence, tastelessness, and going stale?

It seems to me that there is a simple and compelling answer to this question: Heidegger is working out a phenomenological concept of what we now call *conformism*. It should be clear enough how this accommodates the earlier observations and connotations. But why is it essential to dasein and especially to everydayness? Why should conformism be an *existentiale*?

Return to languages, as we used them earlier to illustrate the basic structure of dasein. Several points stand out. First, people have to learn their native tongues, including both the ability to understand what others say and the ability to make themselves understood by others. Second, those "others" are arbitrary colinguals: by and large, any two speakers of the same language can (even at first meeting) converse effortlessly on a wide range of topics—whereas monolingual speakers of different languages cannot. Therefore, third, there must be a great deal of consistent commonality in how the learners of any given language have learned to act and respond.

How is such commonality inculcated and maintained? Surely, something like conformism—both in one's own behavior and in one's expectations of others—is an essential component in that process. And, once the point is grasped in connection with language, it becomes obvious that it extends quite broadly to the determinate character of human ways of life as such and for the same basic reasons. Where would commerce, sports, politics, courtship, highway driving, or dinner parties be if people could not count on one another to act and respond—relative to their current situations—in more or less standardized ways? Conformism is an existentiale because dasein would be impossible without it.

The upshot is that individual people are largely "standardized"—and not just in their public behavior, entitlements, and obligations but also in their private convictions and preferences, their tastes and habits, their hopes, fears, and dreams and not just from a third-person perspective qua others but also from the first-person perspective as "I myself" in each respective case. In ordinary everydayness, cases of dasein mostly (and rightly) understand *themselves* as ordinary, everyday people.

As noted at the outset, however, the "who" of everyday dasein cannot be identified with these ordinary people, whether singly or ensemble. The "who" is on a par with the world in the basic makeup of being-in-the-world. Hence, like the world, it functions at a higher structural level than any intraworldly entities—including people.

But, then, what is the point? If people qua people, with all that has just been said about them, are intra*worldly*, why is the world not enough? Why do we need the *"who"*?

Descartes did not just *say* "I am . . ."; he was also *right—deeply* right. I do not mean, of course, that he wrote while he was still alive or even that his claim was therefore true. Rather, in expressing himself as *"I myself,"* he expressed something deeply right about dasein as such. (Grammatically, we say he wrote in "the first person," but the lens of grammar is shaped by the exigencies of everydayness.) The phenomenon of the "I myself," what Descartes really (and rightly) expressed, is essential to dasein. Only when you add such an I myself to "just another other" do you get a case of dasein.[6]

[That insight indicates *why*] the parallels between equipment and people as two sides of the same coin are not exact, as one might suppose. Indeed, part of the point here is that people—*others*—are intra*worldly*. They belong on the *world* side, right along with equipment. But that point, true as far as it goes, still leaves out something quite essential. For people, unlike any equipment, there is a fundamental distinction between the first- and third-person perspectives—the distinction between I myself and others. Finally, therefore, the I myself is the essential element in the *who* that is the counterpart of the world in the makeup of dasein.

6.5 THE "ANYONE" AS THE "WHO" OF DASEIN

Dasein is not people. In my experience, this cannot be said too often. People—others—are intraworldly entities. Though they are ontologically distinct from equipment and things (co-dasein versus being-available or being-occurrent), they are on a par with them as intraworldly.

Yet, the who of everyday dasein is neither these ordinary, normal people themselves nor anything like an amalgam or average of them. Indeed, I think Heidegger's point is best expressed with a grammatical device introduced by Wilfrid Sellars—namely, what he called a "distributive singular term" (Sellars 2007, ch. 4, 7). The canonical example of such a term is 'the lion,' in a sentence like "The lion is tawny," such as might appear in an encyclopedia or a wildlife guidebook. Clearly, in such a context, the expression 'the lion' would not denote any *particular* lion; nor could it mean *all* lions (since, after all, a few lions are albino, and so on). Rather, it refers to

---

6. The fourth and fifth sentences of this paragraph were inserted in the manuscript as separate paragraphs, with the two together set off from the surrounding text as if they were to be developed further or possibly moved elsewhere within the text. The sentence that follows them is interpolated from a variant draft of another part of the chapter.—*Ed.*

the *typical* lion: your ordinary, normal, everyday lion. What Heidegger wants to specify as the *who* of everyday dasein is "the person," or, more precisely, "the I-myself," where the quoted phrases are understood as distributive singular terms.

Lacking that conceptual innovation, however, his route to the point is different and, indeed, rather more fraught:

> But this conformism [*Abständigkeit*] that belongs to being-co implies that dasein, as everyday being-co-one-another, stands *beholden* to others. It itself *is* not; the others have taken its being away from it. Dasein's everyday being-possibilities are up to the others to decide. These others, moreover, are not *definite* others. On the contrary, any other can represent them. What is decisive is just that inconspicuous domination by others that has already been taken over unawares from dasein as being-co. One belongs to the others oneself and enhances their power. "The others"—whom one so calls in order to cover up one's own essential belonging to them—are those who, initially and usually, *"are there"* in everyday being-co-one-another. The who is not this one nor that, not one oneself nor some of them nor the sum of them all. The "who" is the neutral, *the anyone* [das Man].[7] (SZ 126)

This "anyone" is the who of everyday dasein, the counterpart of the everyday world in the basic makeup of everyday being-in-the-world. It is *"the* I-myself" (in the sense of a distributive singular term).[8]

---

7. In German, the word '*Man*' is used to indicate, indefinitely, any normal person— much as we use 'one' or 'you' in sentences like: "One needs a good coat in Alaska" or "You can't win them all." I do not translate '*das Man*' with 'the one' because that phrase often suggests something unique or even exalted.

8. The following paragraph, including the three quotations, has been interpolated from a section of the manuscript titled "Outtakes from Section 6.4." The current section 6.4 has been composed from two separate but parallel versions that were both included in the manuscript along with the "outtakes." This editorial strategy presumes that Haugeland was still working on this section and hoped to include some or all of the material from the "outtakes" in a final version of the section. There is no way to know whether he would have included all of this material or what additional explication he would have provided. The rationale for inserting these passages here is that they each explicate the claim that "this 'anyone' is the who of everyday dasein." Moreover, the three-part strategy outlined at the end of the interpolated passage is in fact the strategy Haugeland followed in the original main text.—*Ed.*

So, like the everyday world, the anyone is not itself an entity but rather (as already mentioned) a constitutive moment of one—namely, of a living way of life that embodies an understanding of being (= dasein):

> In this inconspicuousness and un-nail-down-able-ness, the real dictator-ship of the anyone unfolds. We enjoy ourselves and have a good time as *anyone* enjoys. We read, see, and judge about literature and art as *anyone* sees and judges; but we also shrink back from "the great mass" as anyone shrinks back; we find outrageous what *anyone* finds outrageous. The any-one . . . prescribes the sort of being of everydayness. (SZ 126ff.)

> *The anyone is an existentiale, and, as an originary phenomenon, belongs, to the positive makeup of dasein.* (SZ 129)

> *Owned self-being* is not based on some exceptional status of the subject, detached from the anyone, but is rather an *existentiell* modification of the anyone as an essential *existentiale*. (SZ 130)

Like the world again, the anyone is a rich and complicated phenomenon that needs to be spelled out. First, we need to characterize it more care-fully; second, to specify how it is instituted and maintained; and third, to say something about its place in the existential analytic and fundamental ontology.

[A more careful characterization of the anyone begins by asking] how this proposal can be reconciled with the passage quoted earlier in section 1:

> It could be that I myself, in each case, am precisely not the who of everyday dasein. (SZ 115)

The answer, I think, is clear. The phrase "I myself in each case" intends each respective case of dasein as a distinct I-myself—as if each of them him- or herself might be "the" who of everyday dasein. This is what the quoted pas-sage is calling into question. The proposal I am making, by contrast, does not (directly) involve *any* individual cases of dasein. "The I-myself," taken as a distributive singular term, does not refer to individuals but rather to the typical, ordinary I-myself. The quotation does not bear on this proposal at all.

Of course, "the" ordinary, normal "I-myself" admits of great variety in particular cases (lots more than lions). The point is not that everybody is exactly alike but only that there is a considerable *basic* commonality within and by virtue of which boundless variations can then flower. (Even if we all speak the same language and thus hold much in common, we do not all say the same things.) The house of the anyone has many mansions.[9]

Though it is invisible and intangible, it would be a mistake to treat the anyone as an abstraction. It is neither a genus of which individual selves are instances nor any feature that they all share. Rather, it is more like an implicit model or prototype built into the evolving communal way of living itself—the practices, the institutions, the tacit expectations, even the artifacts. And, as thus implicit, it can be covertly yet potently effective in shaping the lives of individuals.

We have already mentioned conformism as a "mechanism" for social shaping and ordinariness as what it fosters. To these, Heidegger adds *leveling-down:* a tendency to render the exceptional unexceptional. This is not the same as conformism, which serves to moderate peculiarity and change, but is rather an unacknowledged modification of ordinariness itself, so as to co-opt and assimilate them. Thus, retroactively, any genuine innovations turn out to have been "normal all along," and the boat of everydayness has not been rocked after all.

Conformism, ordinariness, and leveling-down in turn go to make up publicness (*Öffentlichkeit*), in the sense of "out-in-the-open-ness": easy accessibility to everyone in the clear light of everydayness. This "clarity" is achieved, however, not so much by hard work and insight as by comfortable acquiescence and consensus. What is publicly understood with such universally acknowledged assurance is nothing other than what "everybody knows": plain common sense.

Several difficulties complicate a just appreciation of publicness. First, it is simply too easy to denigrate conformism and ordinariness. We are all familiar with the adolescent who says: "I want to be *different*—like all my

---

9. This sentence should probably be understood as an allusion to the biblical text John 14:2 ("My Father's house has many mansions.") *via* Brandom (1994, 55): "The normative house has many mansions." Yet if so, Brandom and Haugeland are indicating quite different forms of multiplicity. The Brandom passage refers to multiple forms of normativity in order to identify his more specific focus on discursive or conceptual normativity. Haugeland is instead indicating how normative conformism can generate an extraordinarily rich variety of behaviors and roles (Haugeland nevertheless refers elsewhere (p. 19n2) to a different Brandom text (1979, section III) on precisely the point that he here expresses with "the house of the anyone has many mansions.").

friends."[10] [Such facile criticisms overlook that] the attractive and valuable effect [of publicness] is to relieve individuals of the burden of thinking things through for themselves. That really is valuable, of course, since it saves later thinkers from a lot of redundant effort and enables them to build on what has gone before. Such shared, cumulative knowledge, including traditional lore and practical know-how, is both essential to the possibility of dasein at all and the foundation of its unprecedented power.

Yet that same relief from the burden of thinking for oneself is equally a prescription for banality and stagnation (not to mention prejudice and bigotry). The crucial insight is that these two fruits of public common sense—not having to reinvent the wheel, coupled with a smug intolerance of anything but the same old wheels—go inseparably together. You do not get one without the other.

Finally, and most important, this common, public intelligibility extends also to the everyday self and its own *self*-understanding:

> The self of everyday dasein is the *anyone-self,* which we distinguish from the *owned*—that is, explicitly grasped—*self.* (SZ 129)

> *Initially,* it is not "I" that "am," in the sense of my own self, but rather the others, in the way of the anyone. It is from out of this anyone and as this anyone that I am initially "given" to "myself." Initially, dasein is anyone, and usually it remains so. (SZ 129)

---

10. The most developed version of section 6.4 ends abruptly here, but the passage is repeated in section 6.5. What follows are passages from the "outtakes from section 6.4," some of which were also repeated in section 6.5, which seem to spell out the "difficulties that complicate a just appreciation of publicness." Presumably, Haugeland would have further elaborated on what he describes as the "final and most important" feature of "common, public intelligibility," a feature that the manuscript explicates with only the two quotations that now end section 6.5.—*Ed.*

7

Being-in as Such

We've just finished big chapters about the world and the who, and also about equipment and others (intraworldly entities). We've exhibited the anyone (understood as a distributive singular term) as the neutral "I-my-self" of people *qua* cases of dasein. And we've used "comportment toward entities as entities" as a general expression for letting them show up. Now we have to talk about the "relations *between*" them (except that the coin meta-phor turns "relation" inside out). Put another way, what is conspicuously lacking is any account of *how* that comportment lets entities show up as *entities*. Yet that is clearly the heart of the matter—the being-in *as such* of being-in-the-world.

7.1 WHY NOT CONSCIOUSNESS?

'Consciousness' is not one of Heidegger's words.[1] This is surely remarkable, given its centrality in the modern era—including for three of the philoso-phers with whom Heidegger is most in dialogue: Descartes, Kant, and Husserl.

There is no denying, of course, that people are conscious and, indeed, in a way that differs significantly from dogs and cats. The issue, rather, is a

---

1. Haugeland wrote a marginal note in his "working copy," concerning the question posed in the heading for this section: "The main answer to this question is that conscious-ness is a phenomenon of individual people (e.g., Descartes, Husserl, Brentano, et al.)."—*Ed.*

philosophical conception of consciousness that is deeply implicated in the modern understanding of (what Heidegger calls) comportment toward entities as entities. We need to see why.

The traditional concept of consciousness includes a number of diverse elements, and their combination is what gives it its power and thereby makes it tendentious. For the mere subsumption of these various elements under a single technical term implicitly propounds a substantive thesis that they all belong together in a unitary phenomenon. Thus, even in just using the term, one tacitly endorses that thesis.[2] To deny the thesis, therefore, is also to reject the word.[3]

We have yet to see, however, what that combination of elements is or why it might be tendentious. Since Heidegger himself does not actually say any of this, I will articulate briefly what (as I am supposing) he might have said—beginning with the alleged "diverse elements" in the traditional conception of consciousness. Here is a list of candidates:

Innerness: Consciousness is an *"inner arena"* populated with
  nonspatial contents—in contrast to the world, which is "outer" and
  has spatial contents.
Immediacy: Consciousness has *direct* and *"privileged"* access to all
  (and only) its own inner contents.
Evanescence: Consciousness is *fleeting:* always new in every passing
  moment and "flowing away" like a stream.
Experience: Consciousness is the locus of *sensations* and *passions*
  (the "qualia" that "zombies" are supposed to lack).[4]
Intentionality: The contents of consciousness can *intend* or be *directed*
  at objects (even ones that are not there).
Affect: The contents of consciousness (and/or what they intend) can
  "matter" or be *important* to it.
Agency: Consciousness is in the "driver's seat" of life—the intelligent
  agent of rational decision and action.

---

2. In other words, in N. R. Hanson's phrase, the term 'consciousness' is "theory laden."

3. Note that Haugeland takes Heidegger to reject 'consciousness' as a technical term in philosophy. The question of the extent to which ordinary, nonphilosophical uses of the term implicate its philosophical meanings is not here addressed.—*Ed.*

4. Haugeland's marginal notes group these first four items together with the heading "The character of consciousness 'in itself.'"—*Ed.*

Autonomy: Consciousness, as *self*-consciousness, is a *"me"* in a sense that entails *"mineness"* or *"ownership"*—hence also proprietary rights and responsibilities.

Though all the entries on this list are different, they fall fairly readily into two groups. The first four—innerness, immediacy, evanescence, and experience—all acknowledge consciousness as a sort of inner venue, separable in principle from the "outer" world. The latter four, by contrast—intentionality, affect, agency, and autonomy—all involve concrete worldly life.

Heidegger, of course, does not compile any list like this, nor does he, *a fortiori,* divide it into two groups. I do not imagine that Heidegger would repudiate any of the entries on that list. But I do suggest that he would regard the first four as effectively irrelevant to the existential analytic of dasein; whereas the second four, appropriately reconceived, are all essential. He thus rejects the implicit assimilation of the first group of phenomena to those in the second group, for that is what can make it *seem obvious* that intentionality, say, or affect or autonomy is inner or immediate or some sort of experience. The operative difference is that the former have nothing intrinsic to do with being-in-the-*world*, whereas the latter are integral to it.[5]

7.2 INTRODUCTION TO BEING-IN AS SUCH

Being-in is the current, concrete *living*—by people in the world—of a living way of life that embodies an understanding of being. Thus, to return to our earlier examples, it is not Italian (the living language) or chemistry (the living science) but rather *speaking* Italian and *practicing* chemistry. That is what it is actually to *live* those ways of life, and that is what (more generally) being-in as such is. If there were no such living, the way of life itself would not be "alive"—it would not *exist*—so there would be no livers of it and no world in which it is lived. In other words, there would be no *dasein*

---

5. The two preceding paragraphs are composed from two different versions of the conclusion of this section, one from the manuscript found on Haugeland's computer and one from the printed manuscript of some chapters that he labeled as his "working copy." The first of the two paragraphs, as well as the first and penultimate sentences of the second paragraph, are taken from the working copy.—*Ed.*

(at least of that sort) at all. This is why being-in as such is the "heart of the matter."

In his own prologue to the being-in chapter, Heidegger introduces three new technical concepts: the *there*, the *clearing*, and *disclosedness*. He offers little by way of explanation for any of them but rather just seems to identify each with dasein itself—which might further suggest that they are themselves identical. On closer examination, however, the relations are more subtle.

Dasein is "itself, in each case, its 'there' [*sein 'Da'*]" (SZ 132). This there is "where" dasein in each respective case is being lived, where it currently is in the living of its life. This "there" is, of course, worldly—dasein is always lived in the world—but it is idiosyncratically "local" in a way that the world as such is not. We all share our world (or worlds) with others, but we are not all at the same "places" in them. Someone's "there" is not just the world at large but rather *where* that person in particular *is*, "here and now."

Thus, we can put the point another way: each life at each moment is always already concretely *situated*. Yet, importantly, this sense of 'situation' is not exclusively or even mainly spatial. On the contrary, it is one's "current situation" with friends and lovers, projects and progress, finances and obligations, regrets and aspirations, career and reputation, and so on. Such and their ilk are what make up—differently from person to person and from day to day—the concretion of everyday living in situ. And it is our respective life situations in this rich sense that Heidegger calls "the there": the there that dasein *in each case* is. (Literally, *da sein* = being there.)

Dasein is "in itself, as being-in-the-world, cleared [*gelichtet*]—not by any other entity but rather such that it itself *is* the clearing [*Lichtung*]" (SZ 133). The root word is 'light' ['*Licht*'], and Heidegger explicitly invokes the Cartesian "light of nature" (hence implicitly also the "brightness" of clear and distinct ideas). But that gesture is merely a feint: the point is not to endorse Descartes's metaphors but rather to turn them inside out.

As the earlier translation already suggests, what the noun '*Lichtung*' really means in everyday German is not illumination but rather a *clearing*— as in the midst of a forest, a storm, or a fog. The intended implication, of course, is still that entities within the clearing are "clearly" manifest and visible. But in this version, the pivotal word, 'clearly,' does not mean brightly lit. Rather, it means something like visible via a clear line of sight—not blocked from view. Thus, one can see better in the clearing not because the light is better but because the occluding trees or water droplets have been "cleared out of the way."[6]

Given that much, further differences from Descartes fall into place. The light of nature, for instance, shines in the soul. It is a private, inner light, and what it lights up are private, inner ideas. The clearing, by contrast, is in no way private or inner but essentially public and "outer." What shows up in it is the being-in as such of dasein's being-in-the-world: the concrete living—amidst equipment and co-others—of the way of life that dasein is.

Finally, though more tentatively, I think the image of the clearing intrinsically implies finitude—indeed, in a double sense. First, any clearing obviously extends only so far; it is always still surrounded by the rest of the forest. (There may even be other clearings elsewhere, corresponding to other ways of life.) But second, and ultimately more important, no clearing is forever. The forest always encroaches and grows back, so that any clearing can last only as long as it is continually recleared, lest it be overgrown again and disappear.

"Dasein is its disclosedness" (*SZ* 133). The clearing, in fact, is rarely mentioned in *Being and Time.* Disclosing and disclosedness, on the other hand, come up centrally and often. Taken literally, 'disclosing' suggests "opening-up" and thus revealing or making visible (not unlike "clearing"). Indeed, Heidegger himself says this:

> 'To disclose' and 'disclosedness' will be used as technical terms in the passages that follow and will signify 'to lay open' and 'laid-open-ness.' (*SZ* 75)

But what is it to disclose or lay open? Surely at least this: it is to release or extricate from some sort of closed-off-ness, such as concealment, disguise, or even just unnoticedness—and thereby, to *let* something emerge or come forth "out into the open" (the "plain light of day"). The figure of *allowing* phenomena to come into view—whether they were previously hidden, distorted by prejudice, or simply overlooked—runs deep in Heidegger. (It is the heart of the phenomenological method.)

---

6. In the margins of his working copy, Haugeland wrote: "*See SZ 146f.: Sight* corresponds to the clearedness that characterizes the disclosedness of the there (has to do with access)."—*Ed.*

Yet, there remains an ambiguity. Modern philosophy, up to and including Kant, did not decisively distinguish knowledge from understanding. They were alike conceived as a kind of grasp or apprehension, validated by one standard or another ("clarity," as it might be). Heidegger, by contrast, sharply separates discovering from disclosing. The former has to do with knowledge of entities—including the noncognitive knowledge embodied in inarticulate "know-how."

To disclose, by contrast, is to make sense of—hence, to render intelligible. But two themes intersect here, and it is important to keep them straight.[7]

Officially, what dasein discloses to dasein is dasein itself, and, it discloses itself to itself *as* a living way of life that embodies an understanding of being. In that formula, the living way of life is the embodiment (the "implementation," as it were) of that understanding. But it is the understanding of being thus implemented that makes it *dasein*. Accordingly, the disclosedness of dasein to itself is tantamount to the disclosure (rendering intelligible) of being.

In the chapter that follows, we will work through the basic structure of disclosedness as embodied in a way of living—what Heidegger calls "being-in as such." The discussion has two main parts: first, a general account of being-in as such that is neutral between owned and unowned dasein, and then, second, a briefer treatment specific to unowned dasein. (Later chapters will then present a rich and detailed exposition of owned disclosedness.)

As implemented in being-in-the-world, disclosedness has a threefold structure. The basic moments of this structure are called *findingness* [*Befindlichkeit*], *understanding*, and *telling* [*Rede*]. Eventually, it will behoove us to ask: "Why *three?*" and "Why *these* three?" But first we must go through them *seriatim* and see what, respectively, they are and how they work. Only then will it be possible to ask what, as a unified structure, they amount to.

---

7. This paragraph in the manuscript ends here, is followed by a gap of three or four lines, and then resumes in the middle of a hyphenated word, presumably "disclosedness." The partial paragraph that follows seems to be an alternative version of the opening sentence of this paragraph. That partial paragraph has been omitted, and the gap closed, but that closure should be read with caution: it is unclear whether Haugeland intended the next paragraph to articulate the two intersecting themes indicated here.—*Ed.*

7.3 FINDINGNESS AND THROWNNESS

'Findingness' is my contrived rendition of Heidegger's *'Befindlichkeit.'*[8] The verb *'befinden'* means to deem or judge something to be thus and so—as when a court finds a case to be without merit, or students find a seminar stimulating. In the reflexive, it means to be (or be found to be) in such and such a condition or situation. Thus, the ordinary greeting *"Wie befinden Sie sich?"* asks: "How do you find yourself?" in the sense of "How are you?" "How are things going?" "How's life treating you?" and so on. Now, questions like these are mostly addressed to *cases of* dasein (individual people), and what they ask about is the current *"there"* of the addressee— that person's "life situation" here and now. But, much as I said earlier about the there, I think greetings like the foregoing and the sort of "found" situation or condition they ask about make perfect sense for larger integral units like families, teams, or companies.

Be that as it may, *thrownness* is the character of dasein that such questions always already have answers—answers that, somehow or other, it has to live with. And *findingness* is the character of dasein that it always already has some sense of what those answers are: it *finds* itself thus and so.

In the word 'thrownness,' the form of the embedded verb is as important as the verb itself: it is in both the past tense and the passive voice. Thus, dasein has always already *been* thrown. And the implication that this having been thrown is something that has happened to it—or, at any rate, something it is now stuck with—is clearly intended. For Heidegger also speaks (both here and elsewhere) of dasein as being *delivered over* to itself or its there: abandoned to its own devices, as it were.

Whatever the formulation, thrownness clearly entails some sort of "factual determinacy" in dasein: its living—including its having lived and being able to live—in these ways *rather than* those. But since this determinacy can only be a matter of the *how* of its living, it cannot be the same ontological category as the factuality of things. Indeed, it is not strictly a category at all but rather an existentiale. Heidegger calls it *facticity.*

---

8. Macquarrie and Robinson render *'Befindlichkeit'* as 'state-of-mind,' one of their least fortunate choices: it is neither a state nor "of mind." Stambaugh's 'disposition' (Heidegger 1996) is better in these regards, but it misleadingly evokes reductive, behaviorist doctrines (such as Ryle's 1949), and it misses the point that one finds oneself so disposed.

What dasein has always already been delivered over to and stuck with is *itself,* qua *there*—its current factical situation in the fullest sense. Every such situation is replete with its past and pregnant with its possible future. If you are now a licensed accountant, for instance, that is only because you once studied accounting and passed a licensing exam. The studying and exam passing are no longer part of your current there, but having done them and so now being an accountant certainly are. Likewise, if that license puts you in a position to apply for certain jobs, then actually applying for them may or may not belong to your current there, but being in a position to do so certainly does. Thus, finally, saying that dasein is "stuck with" its current situation does not at all mean that it cannot move on. On the contrary, it means that it *has to*—and *can only*—move on *from there.*[9]

At each moment, dasein is its there—its current life situation. And its thrownness is *that it is and has to be* this there, here and now (SZ 135):

> This being-character of dasein, veiled in its whence and whither, yet in itself so unveiledly disclosed, this "that it is," we call the *thrownness* of this entity into its there—thrown, indeed, in such a way that, as being-in-the-world, it is the there. The expression 'thrownness' is meant to suggest the *facticity* of its being *delivered over.* (SZ 135)

Dasein always must and can only ever go on from wherever it already is; there are no alternatives.

As factically thrown into its there, dasein always has some "sense of" or "feel for" or "appreciation of" how it is doing or how life is going for it. This "sense," as already noted, is called *findingness,* and (along with understanding and telling) it is one of the three constitutive moments of disclosedness.

Heidegger introduces his own discussion by saying this: "What we indicate *ontologically* with the term 'findingness' is *ontically* most familiar and everyday: mood, being attuned" (SZ 134). Thus, mood and attunement are not the same as findingness itself but illustrative ontical manifestations of it. Nevertheless, they are a particularly good place to start and for several reasons. First, they are a distinctively "direct" or "unmediated" uptake of how things are going—whether locally or more globally. Second, they tend to be relatively "pure" in the sense of being inarticulate and therefore resis-

---

9. Haugeland's working copy marks the four preceding paragraphs with this comment: "These sound as if they apply only to individual people." He presumably intended to revise them to dispel that impression.—*Ed.*

tant to intellectualization or confabulation. Finally, moods are peculiarly unbidden and compelling, making them especially vivid as manifestations of life's beholdenness to its current there (intraworldly entities and situations).

It should be noted that the German word for mood, 'Stimmung,' is somewhat broader than ours, encompassing some phenomena that we might rather call affects or emotions (such as fear—as we will see in a moment). The word itself is cognate with the verb 'stimmen,' which means either "to tune" (e.g., a musical instrument) or "to be in accord with" (e.g., the facts[10]). In these, the common note of "consonance" is conspicuous. That is why Heidegger can so easily use the verbal nouns 'Gestimmtheit' and 'Gestimmtsein' ("attunement," "being attuned") as alternatives for 'Stimmung' in a way that conveniently broadens its sense.[11]

The exposition of findingness has three parts and is followed by a specific example.

First: dasein is its there by way of finding itself *in its throwness*. This is, of course, neither a perceptual nor a cognitive finding (though it may be more or less explicit). Rather, qua mood or attunement, it primarily takes the form of dasein's facing up to its current situation or evasively turning away from it—mostly the latter.[12] In a memorable line, Heidegger says that, in a mood, the *that-it-is* of dasein's there "stares it in the face with the inexorability of an enigma" (SZ 136).

Second: moods/attunements disclose being-in-the-world as a whole—that is, as the whole unitary structure of who, being-in, and world. In particular, they are neither specifically "inner" (psychological) nor specifically "outer" (worldly) but instead arise in the course of concrete interactive living amidst things and co-others. But that means that findingness itself is the fundamental form of—indeed, first makes possible—directing oneself toward something (in other words, intentionality).

Third, and the most important for understanding the worldishness of the world: moods and attunements are the basic way in which intraworldly

---

10. Note also that 'Übereinstimmung' is the standard philosophical term for correspondence, as in "the correspondence theory" of truth.

11. Haugeland's marginal note in the working copy: "How about: 'affective attunements'?"—*Ed.*

12. Haugeland's marginal note in the working copy: "Well . . . why? You can't just *say* this."—*Ed.*

entities *affect* us. This does not mean causing effects "in" us but rather eliciting affective responses from us. These are the responses that make concepts like 'carefulness' and 'caringness' intelligible. In findingness as affect, things *matter* to dasein: the hammer is missing, business is booming, a friend lets you down, your health is improving—these are not just "facts" that we register but things that we care about.

The point is not that, without affect, human lives would be drab, aimless, or somehow merely mechanical. The point is that they would not be possible. If nothing ever mattered, nobody would ever do anything, and there would simply be no "way of life" (to embody an understanding of being) at all.

Any number of moods or attunements might be brought forward to illustrate this account: eagerness, dejection, puzzlement, exasperation, pride, wariness, satisfaction, and so on. Heidegger's choice, fear, is as good as any, but it also has an ulterior motive. Later, and for substantive philosophical reasons, he will offer a parallel analysis of anxiety, and it will be useful then to have discussed fear already, so that he can clearly distinguish the two.

For our purposes, it is not necessary to go through this example in particular detail. Suffice it to say that fear has a three-fold structure as follows:

First, there is the before-which ("in-the-face-of-which") of the fear—namely, whatever it is that is frightening. It might be a fire, a bear, a bandit, a job evaluation, or any other ontical phenomenon that might show up as menacing. To say that it is menacing is to say that it threatens some imminent, determinate harm but that it has not yet delivered that harm—and so there is still a possibility that it will not. Finding itself faced with such a threat is a manifestation of dasein's *thrownness* into its there.

Second, there is the fearing or being afraid as such: the affective disquiet or recoil in which something intraworldly is set free as a *definite danger* (possible harm) to us *here and now*. It is not just that there is something bad that might really happen but also that we *feel* it as looming or closing in on us. This is an affectively charged manifestation of being-in-the-world as a whole—a particular way in which dasein lets intraworldly situations (amidst entities and co-others) *matter.*

Third, there is the *on-behalf-of-which (Worum)* of the fear—namely, "the very entity that is afraid: dasein" (*SZ* 141). Of course, one can fear for any number of things: one's house (in the face of a fire), one's safety (in the face of a bear), one's money (in the face of a bandit), or even one's career or reputation (in the face of an evaluation, say). Indeed, one can even fear for the safety (or house or whatever) of *someone else*. The point is that, whatever dasein fears for—whatever it is concerned about and takes to be at risk—what it fears *on behalf of* is *itself.*

7.4 UNDERSTANDING AND PROJECTION

Findingness is the first of the three constitutive moments that Heidegger works out in the disclosedness of the there, the existential structure of being-in as such. The second, roughly counterposed to findingness, is understanding. Unlike 'findingness,' 'understanding' is a perfectly ordinary word and also one that has been much used by philosophers. Heidegger is by no means dismissive of this background, but his aim is to develop a more basic understanding of understanding—one from which its familiar manifestations can then be seen as derivative.

This is not the first time that the notion of understanding has come up for us. All along, for instance, I have been glossing 'dasein' as a way of living that embodies an *understanding* of being. Moreover, Heidegger's own specification of the overall aim of *Being and Time* is "to reawaken the question of the sense of being"—which is to say, the question of how being makes sense—within the horizon of time. Finally, the disclosedness of the there (the topic of the present chapter) is tantamount to its being rendered intelligible. I think it is not an exaggeration to say that, along with being, dasein, and time, understanding is among the most important concepts in the book. Indeed, as the foregoing indicates, they are all deeply interconnected.

We begin with an introductory observation about how the word 'understand' is sometimes used—namely to attribute a kind of competence or ability to manage in some domain. For instance, an experienced but untrained and inarticulate auto mechanic might be said to "really understand" cars if—even without being able to say how—she is good at making them run well. Understanding a band saw or a carpenter's plane is *knowing how* to use them or at least how they can be used. Finally, the most basic form of understanding a game or a natural language is being *able* to play it or converse in it fluently and competently.

The claim is not, of course, that there can be no explicit, theoretical understandings or explanations of such phenomena or that there are no domains in which theoretical explanation is essential but only that understanding qua know-how is always fundamental. (Even theoretical explanation itself inevitably presupposes competent know-how—namely with its own theoretical/explanatory apparatus.)

All of these examples have been ordinary and ontical. In this regard, they are analogous to ordinary moods. But there is another sense in which understanding as such is analogous to findingness as such, and at this more structural level, understanding is, like findingness, an existentiale. Understanding and findingness are, as Heidegger also puts it, *equioriginary*. And it is in this originary, existential sense that findingness and understanding are two of the three constitutive moments of the disclosedness of being-in-the-world. All the same, understanding is an essentially richer phenomenon than findingness.

Understanding as an existentiale is still a kind of know-how, but the relevant competence is to live a way of life that embodies an understanding of being—that is, to exist as a case of dasein. Heidegger says this in several ways: "dasein is in each case what it can be" (*SZ* 143); "possibility . . . qua *existentiale* is the most originary and ultimate positive way in which dasein is characterized ontologically" (*SZ* 143ff.) or simply that dasein "*is* its possibilities as possibilities" (*SZ* 145).

But, to hear these aright, one must appreciate that 'possibility' does not mean "mere" possibility—the Leibnizian sense in which possibility is a *lower* status (or *weaker* claim) than actuality. On the contrary, "possibilities" must here be understood *positively* as capacities or capabilities: what dasein is able to do.[13] Thus, Heidegger can also put the point by saying that dasein is, in each case, its ability-to-be *(Seinkönnen).* And this formulation is really better, both because it does not risk the confusion about what "possibility" means and because it emphasizes the fundamental connection with competence.

We must ask, however, what else this understanding qua competence involves. Return to the inarticulate car mechanic: we say that she understands cars inasmuch as she is able to make them run well. But what, more specifically, must she grasp about the innards of the car itself if she is to have that ability? Surely something like this: she has to know how they have to be able to work together in order to amount, ensemble, to a functioning car.

---

13. The modal dual of possibility in this sense is neither mere inability nor ability not to but rather necessity qua force or compulsion: the *inability not to.*

In other words, in her understanding of cars, "abilities" are essentially involved at two distinct levels: first, there are the abilities that the mechanic herself must have, but second, and just as important, there are the functions and capacities of the car parts and systems themselves. So, in effect, her abilities amount to an understanding of their abilities. This structure is not new to us. Recall that the most basic understanding of equipment is knowing how to use it properly and effectively, and skillful know-how is nothing if not an ability. But also, what is mastered in such practical mastery is what the equipment itself is capable of—its service*ability* or us*ability*.

Nor is that all. Even physical nature is rendered intelligible—explained—by subsumption under modal laws (which is to say, laws delimiting what is physically possible). While the "deductive-nomological" model of scientific explanation postdates *Being and Time* by some years, Heidegger roughly anticipates it by connecting the intelligibility of natural entities with what Kant called "the conditions of their possibility."

So far, we have been exhibiting understanding phenomenologically: presenting various typical instances and descriptively pointing out some of their characteristics. Now, however, we turn to something more like a theoretical account. "Why," Heidegger asks, "does understanding . . . always press forward into possibilities?" And he answers: "Because it has in itself the existential structure that we call '*projecting*'" (SZ 145).

Thus, just as 'thrownness' is a technical term for the basic character of dasein that is manifest in findingness, so 'projecting' is a technical term for the basic character of dasein that manifests itself as understanding. What is more, the two terms are semantically related inasmuch as 'projecting' literally means "throwing forth" or "throwing forward." (German has the same root, '*werfen*': "to throw.") Thus, verbally, the contrast is between *having-been*-thrown (past and passive) and throw*ing-forward* (futural and active). But what is the point of these verbal devices?

The topic of the present chapter (the disclosedness of being-in as such) is dasein's *making sense* of entities (itself included) as entities and as the entities they are. Initially, one might suppose that making sense is the exclusive province of understanding. Yet if that sense making were not concretely situated and "beholden" to the entities themselves, it would float free as mere fantasy. The thrownness manifested in findingness just is this requisite (and inevitable) *beholdenness* to situated entities as they already are.

Still, dasein's finding itself thrown into the midst of entities does not suffice for the disclosedness of its being-in as such. Projective understanding, while not the whole story either, is certainly no less essential for the basic "making sense of" that disclosedness amounts to. Moreover (as we will see soon enough), there is also a third factor that is equioriginary with findingness and understanding: only in concert can they constitute dasein's disclosedness.

In the meantime, we have yet to explain projection as the existential structure of understanding. There is a conspicuous difference between the past and the future. The former is already done: it is "fixed" in the sense that there is no going back and changing it. (This is part of the point of thrownness.) The future, by contrast, is not yet: there remain options—what Heidegger calls "room for maneuver." But options in a vacuum are useless (nugatory). If there is no basis for going on in one way rather than another, one might as well (as we say) flip a coin.

Now projection, as the counterpart of thrownness, has to do with this question of how to go on—how to come to terms with the "not yet." And Heidegger distills the basic alternatives down to two:

> Understanding *can* devote itself primarily to the disclosedness of the world; that is, dasein can, proximally and for the most part, understand itself in terms of the world. Or else understanding throws itself primarily into the "for-the-sake-of-which"; that is, dasein exists as itself. Understanding is either owned, arising out of one's own self as such, or unowned. (*SZ* 146)[14]

> [U]nderstanding . . . has in itself the existential structure we call projecting. It projects dasein's being onto its for-the-sake-of-which just as originarily as onto significance as the worldishness of its current world. The projective character of understanding constitutes being-in-the-world in regard to the disclosedness of its there as the there of an ability-to-be. (*SZ* 145)[15]

Thus, the understanding of equipment that consists in knowing how to use it is a special case. Other special cases would include the projection of

---

14. Haugeland does not specifically include this passage but only provided a reminder to himself to find the relevant quotation on SZ 145; context strongly suggests that this is the passage he had in mind. There is a gap in the manuscript before the next quotation, suggesting that Haugeland planned further explication built around that quotation.—*Ed.*

15. Macquarrie and Robinson omit the words after 'disclosedness' and run this sentence together with the next.

physical systems onto the possibilities delimited by physical laws (thereby rendering intelligible their progress through space and time); the intelligibility of chess pieces and positions via projection onto the rules that determine how the game can proceed; and so on.

The reason Heidegger uses the term 'possibility' at all in this context rather than simply sticking with competence and ability throughout is precisely that 'possibility' is a more generic term—in the sense, indeed, that it pertains to *all* intelligible entities as such.[16]

16. The manuscript ends at this point, with substantial parts of chapter 7 unwritten. Haugeland's plan for the chapter, stated at the outset, suggests that after elaborating on these remarks about projection onto possibilities, he would also have included in this chapter his discussions of interpretation, assertion, language, and telling *(Rede)*, as well as a briefer characterization of unowned, "falling" dasein, characterized by curiosity, ambiguity, and "idle talk" *(Gerede)*. Many of these topics are taken up in other papers in the volume, notably "Dasein's Disclosedness," "Reading Brandom Reading Heidegger," "Letting Be," and "Truth and Finitude."

Glossary of Haugeland's Translations from *Sein und Zeit*

Suggested alternative translations for some of Heidegger's terms in *Being and Time* (prepared for University of Chicago Humanities MA students, Fall 2005).

Macquarrie and Robinson	Haugeland's Alternatives	(Original German)
distantiality	conformism??	*Abständichkeit*
(the) they	(the) anyone	*(das) Man*
ahead (of itself)	forward (of itself)	*(im sich) Vorweg*
anticipate	fore-run	*vorlaufen*
appeal (to)	call upon	*anrufen*
assign or refer	assign	*verweisen*
authentic	owned	*eigentlich*
average	ordinary	*durchschnittlich*
basic state	basic makeup	*Grundverfassung*
be as having been	have (be?) been	*gewesen sein*
be encountered (entities)	show up	*begegnen*
being alongside	being-amidst	*Sein bei*
being-with	being-co	*Mitsein*
circumspection	around-sight	*Umsicht*
circumstances	surroundings	*Umstände*
concern	carefulness	*Besorgen*
constitution	constitution	*Konstitution*
context	nexus	*Zusammenhang*
being-with	co-dasein	*Mitdasein*

152

Macquarrie and Robinson	Haugeland's Alternatives	(Original German)
dealings	dealings (getting-around)	*Umgang*
deprive of its world	de-world	*entweltlichen*
discourse	telling (or talk)	*Rede*
environment	around-world	*Umwelt*
equipment	equipment	*Zeug*
expect	anticipate	*erwarten*
for the most part	usually	*zumeist*
forbearance	indulgence	*Nachsicht*
fore-conception	fore-ception (= fore-grasp)	*Vorgriff*
guilt	responsibility	*Schuldigkeit [Schuld]*
guilty	responsible	*schuldig*
having a mood	attuned	*gestimmt*
having a mood	attunedness	*Gestimmtheit*
having a mood	being-attuned	*Gestimmtsein*
having been	been	*gewesen*
he to whom the appeal is made	(the) callee	*(der) Angerufene*
historicality	(historical) happeningness	*Geschichtlichkeit*
historize, happen	happen	*geschehen*
history	(historical) happenings	*Geschichte*
idle talk	idle telling	*Gerede*
in terms of . . .	from out of . . .	*woraus . . . her*
in the process of having been	beening	*gewesend*
interpret	spell out; construe	*auslegen*
involvement	role	*Bewandtnis*
locus, location	locus	*Ort*
not to be outstripped	unbypassable	*unüberholbar*
null, nugatory	not-ish	*nichtig*
on that former occasion	back then	*damals*
potentiality for being	ability-to-be	*Seinkönnen*
present-at-hand	occurrent	*vorhanden*
primordial	originary	*ursprünglich*
proximally	initially	*zunächst*
ready-to-hand	available	*zuhanden*
situation	location	*Lage*

(Continued)

Macquarrie and Robinson	Haugeland's Alternatives	(Original German)
Situation	situation	*Situation*
solicitude	caringness	*Fürsorge*
source	origin	*Ursprung*
state	(structural) makeup	*Verfassung*
state of mind	findingness	*Befindlichkeit*
summon	call onto (or out-onto)	*aufrufen*
Temporality	temporality	*Temporalität*
temporality	timeishness	*Zeitlichkeit*
then	up then (think: "upcoming")	*dann*
totality	wholeness, totality	*Ganzheit*
upon-which (etc.)	out-onto-which	*woraufhin*
whole	whole	*Ganze* (noun)
whole, wholly	whole, wholly	*ganz* (adj., adv.)
wholeness	(in its) entirety?	*(in seiner) Gänze*
within-the-world	intraworldly	*innerweltlich*
within-time	intratimely	*innerzeitig*
with-which	of-which	*Womit*
with-world	co-world	*Mitwelt*
worldhood	(worldishness)	*Weltlichkeit*
X is an issue	X is at stake	*es geht X um*

THREE

Late Papers on Heidegger

Reading Brandom Reading Heidegger

(2005)

While brilliance and originality surely top the list of qualities shared by Brandom and Heidegger, another commonality is a tendency to treat their predecessors as partial and sometimes confused versions of themselves. Heidegger, therefore, could hardly be indignant on principle if Brandom finds a fair bit of *Making It Explicit* in the first division of *Being and Time*. Nevertheless, some details may deserve a closer look. Here I concentrate on the more recent of the Heidegger essays reprinted in *Tales of the Mighty Dead:* "Dasein, the Being That Thematizes."

The basic premise of the essay is that *"Being and Time* can be understood as propounding a normative pragmatism" (Brandom 2002, 324). That, in turn, is cashed out as comprising two distinctive commitments. First, that the normative is to be understood as conceptually and explanatorily prior to the factual, and second, that the norms implicit in social practice are similarly prior to those made explicit as rules.

Although these two commitments will certainly be familiar to any reader of *Making It Explicit,* extracting them from *Being and Time* is a more delicate matter. 'Norm' is not one of Heidegger's words, nor particularly is 'practice' (though each does occur a few times). That does not mean, of course, that normative pragmatism cannot be read into the text. Indeed, as Brandom justly notes, I was myself, some years ago, one of the originators of such a reading.[1] But even though I still think there is something to that, it

---

1. Haugeland here refers to "Heidegger on Being a Person" above. —*Ed.*

157

no longer seems to me to shed much light on what Heidegger himself is really up to.

In particular, it scarcely connects at all with the principal aim of the work, which is to reawaken the question of the sense of being, nor does it make more than incidental contact with important topics like anxiety, care, truth, death, conscience, authenticity, resoluteness, historicity, and time. Thus, much that is central to Heidegger's own purposes is entirely missed by this exegetical strategy.

Arguably, however, these larger and later issues are irrelevant to the more focused concerns of "Dasein, the Being That Thematizes." Yet, before turning to specifics, we might be puzzled by that title itself. The most important distinction in early Heidegger is that between being (Sein) and entities (Seienden)—soon to be called "the ontological difference." Macquarrie and Robinson (the translators Brandom mostly relies on) are quite scrupulous in marking this distinction with the aforementioned contrasting terms. Yet, in the present conspicuous instance (the title is actually lifted from the text—SZ 363), Brandom departs from their consistent practice and renders 'Seiende' with "being."[2] Why?

It is hard to say, but I suspect it is connected with an even more troubling confusion that begins on his second page. There, he explicitly takes 'dasein' to denote not an entity but rather a kind of being. In other words, he gets it on the wrong side of the ontological difference. Here is an illustrative passage:

> Heidegger sets out these commitments in the form of an account of the relations among three fundamental ontological categories, or more officially, regions of being within which different sorts of entities are disclosed: *Dasein, Zuhandensein,* and *Vorhandensein. Dasein* is the kind of being we ourselves have. (Brandom 2002, 325)

Of course, if that were correct, then Heidegger himself should have written *"Sein"* instead of *"Seiende."* But he did not—and rightly not.

Although I cannot be certain, I do have a conjecture about what is going on. Unlike many readers of *Being and Time,* Brandom is commendably sensitive to the fact that "dasein" is not only not synonymous but not even

---

2. In the two places in the text where Brandom quotes his own title (Brandom 2002, 329 and 347), he subjoins "entity" (in parentheses) after "being." That seems only to compound the confusion.

coextensive with the ordinary term 'person.' Indeed, the grammar is different: unlike "person," "dasein" is not used with what Quine called "the apparatus of divided reference" (indefinite articles, the plural, and so on). But, similarly, the term *"Sein"* and its derivatives *"Zuhandensein"* and *"Vorhandensein,"* are not used with that apparatus, either. So 'dasein' would seem to fit right in with them (indeed, even etymologically).

All the same, it does not. Without question, dasein is not a kind of being but rather an entity. There are many ways in which this could be documented, but the quickest and most conclusive is that the grand finale of division I (§42) is a specification and an articulation of the being of dasein. In particular, the being of dasein is care, and its articulation is existence, facticity, and falling. But being 'is' always and only the being of some (possible) entity or entities. So, dasein is an entity.

Yet, there remains something peculiar about this, as Brandom may be sensing. It is beyond question that dasein is somehow intimately connected with people. It is Heidegger's basic technical term for whatever it is that is special about us. But if it is neither an ontological term for our being nor an ontical sortal that denotes precisely us, then what is it? And, in the meantime, if not "dasein," then what are Heidegger's terms for people and their being?

The official term for people is "others" (oneself included) (SZ 118, 126), and the being of others is co-dasein ('Mitdasein': SZ 118, 120, 125, 140; BP 396). Unlike 'dasein', therefore, 'co-dasein' is an ontological term: it names the being of people. The key to understanding this correctly is to appreciate that others (which is to say, we people) are intraworldly entities. That is, we show up to each other as entities within the world, much as do available equipment and occurrent things. Of course, we ourselves are neither available nor occurrent entities but rather co-dasein entities.

And it is here, I think, that normative pragmatism makes its closest approach to *Being and Time.* For what norms and practices are all about is intraworldly entities, especially equipment and people, and (as Heidegger makes painfully clear) to be an entity whose being is co-dasein is—initially and usually—to live as a normal member of a norm-governed community. Yet, as I will explain momentarily, this cannot be either the whole story or, in the end, even a major part of it. Rather, if I may venture a rough simile, normative pragmatism is to the central concerns of *Being and Time* something like what the capacity to acquire and instill reliable differential responsive dispositions is to the central concerns of *Making It Explicit.* That is, it is an enabling prerequisite for the main topic to get off the ground, but it is not itself part of that topic.

As already mentioned, Heidegger's main topic is "the being-question." The reason dasein gets so much attention is that, more or less by definition, it is the entity that embodies an understanding of being. But it is crucial to appreciate that this is not a stipulative definition of, say, the term "dasein." When Aristotle "defined" man as the talking animal or, again, as the political animal, he was not laying down necessary and sufficient conditions for the correct application of a predicate. Rather, he was attempting to spell out, in a compelling and illuminating way, what is most characteristic of these conspicuously peculiar entities. And that, I suggest, is what Heidegger is up to as well, but with an additional level of analysis.

Dasein is neither people nor their being but rather a way of life shared by the members of some community. It is ways of life, in this sense, that have the basic structure of being-in-the-world. (People certainly do not have that structure—they are intraworldly.) Insofar as there is an understanding of being, it is embodied, initially and usually, in such a way of life—which is then dasein. And this is why Heidegger is so interested in anxiety, being-toward-death, and conscience, each of which individualizes dasein. The resulting individualization is what he calls authenticity or ownedness. Dasein, and more particularly the understanding of being that it embodies, is owned by some individual person—in the sense of taking responsibility for its tenability.

A pretty good analogy, one that Heidegger himself mentions several times, is language. Languages are, of course communal, but they are not to be identified with the communities in which they are spoken or with the individual speakers who speak them. Rather, languages are communally shared "ways of speaking." Similarly, dasein is a communally shared way of living of a specific sort—namely, one that embodies an understanding of being.

With these preliminaries in place, we can now turn to Brandom's exegetical arguments in more detail. He introduces his main thesis with a 'layer cake' metaphor. Each layer is a kind of being: dasein on the bottom, availability in the middle, and occurrentness on top. (Remember: he understands dasein as the being of people.) The idea is that the higher layers clearly presuppose those below them: availability is unintelligible without dasein, and so on. But whether the lower layers similarly presuppose the upper ones is less obvious. He grants, however, that dasein is unintelligible without availability, so the only remaining question is whether these two together presuppose occurrentness. And his answer is a resounding 'Yes!': you get none of the three without all three.

Yet the claim is oddly hedged. It is not that there could not be a normative community whose members understood themselves and each other as fellow members and their paraphernalia as equipment (or something much like it), while understanding no entities as occurrent. That, after all, is what basic normative pragmatism accounts for (and besides, "talking doesn't develop *ex nihilo*"—Brandom 2002, 334). The claim is rather that, according to Heidegger, unless those creatures also understand some entities as occurrent, they do not "count as" or "qualify as" dasein (Brandom 2002, 329, 330, 331, 332, 336). In other words, the point reduces to a terminological restriction. Heidegger himself, of course, never explicitly stipulates such a restriction—that is not his style. But Brandom maintains that he implicitly commits himself to it, and showing that this is so is the principal aim of the article.

There is one primary argument for this conclusion, plus two subsidiary variations. I will concentrate on the former. Brandom summarizes it in four steps (Brandom 2002, 331):

1. There can be no dasein without talk *(Rede)*.
2. There can be no talk without idle talk *(Gerede)*.
3. There can be no idle talk without language *(Sprache)*.
4. There can be no language without assertion *(Aussage)*.

The reason the final point is supposed to be sufficient for the intended conclusion is that, as Brandom says in a number of ways, "the capacity to use assertional language . . . essentially involves the capacity to treat things as occurrent" (Brandom 2002, 347; cf. 324, 327–32, 341ff.).

We can grant the first thesis, that there is no dasein without *Rede,* since, along with *Befindlichkeit* and understanding, *Rede* belongs to the constitution of being-in as such. The reason this does not settle the matter is that, as Brandom points out, Heidegger means more by *"Rede"* than just talking or verbal communication. Also, and perhaps more fundamentally, *Rede* is characterized as the articulation of intelligibility or significance—where 'articulating' means something like 'carving at the joints' or, less figuratively, "telling apart" and making relevant distinctions. So there remains a question of whether it might be only in this latter sense that *Rede* is integral to being-in as such. The rest of the argument is intended to foreclose that possibility.

The second step is that there can be no talk or telling without idle talk. Brandom says that idle talk is just the everyday form of talking and hence the "background" for all other forms (Brandom 2002, 336). But that cannot be right. In the first place, it would trivialize the claim that there is no talk without idle talk. But, more to the point, there is lots of everyday talking—most of it, I should think—that is not 'idle' at all: it is just ordinary and routine. Indeed, citing one of the connotations of "*Gerede,*" Brandom says that the essence of idle talk is gossip, but surely he does not think that ordinary, everyday talking is all essentially gossip! On the contrary, idle talk is talk that is not performing its proper, ordinary function and is therefore an incomplete or "defective" variant. As the English expression suggests, idle talk is talk that is "idling"—like an engine that is disconnected from, and so not doing, the work it is really for.[3]

This leaves us with the question of what talking is "really for." Surely, it is "for" communicating with others, sharing insights, coordinating activities, drawing distinctions, making plans, imparting understanding, and so on. But Heidegger says something more specifically philosophical and by way of a direct contrast with idle talk.

> Talking, which belongs to the essential being-makeup of dasein and which co-constitutes the disclosedness thereof, has the possibility of becoming idle talk. As such, it does not so much hold being-in-the-world open in an articulated understanding but rather closes it off and covers up intraworldly entities. (SZ 169, my translation)

So, at least part of what talking does for dasein that idle talk fails to do is "hold being-in-the-world open in an articulated understanding" and uncover intraworldly entities.

Yet, the role of idle talk is far from entirely negative, for on the same page we also read the following:

> This everyday way in which things have been interpreted [in idle talk] is one into which dasein has grown in the first instance, with never a possibility of extrication. In it, out of it, and against it, all genuine understanding,

---

3. When Heidegger says, "The expression 'idle talk' is not to be used here in a 'disparaging' signification" (SZ 167), he does not mean, of course, that idle talk is just fine and dandy but rather that his purpose in discussing it is not simply to denounce some commonplace human failing (like laziness or dissembling).

interpreting, and communicating, all rediscovering and appropriating anew are performed. (*SZ* 169)

There are two points here. First, when it comes to understanding and interpretation, we inevitably begin with what is implicit in idle talk, but second, and ultimately more important, idle talk therefore affords the requisite starting point for all genuine understanding, interpreting, and communicating. In other words, even though idle talk itself "closes off" and "covers up," it thereby also enables opening up and discovering.

How could idle talk simultaneously close off and cover up, on the one hand, and enable opening up and discovering on the other? The answer is this: for all its promiscuity and shallowness, idle talk serves as a fundamental reservoir of conceptual resources and distinctions. It is one of the basic cultural mechanisms by which the practical and cognitive achievements of the past are preserved and propagated. The fact that they are typically preserved in a watered-down and ossified form is why they often 'cover up' and 'close off,' but the fact that they are preserved at all is why they also enable opening up and discovering anew.

Brandom's third step, that there can be no idle talk without language, is his most detailed and ingenious. The thesis might seem trivial since, on the face of it, there could hardly be any talking at all—idle or otherwise— without some language to be 'talking in.' But that misses the point because what is really at issue is whether all of what Heidegger calls *"Rede"* might be confined to articulative 'telling' (in the sense of distinguishing and telling apart) or whether, on the contrary, at least some of it must be specifically declarative and hence linguistic.

The reason Brandom makes this point first in terms of idle talk is that there happen to be several statements in the pertinent section of *Being and Time* (*SZ* §35) that he can easily tie into the apparatus of *Making It Explicit*—and, in particular, to his beautifully elaborated version of the game of giving and asking for reasons. It is this remarkable connecting up of the two disparate texts that I find so technically impressive. Nevertheless, I will neither work through nor dispute the details because I think it gets off on the wrong foot from the start and thus misconstrues the whole discussion.

A pretty good colloquial characterization of idle talk would be as follows: "blathering on without knowing what you are talking about." My purpose in mentioning this is that the phrase "knowing what you are talking about" is conspicuously ambiguous, and what I want to suggest is that, in effect, Brandom disambiguates it in one way, whereas Heidegger means it in the other.

According to the former—the gloss I am putting in Brandom's mouth—"knowing what you are talking about"—means having good evidence or justification for what you claim. And, bringing to bear the account of giving and asking for reasons, he can then produce an intricate reading to the effect that what is wrong with idle talk is that appropriate justification is neither expected nor, as a rule, to be had. Moreover, in support of that reading, he can cite passages like this:

> What is said-in-the-talk as such spreads in wider circles and takes on an authoritative character. Things are so because one says so. Idle talk is constituted by just such gossiping and passing the word along—a process by which its initial lack of grounds to stand on becomes aggravated to complete groundlessness. (SZ 168; Brandom 2002, 336)

But, in so doing, he ignores the far more numerous surrounding passages like:

> Terminologically, [the expression "idle talk"] signifies a positive phenomenon which constitutes the kind of being of everyday dasein's *understanding* and *interpreting*. (SZ 167)

And:

> Idle talk is the possibility of *understanding* everything without previously making the thing one's own. (SZ 169)

And:

> Idle talk, which closes things off in the way we have designated, is the kind of being which belongs to dasein's *understanding* when that understanding has been uprooted. (SZ 170) [emphasis in each case added]

All of these (along with both of my previous quotations) suggest that what is missing or defective in the idleness of idle talk is not evidence or reasons but rather some adequate degree of understanding and/or appropriate interpretation. And this, of course, is the other way of hearing the charge: "You don't know what you're talking about." The allegation is not that the speaker is making unjustified claims but rather (and perhaps worse) is making claims about something the speaker does not adequately understand. The relevant failing is not lack of evidence so much as being shallow, confused, and/or obtuse—what we sometimes refer to as "just not getting it." (Surely every teacher of philosophy is familiar with this phenomenon.) But if, as I suggest, it is the fundamental phenomenon of idle talk, then latching onto phrases like "so because one says so" and "passing the word along" is mistaking the salt for the soup.

By way of rejoinder, it might seem possible to maintain that understanding something is just the ability to make justified true assertions about it. But, whatever its intrinsic merits, that idea certainly is not Heidegger's. On the contrary, he begins his own discussion of understanding with a reminder of the colloquial usage according to which it amounts to a kind of competence or ability to manage (*SZ* 143). And he then radically develops that into a more general account in terms of projecting entities, (including but not limited to dasein itself), onto their possibilities (*SZ* 145). Whatever exactly we make of that, it is certainly not just a matter of checking one's premises.

The fourth and final step of Brandom's argument is this: no language without assertion. One is tempted to ask: As opposed to what?—questions and imperatives? But the point is rather that all properly linguistic intentionality, regardless of the particular speech act, presupposes the articulation of giving and asking for reasons, and the essential tokens with which that game is played are ones with propositional content—paradigmatically assertions. In my own view, this is a slogan-sized capsule of a profound and powerful insight and, moreover, one of which Heidegger—not having read (say) Frege, Wittgenstein, and Sellars—could scarcely have had an inkling.

That leaves only the title topic of thematizing. According to Brandom, what Heidegger means by this verb is making assertions or stating rules (Brandom 2002, 324, 326, 327). But the definition in *Being and Time* is actually rather different:

> The scientific projection of any entities . . . already lets their kind of being be understood explicitly and in such a manner that it thus becomes manifest what ways are possible for the pure discovery of entities within the world. The articulation of the understanding of being, the delimitation of an area of subject-matter . . . and the sketching out of the way of conceiving which is appropriate to such entities—all these belong to the totality of this projecting, and this totality is what we call 'thematizing.' (*SZ* 363)

Finally, lest anyone suppose that to thematize entities is to treat them as occurrent (something that Brandom often seems to do), consider this brief passage:

> The idea of historiology as a science implies that the disclosure of historical entities is what it has seized upon as its own task. Every science is constituted primarily by thematizing. That which is familiar prescientifically in dasein as disclosed being-in-the-world gets projected upon the being which is specific to it. (SZ 393)

Yet, if there is anything of which it is clear that "the being which is specific to it" is not being-occurrent, it is "disclosed being-in-the-world," and the historical entities that are disclosed therein cannot be far behind.

In sum then: there is no doubt that dasein as we know it thematizes; there is no doubt that it makes assertions; and there is no doubt that it treats some entities as occurrent. But it has not been established that any two of these three are the same; nor has it been established that any of them is prerequisite to "qualifying as dasein."

Letting Be

(2007)

The official aim of *Being and Time* is to reawaken the question of the sense of being—the project Heidegger calls "fundamental ontology." In that work and others from the same period, he employs, as a new technical term, the expression *sein lassen*, "to let be." This is a compound transitive verb, the subject of which (if made explicit at all) is generally dasein or dasein's world and the direct object of which is entities or some species thereof. So, simple uses of the term might be claims like "dasein lets entities be" or "the everyday world lets equipment be." Moreover, there are also a number of broadly related verbs used in similar ways, such as *begegnen lassen*, "to let show up"; *bewenden lassen*, "to let have-a-role"; *entlassen*, "to release"; and even *freigeben*, "to set-free." Again, in all these cases, the active subject (if mentioned at all) is typically dasein or its world, and the passive objects are entities of some sort.

Various of these points are illustrated by a well-known paragraph from section 18 (worldishness) of *Being and Time* and a shorter one from section 26 (others and *Mitsein*):

Ontically, to let-have-a-role means this: within some factical carefulness, to let something available be thus and so, as it thenceforth is, and in order that it be so. We take this ontical sense of "letting be" as fundamentally ontological. And that's how we interpret the sense of the antecedent setting-free of what is intraworldly available from the outset. To let "be" antecedently does not mean to bring something first into its being and produce it

167

but rather to discover "entities" already in their availability and, so, to let entities with this being show up (*SZ* 117).

And:

> Dasein's world sets free entities that are not only quite different from equipment and things but which, in accord with their sort-of-being as dasein themselves, are "in" the world by way of being-in-the-world—the world in which they at the same time show up as intraworldly. These entities are neither occurrent nor available but rather are just like the very dasein that sets them free—they are there too, co-there. (*SZ* 154)

The latter passage not only explicitly mentions dasein's world as the subject of the verb but also makes clear that its objects are not limited to available equipment—since other people and occurrent things are likewise explicitly mentioned.

Now, the first substantive point I want to make is that this is very weird. What could it mean to say that dasein's world "lets entities be" and "sets them free"? Free from what? And what would happen if it stopped doing that? Would all entities cease to be—or cease to be free? But dasein's world is only insofar as dasein is. Does that mean that if there were no dasein, there would be no entities at all? To be sure, some of these questions may be misguided, but, unless we confront them, we will never find out how or why. If we do not acknowledge at the outset how odd and alien Heidegger's claims are, we have no hope of figuring out whatever it was he was trying to say.

So I propose to take it very slowly and see what sense we can make, step by step—starting with a brief survey of how the verb phrase "let be" is used in English. It seems to me that, very roughly, we can distinguish four basic senses—which might be called the acquiescing, allowing, enabling, and effecting senses—as follows:

> *Acquiescing:* This is what we mean by "let it be," when we advise someone not to struggle with something—for instance, not to respond (to an insult), not to intervene (in a fight), or just not to keep trying (with some hopeless effort). (The title of the Beatles' song has this acquiescing sense.)
>
> *Allowing:* To let be can mean to permit—in the sense of not preventing—as when the Robinsons let their children be a little rowdier on Saturday nights.

Enabling: Or it can mean to permit in another way, as making possible—as when a new highway lets a city be approached from the south or a dam lets the spring floodwaters be held for the summer crops.

Effecting: Finally, to let something be can be to bring it about or make it so—as when God said, "Let there be light" (and there was light). But it is the same sense, I think, when a geometer says, "Let *C* be the midpoint of line *AB*" or ballplayers say, "Let this sidewalk be the goal line."

Now, though Heidegger's word—*lassen*—is cognate and mostly synonymous with the English *let*, they are of course not fully equivalent in all contexts. Even so, I suggest that distinguishing these four senses will be all the "dictionary work" we need. For fundamental ontology makes us push and twist our vocabulary in any case, and English words are as malleable as any.

2. LETTING EQUIPMENT BE

We can begin with the same special case that Heidegger himself does: everyday intraworldly equipment. It is in this context that he introduces the other two *lassen* verbs mentioned earlier: *bewenden lassen* and *begegnen lassen*. But it is not so hard to see how these work, so long as we are careful about the rest of the terminology, too. In sections 15 and 18, respectively, *Zuhandenheit* and *Bewandtnis* are both defined as the *being* of equipment. But they are not the same. The difference between them is what Heidegger calls the articulation of being into that-being and what-being (compare the actuality/essence distinction—of which more later). The that-being of an item of equipment (what is at stake in whether it is at all or not) is its *Zuhandenheit* (what I call availability). Its what-being (what is at stake in what "kind" of thing it is) is its *Bewandtnis*—which I therefore translate as its (equipmental) role. So: availability is the equipmental analog of actuality, and roles are the analog of essences.

Now, these various roles to which equipmental entities are "assigned" make the sense they make only in relation to one another (hammer/nail/wood, pen/ink/paper, and so on). Heidegger calls the relational character of those assignments "signifying" and the totality of such signifyings "significance." And that significance, in turn, is what makes up the structure of the world—the world of everyday dasein. But, with these points and terms in place, it is not so weird after all to say that dasein's world lets intraworldly entities "have their roles" *(bewenden lassen)* or even that it lets them "show up" as anything whatsoever *(begegnen lassen)*. For the world is defined, in effect, as the totality of all those roles in their essential interrelations. Hence, without it, nothing could show up as—or, therefore, be—anything equipmental at all. Or, to make the same point by means of a special case, who could deny that the "world" of baseball lets certain discernible configurations be strikes, home runs, and the like?

The problem with this kind of case is not that it is unpersuasive (as far as it goes) but that it is too easy. It is not big news that, without dasein, nothing would be a hammer or a home run. But what about entities that have been around since long before there was dasein and still will be long after—entities that are (as we want to say) independent of dasein? This question, however, cannot even be addressed without some grasp of the relevant sense of "independence," and that turns out to presuppose the concept of that-being.

3. THAT-BEING AND PRODUCTION

The articulation of being into that-being and what-being is one of the four basic problems identified in *The Basic Problems of Phenomenology (Die Grundprobleme der Phänomenologie)*. In the chapter of that work addressed to this problem—or, rather, the chapter devoted to the historical background prerequisite to addressing the problem—Heidegger begins with the scholastic distinction between *essentia* and *existentia* and the problem of how they could come together in an entity. In the case of finite entities (creatures), they are officially brought together in the causal act of divine creation: entities are at all in that they are enacted or actualized by God. So, existentia = createdness = enactedness = actuality.

The trouble is: if you just say that this "bringing together" is an "actualizing act" (of "causal creation"), you have not really said anything about what that amounts to or therefore thrown any light on what "being actual" in fact means. It is better, Heidegger suggests, to keep track of the original sense of *existentia* itself and then trace that sense back to its roots in Greek ontology. Thus, the verb *existere* came to mean "to exist" from the more original meaning of *ex-sistere:* to cause to stand out, stand forth, or stand still. With that in mind, we can then ask the obvious question: why would a verb with that original sense come to mean anything like "is actual" or "has that-being"? Prima facie, for instance, its inner semantic motives are quite different from those of the Kantian definition of existence as "absolute position." And here is where returning to the formative Greek sensibilities can shed some real light. Briefly, the Kantian definition makes sense within what Heidegger calls the horizon of *perceptual* comportment; that is, Kant's understanding of "empirical" entities as such takes its guidance from the perspective of their being knowable, going back ultimately to intuition. By contrast, Heidegger suggests, the Greek understanding of that-being—in which the scholastic concept *existentia* is still rooted—makes sense within the horizon of productive comportment.

Though we care more about what Heidegger is going to make of it than how he gets there, what he says is roughly the following. Greek ontology understands *morphe* (the shape or form of a thing) as grounded on *eidos* (the "look" of the thing)—even though, conceptually (not to mention perceptually), the form is prior to the look (*GP*, section 11b). And this surprising ontological ordering can be explained only if we see that the Greeks understood being not within the horizon of perception but rather that of production. Thus, if we consider seeing a pot, then the pot itself must already have its form before the look of it can be taken in by the viewer, so *morphe* is prior to *eidos*. But if we consider, instead, *making* a pot, then the potter must *already* have the look in mind to guide him in giving the requisite form to the clay; hence, the resulting *morphe* itself is grounded in that prior *eidos*.

Morphe and *eidos* are both associated with what-being (ancestors of *essentia*). But what interests us is how this "reversing" of their respective priorities might affect the understanding of that-being *(existentia)*. Within the horizon of perception, the "object" is understood as already existing (actual), and so such existence itself can (only) be grasped as standing-over-against-ness (*Gegenständlichkeit,* objectivity), with no further insight into what that amounts to. Within the horizon of production, on the other hand, the entity to be produced is precisely not understood as already existent—but rather merely what can be—and, more specifically, can, via this very production, come into being (become an entity) for the first time. Thus, existence—that-being—is somehow to be "conferred upon" or "accorded to" something (determined by the *eidos*) that does not yet "have" it. And the idea is that this "according of existence to"—"letting be"—can in turn be a clue to that which is accorded by it (= that-being).

Return to the potter. What exactly does he *do* that lets the pot *be?* Well, of course, he shapes it, dries it, colors it, fires it, and so on. But any or all of those could conclude with an angry smash and a pile of rubble—which is to say, neither produce a pot nor let it be at all. Genuine, successful production of a pot—that is, finishing it, and, in fact, letting it be—is something more like *letting go of* or *releasing* it: that is, handing it over to the customer or putting it in the cupboard, available to be used. And here the connotations of allowing and acquiescing, mentioned earlier, begin to get a grip—as, indeed, does "setting-free."

Yet, even in the special context of craftwork, "letting go of" cannot alone suffice as an account of what the producer does in "according" that-being to the product. For if, as soon as the producer let go, the intended product had crumbled or vanished, it still would not have been *produced.* So productive letting be has to have the further character of setting the product out on its own to stand up and be (persist as) what it is—*establishing* it, so to speak. But, if what is involved in coming-to-be is being set out on its own and established in this way, then we can see how the phrase *ex-sistere*—to cause to stand out or stand forth—could be taken to express it. What is more, we get at least a glimmer of how independence (out-on-its-own-ness) could be not merely compatible but also conceptually connected with letting be.

But, finally, in order to establish and set the product up in that way, the producer has to give it (arrange for it to have) the capacities and capabilities that it will need in order to be on its own. A pot, for instance, may need a certain strength, stability, and waterproofness, and so the potter must ensure that it has them. In other words, in producing, the producer must enable the product to be whatever it is to be and, in so doing, enable it to stand on its own—which is to say, to be or *ek-sist* at all. And precisely within that *enabling* lies the intelligibility of creation as actualization—the possible union of essence and existence.

Therefore, at least within the horizon of production, the enabling sense of letting be is ultimately the deepest.

4. SCIENTIFIC DISCOVERING

It is one thing to say that dasein "lets" its own equipment "be," that it "sets" the products of its own labor "free," but it is quite another to say any such thing about protons, planets, or prehistoric lizards. Yet it is perfectly clear that Heidegger wants to make that claim, too: "[Scientific projection = thematizing] aims at a setting free of entities that show up intraworldly in such a way that they can 'throw themselves against' a pure discovering—that is, can become objects. Thematizing objectifies. It does not first 'posit' entities but rather sets them free in such a way that they become 'objectively' questionable and determinable" (SZ 414). But—we have to ask again—what could it *mean* to say that dasein's thematizing sets protons and planets *free*? What prison are they in? How do we "let" them out? How can we enable them to "throw themselves against" a pure discovering?

Now, what is perhaps the biggest surprise in this context is that these questions do have answers. If you will pardon my tweaking the metaphors a moment longer, we can answer this way: until dasein releases them, entities remain in the darkest of all prisons, the prison of utter obscurity; we let them out by bringing them to light (into the clearing); and we enable them to throw themselves against a pure discovery by erecting a pure discovery in their path and accepting what happens as the result of their coming up against it. Or, less metaphorically, we introduce measuring instruments and accept their "readings" as evidence.

The crucial insight is this: letting entities throw themselves against a pure discovery is neither easy nor even easily recognized when achieved. Thus, when Galileo's peripatetic opponents argued that the specks of light visible in his telescope were not moons of Jupiter but rather mere artifacts of the instrument itself, they were being neither entirely obstreperous nor obtuse—and Galileo knew it. As a point of comparison, suppose a colleague claimed that four invisible "Martians" accompany your every lecture—and produced the videos to prove it (made with a special new camera, of course). Would you not suspect that those "Martians" have more to do with that "special" camera than with your lectures? Likewise, Galileo's contemporaries had all kinds of good reasons to doubt the ostensible "evidence" he was offering them. And therefore, most of the work he had to do was to show, step by step, question by question, that what appeared in the telescope really was something "out there."

And what did it take to do *that*? Well, he made multiple telescopes and showed that what you saw was the same, no matter which one you used. He showed and explained how they were constructed and why they would let distant objects seem closer and larger. He invited people to look at distant *terrestrial* objects—objects the existence and appearance of which they could independently confirm. He showed that not only did those specks stay with Jupiter as it moved against the fixed stars but also that they themselves visibly moved relative to Jupiter in just the way they would if they were separate bodies orbiting it. Only after all of this, and more besides, could people so much as see what was in some sense "right before their eyes."

It is this sort of work—often *hard* work—that Heidegger means by "letting entities show up" *(begegnen lassen)* and, more specifically, letting them "throw themselves against" *(entgegenwerfen)* a pure discovery. Such "letting" is clearly more than mere allowing or acquiescing-in; it is also and especially *enabling*. In fact, in the sense in which discovery (observation) is essentially an acquiescing-in-accepting-of-whatever is discovered, acquiescing itself is part of what is enabled.

Now, in German, the words themselves lubricate the transition from *begegnen lassen* and *entgegenwerfen* to *Gegenstand* and *gegenständlich*, but, philosophically, those moves still have to be paid for—in other words, explained and justified. It is one thing to say that dasein enables entities to show up, but it is quite another to say that it enables them to be—or, be objects—at all. Yet the latter, I am convinced, is the claim he is really trying to make—or, more cautiously, was setting himself up to make in division III.

5. SCIENTIFIC LAWS

It might seem that Heidegger explicitly repudiates the thesis I just attributed to him. For he says in section 43: "If dasein does not exist, then 'independence' 'is' not, either, nor 'is' the 'in-itself.' . . . It can be said *then*, neither that entities are nor that they are not. But *now*, so long as the understanding of being is, and with it the understanding of occurrentness, it can perfectly be said that entities will still continue to be then" (*SZ* 255). And he adds in the next section: "*'There is' truth only so far and so long as dasein is.* Only *then* are entities discovered, and they are disclosed only *so long as* dasein *is* at all" (*SZ* 269). Finally, on the following page: "That, prior to Newton, his laws were neither true nor false cannot mean that the entities those laws discoveringly point out were not [there] prior to him. Through Newton, the laws became true; with them, the entities in themselves became accessible to dasein; with the discoveredness of these entities, they show themselves as precisely the entities that already were previously" (*SZ* 269). This all sounds straightforward enough: there are (past, present, and future) whatever entities there are, whether dasein is there—to "let" them be—or not. What depends on dasein, when it exists, is not what there is at that time but only what can be said, pointed out, or accessed then—hence, what can be *true* or *false*. So, for instance, the force of gravity did not come into existence the day Newton discovered his law about it; rather, it just showed itself for the first time but showed itself as an entity that had been there all along and would also continue to be. What could be more obvious?

All the same, it is a little odd to say that the law of gravity was not true before Newton discovered it, especially since one of the things he did with it was retrodict various eclipses, comet sightings, and the like back to antiquity. In the meantime, there remains the question of what to say about *Einstein's* discovery that there is (was and will be) no force of gravity after all—just curved space-time. Does this mean that, through Newton, his laws *became* true but *only for a while?* But that seems *crazy:* if Newton's laws were ever true, then they always were and always will be; that is the kind of laws they are—and the same goes for Einstein's.

(It may be worth noting that this line of questioning about *physical* being and time is not disconnected from the text *Being and Time.* In section 3, Heidegger motivates the entire project of fundamental ontology in terms of its relevance to foundational crises in the sciences, and, though briefly, he explicitly mentions physics and the theory of relativity as one example. So it is hard to believe he did not have that issue in the back of his mind when making the claims we are now considering about Newton.)

So how *does* physics (Newtonian physics, say) let physical objects *be*—"stand on their own, over against us"? Well, everything said earlier about Galileo still applies; Newton had to do that kind of hard, justificatory work, too. But, with Newton, a further and an even more fundamental element comes clearly into view: those very laws about which Heidegger makes such an odd claim. These laws, I will argue, are one version of a more general sort of factor that is essential in every understanding of being and every way of letting entities be. The advantage of proceeding via scientific laws is that the form of their contribution is especially clear.

In order to let entities be, dasein must somehow discover them—which, in science, generally means to observe or measure them. But observation and measurement make sense only if there is, in principle, some way to distinguish between *correct* and *incorrect* results. Now, some invalid results may be detected by flagging technical errors or equipmental failure. But the only fundamental way to establish that something must be wrong is to show that some plurality of results are not mutually compatible. And that, finally, presupposes antecedent constraints on what combinations would and would not be possible—which is to say, *laws*.

Thus, Newton and his colleagues could have far better astronomical data than could Galileo not simply because of technical advances but rather and mainly because they had much better laws. Knowing, as they did, with far greater accuracy, what had to be the case, they could calibrate and fine-tune their instruments and techniques in ways their predecessors could scarcely dream of.

Superficially, there might seem to be a problem here with the credibility of the theory depending on the empirical evidence for it, while the accuracy of that evidence, in turn, is made possible by the theory. But—without even appealing to Heidegger's fondness for circles—we can see that the worry is misplaced. For, no matter how the methods are fine-tuned in general, they still have to produce particular results in practice, independently of any particular predictions, and that still leaves room for empirical failure. The point can be put more generally this way. It is in some sense "easy" to concoct a rich and powerful descriptive vocabulary. It is in some sense "easy" to concoct precise, general methods for investigating the entities putatively so describable. And it is in some sense "easy" to concoct strict laws constraining the results of those investigations. What is not at all easy is to do all three at once in such a way that, when those investigations are assiduously carried out, the actual results are consistently in accord with the laws. Now, according to me, succeeding at that difficult but not impossible threefold task is the general form of discovering entities and letting them be—at least in the special case of scientific investigations. The crucial role of laws is to *restrict* what there can be by ruling out various conceivable combinations. Only by virtue of that restrictive function can subsumption of particulars under laws render the actual intelligible—that is, explain why one thing happened rather than another. I take this to be the scientific version of what Heidegger means more generally when he allows that *understanding* entities is projecting them onto their *possibilities*.

6. SCIENTIFIC CHANGE

If the preceding is the general form of scientific letting be, and if the that-being of scientifically discovered entities is *Gegenständlichkeit*—being-an-object or objectivity—then the relevant sense of letting be is again the enabling sense. For the upshot of subsumption under laws is to *enable* entities to *stand up against* observations and measurements—that is, to defy and repudiate them. And the crucial prerequisite for this defiant repudiation is, as we have seen, the law-mandated impossibility of certain combinations of observed characteristics or measured magnitudes.

More particularly, we now see how, through Newton and his laws, the entities of Newtonian physics became accessible as the entities they already were and would continue to be. What remains utterly opaque, however, is what could be meant by saying that, through Newton, his laws became true—not to mention the inevitable follow-up question of whether they became neither-true-nor-false again through Einstein. What is worse, with this opacity, the force of the seemingly clear "as they already were and would continue to be" becomes pretty murky after all. What could Heidegger have been thinking?

I think *Being and Time* will support an extrapolation in terms of which this question might be answerable. (Whether the answer could ever be acceptable is another issue.)

Remember first that there are different sorts of time in *Being and Time*, including originary time, world time, and vulgar time. Originary time is not sequential at all. Simplifying ruthlessly, I understand it as the temporal character of a commitment to an understanding of being. When Heidegger says that, through Newton, his laws became true, he is referring to the undertaking of such a commitment. Thus, it is ultimately that undertaking which lets the Newtonian entities be. These entities are, of course, in time—and also in space. But this time does not at all have the character of a commitment (or even the significance and datability of dasein's everyday world). Rather, it has only the mathematical character of so-called Newtonian space-time. And it is in this time that those entities show themselves as precisely the entities that already were previously and, moreover, will continue to be.

Now, when Einstein comes along, he has a different commitment to a different understanding of physical being, which, in turn, likewise lets entities be. These entities also show up as ones that already were previously and will continue to be—though, of course, in *relativistic* space-time. It is a difficult and vexing problem to say just what the relationship is between the respective sets of entities, but simple identity seems ruled out.

The easiest (and therefore most tempting) line is to say that, really, only one set of laws has ever been true and only one set of entities—the entities that those laws let be—is actual, in some timeless sense of "is actual." Thus, what Einstein showed us is that, contrary to what we thought, Newton's laws were never true and the Newtonian universe of entities was *never* actual. Rather, it has always been only Einsteinian.

One problem with this interpretation is that it is incompatible with what Heidegger explicitly says. Another problem is that it is unlikely to be a stable position. For, by the same reasoning, we would have to say, *even now,* that it has *really* always been only an X-ian universe, where X is Einstein's successor—or, rather, the ultimate end of the line in that successorship, assuming there "is" such an end and science lasts long enough to get there.

Why would that idea ever strike anyone as the easiest and most tempting thing to say? I suspect that it is more of the legacy of scholasticism. The original and final science—the only one that has ever *really* been right—is God's science: the *scientia* of omniscience. This *scientia* is supposed to be absolutely and eternally correct, literally by fiat—the effecting sense of "letting be." No one who has ever tried to think about it could imagine that "getting over" this legacy is or will be easy. It will require at least a profound reconception of reality as such—which is to say a new and deeper understanding of being.

What I have tried to show is that the idea of *letting be,* taken not as effective and divine but as enabling and human, is an integral part of that larger endeavor.

Death and Dasein

(2007)

I take at face value the professed aim of *Being and Time:* to reawaken the question of the sense of being. The formulation itself implies that the "being-question" used to be awake (presumably among the Greeks) but has since somehow fallen asleep or gone dormant. Reawakening it would have to mean taking it up again as a serious and vital question on which genuine progress could be made. How much progress Heidegger in fact made, or thought he made, I cannot say, but presumably some.

Our entrée into the topic here must be via the phenomenon of dasein and for two related reasons. First, dasein is the one and only sort of entity that understands being, and, second, dasein is the one and only sort of entity that dies.[1] It may surprise some of you that I say dasein is the only sort of entity that dies, but (so far) that is just a matter of Heidegger's technical terminology. The terminology is not gratuitous, however, for it reflects a substantial point about dasein, to which we will turn in due course. But first, let me introduce some other technical terms that will begin to put these in context.

In his chapter titled "The Possibility of Dasein's Being a Whole and Being toward Death," Heidegger makes a distinction between death—in what we will see is a special "existential" sense—and two other (prima-facie

---

1. This talk was prepared for and delivered at a conference on death, in memory of the late Carol White, author of *Time and Death* (2005), a former member of the Philosophy Department at the University of Santa Clara, and, indeed, my Berkeley classmate in the early 1970s.

related) phenomena, which he calls 'perishing' and 'demise.' These are not important in themselves but only in that they are different from death.

Perishing is a biological phenomenon, namely, the event that occurs at the cessation of organic functioning in an organism and thus (usually) the onset of organic decay. So far as we know, all organisms—including all specimens of *Homo sapiens*—eventually perish.

Demise, by contrast, is exclusive to people. Now, by "people," I do not mean specimens of *Homo sapiens* (though they are that, too) but rather what Heidegger calls "others," namely, members of normative communities, who understand themselves and one another in terms of their respective social roles and statuses in those communities; demise, then, is the cessation of that ability to participate. So, demise, like perishing, is an event—indeed, one that usually happens at the same time.[2]

Others are, to be sure, intraworldly entities and, in that regard, entirely on a par with equipment and "mere" things. But, of course, their way of being is neither the availability of equipment nor the being-occurrent of things—any more than those two are the same. Rather, others have yet a third sort of intraworldly being, which Heidegger calls "co-dasein" [*Mitdasein*]—and not so different in sense, I think, from "being-communal." (There is a brief sketch of the ontology of others in SZ §26, just before the section on the anyone).

Here are two further points to keep in mind about others. First, and despite the seeming implications of the term, all people are others, including, in particular, oneself. As I like to put it, one is oneself just another other. Second, others—that is, people—are not "daseins." This bears some emphasis since many readers (especially new readers) are confused about it. The point actually follows from the fact that the being of others is co-dasein, given that the being of dasein itself is existence. But that might bear some elaboration.

Several times, including at the beginnings of SZ §§9 and 12, Heidegger formally indicates dasein as "in each case mine" [*je meines*]. (Formal indication is pointing at or calling attention to something that is already manifest and so not in need of determinate characterization—so you can simply "point it out").

---

2. Robert Brandom's (1994) important work on linguistic communities is entirely about the normative statuses of others in Heidegger's sense.

Now, the phrase "in each case" is Macquarrie and Robinson's rendition of the little particle '*je*,' which might also be translated as 'respectively' (and maybe in some other ways). But Macquarrie and Robinson's version is serendipitously useful because it permits us to invent the phrase "case of dasein," which roughly captures the crucial relation between dasein and people, given that they are not at all the same (not even extensionally). Cases of dasein are individual people, and it is they who are respectively mine. So, the terms "case of dasein" and "person," if not synonymous, are at least coextensive.

But this still does not tell us what dasein itself is, still less why the phenomenon of death looms so large in the existential analytic of it. In ordinary German, '*Dasein*' is an abstract noun, usually meaning existence or life, but (like those English counterparts) it can also have a more concrete—even "grittier"—sense, as in expressions like "the squalid *existence* of the barrio" or "*life* in the infantry." Since, in Heidegger's technical usage, dasein is an entity—indeed, a temporal entity—I suggest that his intended sense is more akin to the concrete uses given earlier than to the abstract ones. Finally, and again like those uses of 'existence' and 'life,' '*Dasein*' is (almost) never used as a "count noun" (one does not speak of a dasein or three daseins), but neither is it an ordinary "mass noun" (one does not say how much dasein there is, any more than one says how many of them there are).

Yet, for all its peculiarity, dasein is an entity: something that there is. And, as I just mentioned, its way of being is 'existence.' What does that mean? Predictably, it does not mean being actual or real in any traditional sense. The official answer is this: to exist—that is, to be dasein—is to understand the being of entities, or (equivalently) to understand entities as entities. But those help only if we know what it is to have such understanding.

Here are three basic points to get us started. First, existing is not a cognitive or an intellectual achievement, still less an exercise in theoretical ontology. Second, all ordinary adults already understand various sorts of entities in their being—which is to say, they understand the being of those entities, at least effectively or practically. But third, and by contrast, small children and nonhuman animals have no understanding of being at all.

Now, we know from the world chapter that understanding equipment, as the equipment it is, amounts to being able to use it in its proper equipmental roles, and understanding the being of equipment is understanding it as available for use in those roles. Likewise, we know from the "who" chapter that everyday understanding of oneself and others, as the people they are, is knowing how to interact ("live") with them in the light of their proper social roles, and understanding the being of others (oneself included) is understanding them as co-dasein *(Mitdasein)*—which is to say, as fellow members of some (human) community.

Therefore, though Heidegger does not mention it, both of these accounts are clearly grounded in social norms. Accordingly, such norms are essential to dasein. But it would be a grievous mistake to suppose—as I once did[3]—that social normativity is therefore the essence of dasein. Everydayness, to be sure, is saturated with norms, and everydayness is essential to dasein. Dasein's possible ownedness ("authenticity"), by contrast, cannot be understood in social-normative terms at all. Though it presupposes everydayness, it also essentially leaves it behind (as we shall soon see).

How, then are we to understand dasein itself—given that it is quite distinct from people? (They are not even individuated in the same way.) I say that dasein is:

(i) a distinctively human way of living that
(ii) embodies an understanding of being and for which
(iii) individual people ("cases of dasein") can take responsibility.

Now, that is a mouthful even just to say, never mind to swallow and digest. So, I propose to work through it by way of a special case that Heidegger himself effectively endorses.

In a handful of places, he says or suggests that sciences (and also languages) exist.[4] But since existence is the way of being peculiar to dasein, that implies that sciences and languages are daseins—which implies in turn that the aforementioned three points characterize them as well. And I myself take that implication at face value: I think it is what Heidegger means; moreover, I think he is right.

Here, I focus more on sciences than languages because their manifest structure is essentially richer. In particular, developed sciences always include their own specialized languages, whereas ordinary languages need not be associated with any special discipline (scientific or otherwise). But further, and more significant, each science necessarily includes—besides

---

3. See "Heidegger on Being a Person," part one, this volume.—*Ed.*
4. See *SZ* II, 166,357, 392; *GP* 296.

the scientists themselves—a rich repertoire of skills, practices, and equipment, thereby exhibiting the basic structure of being-in-the world.

The deeper point of talking about sciences, however, is that they exhibit with striking clarity another fundamental characteristic of dasein—one that is easily overlooked and, indeed, systematically suppressed by *das Man:* sciences and languages, like any dasein, can die. Etruscan, for instance, is a dead language, and alchemy is an equally dead science. How do languages and sciences die? Clearly, they die when (and because) they can no longer be spoken or practiced—death is the possibility of no more possibilities.

While the idea of scientific crisis and breakdown is relatively familiar and obviously integral to the enterprise as such, we need to examine in more detail what it is and how it comes about. In other words, what we need to exhibit is the deep similarity between the basic character of scientific investigation and the basic character of dasein, specifically with regard to death and the finitude of being.

The structural fulcrum, I think, lies in the notion of understanding, which is obviously fundamental on all accounts. Heidegger (who has more on his mind than just science), characterizes the understanding of entities as projecting them onto their possibilities. But since possibility is just the logical dual of necessity, and necessity is the canonical mark of explanatory laws, we are working with essentially similar conceptions of intelligibility.

What has not yet been clarified, however, is why modal notions like possibility and necessity are the cornerstone of that intelligibility. Everything turns, I think, on opening up a space (or "region") in which observations could contravene the laws—in other words, a space in which the actual could turn out to be impossible. That, of course, sounds paradoxical, but the point is just that there must be two different senses of 'possibility'— and we have to accommodate them both.

On the one hand, there is what might be shown or found by experiment or observation, and, on the other, there is what the laws demand or allow. And what is metaphysically significant is that, a priori, these need not agree. Hence, if they do agree—consistently, precisely, and over a wide range of cases—then there is reason to believe we are genuinely on to something. This, I maintain, is the essential foundation of scientific objectivity. The very fact that there can be no antecedent guarantee of empirical/theoretical agreement shows that such agreement, when it does consistently emerge, is objectively revelatory.

Now, Heidegger does not have much to say about scientific objectivity, but he certainly talks about projecting entities onto their possibilities, and he certainly grounds their intelligibility in such projection. Moreover, there is every reason to believe that he intends his general characterization to extend to various special cases, including scientific understanding. And that is at least part of what emboldens me to press the same analogy in the other direction—that is, to illuminate the existential analytic from the perspective of scientific investigation.

The basis of the aforementioned point about objectivity was that, a priori, theory and observation need not agree; so, it is not gratuitous when they do. But it is at least as important when they do not, for that shows unequivocally that something is wrong. And this is really the more fundamental phenomenon. For, in the face of such anomalies, it is incumbent on responsible scientists to figure out what is wrong and how to correct it. Indeed, a great deal of everyday scientific practice takes the form of solving problems which—for antecedent reasons—"ought" to be solvable. And, of course, mostly they are—eventually. Such successes vindicate both the theory and the practice.

Now, I said earlier that existing is living—or, more carefully, being-lived—in a specifically human way. And what is specifically human about that way of being-lived is twofold. First, the being-lived of dasein (by people = cases of dasein) "embodies" an understanding of being; second, that way of being-lived includes the possibility of taking responsibility for itself—specifically, for the understanding of being that it embodies. And this characterization of existence gives us—at least schematically—another angle on what dasein is, for dasein is the entity that exists.

Two points bear notice in this formulation. First, the phrase "way of living" is neutral between a common way of living (shared by the members of a community) and an individual's way of living. (This roughly reflects the distinction noted earlier between dasein and cases of dasein.) Second, only the possibility of someone taking responsibility is prerequisite for dasein; whether anybody does so is a further matter. This reflects the difference between owned and unowned dasein.

It must be conceded, however, that the idea of taking responsibility for an understanding of being is fairly strange, and all the more so if what is said to "take" that responsibility is a "way of living." But it is just here that focusing on scientific dasein can be particularly helpful and illuminating.

Any science worthy of the name must provide at least these three things: first, a vocabulary in which the relevant phenomena can be appropriately described; second, a number of accepted ways of ascertaining or discovering which of those descriptions are true; and third, a set of modal constraints on what must or cannot be true of those phenomena.

Cursory though it be, that is a pretty standard philosophy of science. Given the vocabulary, experiment and observation are the ways of determining what is the case, and the laws of nature provide the modal constraints. Explanation—the canonical route to understanding (as opposed to mere knowledge)—is the subsumption of observed particulars under modal laws.

Heidegger, too, essentially connects intelligibility with modality. Understanding entities, he says, is projecting them onto their possibilities. But he is more interested in understanding the being of entities than in understanding those entities themselves. Still, this is not as big a difference as it seems inasmuch as the being of entities is effectively determined by the relevant modal constraints (and vice versa).

Here again, the special case of scientific engagement may prove illuminating. The domains of scientific investigation are what Heidegger calls regions of being. The domain of physical investigation, for instance, is entities in the ontological region of the physical. The point of the terminology is that entities in one region *are* in a different "way" than the entities in a different region are.

This is not as alien as it might at first seem. For, surely, psychological entities *are* in a way that is quite different from the way in which, say, biological entities are and the way in which physical entities are is quite different again. It is not so important philosophically to identify, still less delineate, the various regions as it is to appreciate the phenomenon of regionality as such and its implications for ontology. And, here, the most fundamental point is that regions of being are not free—nor do they come with lifetime guarantees.

I have already mentioned alchemy as a dead science, but I did not ask how it died. No doubt the world-spirit was somehow moving on, but down here on the ground, alchemy went out of business because it could not keep its promises. Does physics make promises? Of course it does—more precise and more demanding promises than any other empirical enterprise in human history. That is why it is the king of the sciences; yet, as we know, kingdoms do not always last.

How can a region of being fail to last? This is the essential question and the one with which I will close. The laws that I earlier identified, along with a descriptive vocabulary and a set of empirical procedures, as determining a scientific region collectively articulate constraints on the viability of such a region. But those constraints can be imposed only by some case of dasein who is resolutely committed to them. By the same token, however, such commitments are essentially risky. And, as the word 'commitment' implies, the scope of the risk—within and across individuals—is antecedently unbounded.

Assuming this unbounded risk, I suggest, is what Heidegger means by being toward death.

Truth and Finitude: Heidegger's Transcendental Existentialism

(2000)

In their lengthy and powerful appendix to Dreyfus's (1991) *Being-in-the-World,* Dreyfus and Rubin argue that the "existentialist" portions of *Being and Time*—those having to do with authenticity, falling, anxiety, death, conscience, guilt, and resoluteness—are an attempt to secularize Kierkegaard's notion of religiousness a, while also incorporating certain features of his religiousness B (though without the latter's essential risk or vulnerability). They conclude, however, that, for all its ingenuity, this attempt results in an inconsistent position and is therefore a failure.

It is undeniable that Heidegger drew most of these terms and much of what he says in their regard from Kierkegaard. I believe, nevertheless, that his uses of them and the larger endeavor within which they fit are farther removed from Kierkegaard's than Dreyfus and Rubin allow. In particular, they are deeply integrated with the explicit and overarching aim of *Being and Time*, which is to reawaken the question of being. For instance, Heidegger says this about *Being and Time* in 1930:

> It was never my idea to preach an "existentialist philosophy." Rather, I have been concerned with renewing the question of ontology—the most central question of Western philosophy—the question of being.[1]

---

1. *PG* 13 (an edited transcript of lectures delivered in 1930 and 1931). This translation and all translations of *Sein und Zeit (SZ)* are my own.

Accordingly, I take it as a sign of the incompleteness (at best) of Dreyfus and Rubin's reading that they do not so much as mention the understanding of being until their last few pages and then only in the context of discussing how Heidegger's position evolved in subsequent decades.

In the present setting, I will undertake neither to summarize the Dreyfus/Rubin interpretation nor to criticize it in any detail. Rather, in the space available, I will sketch an alternative approach that may better unify the various themes in *Being and Time* and perhaps thereby illuminate them severally. In so doing, I will give pride of place to Heidegger's extensive and central treatment of death, surely one of the most striking and puzzling "existentialist" notes in the book. (Indeed, it is so puzzling that the foremost exegetical question is what it is doing there at all—that is, in a technical treatise on the question of being.) Yet I will maintain that death, as Heidegger means it, is not merely relevant but in fact the fulcrum of his entire ontology.

Toward this end, it will be necessary to expound in outline that larger metaphysical project, and here it seems to me that Kant is at least as important and illuminating a predecessor as Kierkegaard. Specifically, Heidegger's inquiry into the disclosing of being as the condition of the possibility of comportment toward entities as entities is a direct descendant of Kant's inquiry into the forms of sensibility and understanding as conditions of the possibility of knowledge of objects as objects. In Kantian terms, this could be called the *transcendental* question of the possibility of *objectivity*. In Heideggerian terms, that would become the *existential* question of the possibility of *truth*.

I. TRADITIONAL AND HEIDEGGERIAN CONCEPTS

Heidegger is inevitably and self-consciously a follower in the Western philosophical tradition. But he is also attempting to advance and hence transform that tradition. This effort entails generalizing and/or transforming various traditional concepts, as well as introducing new ones. The most basic of Heidegger's innovations—in the sense that it is what all the others turn on—is his "reawakening" of the question of being. So that will be my main topic in this introductory section. Before undertaking to explain what "being" means, however, I need to review four of Heidegger's other characteristic words—"entity," "comportment," "dasein," and "disclosedness"—and how they relate to their traditional predecessors.

Entities are all and only what there is: *everything* that there is—no more, no less. Thus, if Quine were right that to be is to be the value of a bound variable, then entities would be all and only the values of bound variables. Now, the term "object" can be used in broader and narrower ways. Heidegger usually reserves for it a recognizably Kantian sense: objects *(Gegenstände)* are the entities that can be known in explicit, theoretical judgments—paradigmatically, the knowledge attained in natural science. He also often calls such objects *occurrent (vorhandene)* entities. But, according to Heidegger, not all entities are occurrent objects. Two other sorts of entity are discussed at length in *Being and Time:* (i) *available (zuhandene)* entities, which include tools and other equipment and paraphernalia, and (ii) *existing* entities (in Heidegger's proprietary sense of "existence"), which include dasein and "daseinlike" such entities as sciences and languages. Thus, all objects are entities, but not all entities are objects. So Heidegger's term is a generalization of Kant's.

Corresponding to that generalization is another. Heidegger is concerned with the possibility of *comportment toward* entities (as entities). Husserl (following Brentano) had already generalized theoretical knowledge to intentionality, which includes other cognitive attitudes besides knowing, such as those characteristic of action and perception. But Heidegger maintains that everyday uses of equipment and interactions with other people are not usually *cognitive* at all even in Husserl's broad sense. Yet they are still ways of having to do with entities *as entities*—that is, not just interacting with things physically (as do sticks and stones) or even just actively and sentiently (as do animals) but also in some way that involves understanding them as what they are. Thus, he speaks instead of comportment-toward, which is even more general than Husserlian intentionality (though still not so general as to include whatever it is that animals do).[2]

The generalization from intentionality to comportment-toward is important not merely because the latter encompasses a wider range of relevant phenomena but also and mainly because, according to Heidegger, the further phenomena that it embraces are more basic. Comportment-toward is not exclusively or even primarily a mental phenomenon but rather, in the first place and usually, an active and competent "taking care of business."

---

2. This implies, of course, that animals do not have genuine intentionality—a thesis that I, like Heidegger, endorse (but will not argue for here).

Cognitive comportments (that is, intentional "attitudes"—including but not limited to knowing) are a special case that is not only different from but also *founded upon* noncognitive comportments—such as skillful engagements. Thus, the generalization is not made simply in the interest of thoroughness but rather in the interest of addressing what is most fundamental.

Dasein is Heidegger's word for what essentially distinguishes the human from the nonhuman (whether animate or inanimate). This is not definitive of dasein but only indicative of its evident scope; in other words, it is not ruled out that there may be nonhuman dasein (perhaps on other planets), but we do not know of any. It is *definitive* of dasein that it is the entity that understands being and hence can comport itself toward entities *as entities*. (This is not the most basic definition of dasein, but it follows from it.) Thus, dasein is a distant successor of the logos and the immortal soul and a not-so-distant successor of the transcendental subject or spirit. (As it happens, I disagree with most readers of Heidegger about the individuation of dasein; in particular, I do not think there is a separate and unique dasein for each person. But that will not matter for most of what follows, so I will not discuss it except in passing.)

Dasein's essential characteristic, as the entity that understands being, is what Heidegger calls *disclosedness*. I am going to argue that disclosedness is a successor, albeit fundamentally transformed, of Kant's transcendental apperception. Apperception, for Kant, is consciousness of an object that is or at least could be conscious of itself as conscious of that object. Apperceptive consciousness is the consciousness that is distinctive and prerequisite to the possibility of synthetic judgment—hence of empirical knowledge. In particular, the fact that it could be conscious of itself in being conscious of an object is prerequisite to the possibility of its being conscious of the object *as an object* at all. This is why apperception is *transcendental*.

There are many conspicuous and important differences between disclosedness and apperception. (I will mention several in a footnote to a later passage.) The reason that I nevertheless want to emphasize their kinship is that disclosedness has the same sort of interdependent duality in what it is "of" that apperception has. Any disclosing is *at once* a disclosing of dasein itself *and* a disclosing of the being of entities. It could not be either without being also the other. But, as we shall see, disclosing the being of entities is the condition of the possibility of any comportment toward them *as entities*, and, moreover, this depends on the fact that it is always also a self-disclosing. Therefore, disclosedness, too, is *transcendental* and for a structurally similar reason.

One disanalogy, however, is quite fundamental. Whereas apperception, as self-conscious, is conscious also of objects, disclosedness, as self-disclosing, does *not* disclose also entities but rather the *being* of entities. This is not a minor difference. If there is any single thesis that can be picked out as Heidegger's most emphatic, basic, and original, it is this: "The being of entities 'is' not itself an entity" (*SZ* 6). This expresses what he calls "the ontological difference"—the difference between being and entities. It is the central thought of Heideggerian philosophy.

Kant could not have seen this profound difference between apperception and disclosedness because he did not thematize the difference between being and entities. For the same reason, he could not have raised the question of being. Heidegger claims that, apart from a few dark glimpses, all of his predecessors since the earliest Greeks have *forgotten* the question of being (and he has an account of how and why that happened). But he also claims that the disclosedness of being (as self-disclosing, too) is the condition of the possibility of any comportment toward entities as entities. That is why the question of being now needs to be *reawakened*—the principal aim of *Being and Time*. Thus, disclosedness lies at the heart of the whole project.

It is all too easy to get baffled or intimidated—not to say exasperated—by the way Heidegger talks about being. But that is not necessary; the basic idea is in fact fairly straightforward. The *being* of entities is that in terms of which they are *intelligible as entities*. The qualifier "as entities" (as I am using it) is short for this: with regard to the fact *that* they are (at all) and with regard to *what* they are. Understanding an entity *as an entity*—and there is no other way of *understanding* it—means understanding it in its that-it-is and its what-it-is. Disclosing the being of entities amounts to letting them become accessible in this twofold intelligibility—that is, as phenomena that are *understood*. When taken with sufficient generality, a pretty good colloquial paraphrase for "disclosing the being of" is *making sense of*.

I can illustrate and clarify this by reciting a familiar special case. Consider the entities that are investigated by fundamental mathematical physics—electrons, quarks, photons, the properties or states they can have, the basic forces by which they interact, and so on. These are all *physical* entities (in a specific sense of "physical"); that is, they are things that there are, according to fundamental physics. Now, in terms of what are these entities *intelligible* as entities *that* are and as *what* they are? Obviously, they are intelligible via physical theory, especially the basic laws that specify how they can and must relate to one another. For instance, *what* the electromagnetic force is—its essence—makes sense in terms of and only in terms of the laws of electromagnetism, and so do electric charge, magnetic moment, and what have you. More subtly, perhaps, but just as clearly: *that* there is such an entity—its *actuality*—is intelligible as its current, particular standing in just such relationships at determinate locations in space and time.[3] In sum, the *being* of the physical—the essence and actuality of physical entities—is spelled out by the laws of physics.

This being, in terms of which those entities are intelligible as entities, is *disclosed* by dasein—more particularly, by what might be called physicist-dasein. (On my controversial reading, physicist-dasein is not individual physicists or something that they all "have" but rather the scientific theory and practice of physics that they develop and carry out, but never mind that.) We, physicists and their disciples, comport ourselves toward physical entities (as physical entities) in terms of what is thus disclosed—that is, in terms of their being. No one could observe or measure an electron or an electric field (or even talk about them) *as such* except in terms of that being as spelled out by the relevant laws. It is only in such terms that they so much as make sense to us as entities at all. In other words, disclosure of the being of the physical is the condition of the possibility of comportment toward physical entities as physical entities.

This example of physics and physical being is mentioned by Heidegger (*SZ* 9ff., 362ff.) but not elaborated. On the other hand, he discusses the being of *equipment* in considerable detail. Everyday equipment is primarily understood in the skillful mastery of its proper use—what we might call a "hands-on" intelligibility. What an item of equipment is (its "essence") is what it is properly to be used for—what Heidegger calls its *employment (Bewandtnis)*, which is tantamount to its equipmental *role*.

---

3. Since these relationships concern what is possible and impossible, the actuality of an entity of one determinate kind can be seen as enabling, requiring, or precluding the actuality of another in accord with their respective physical determinations; hence, physical actuality can also be explicated in terms of (a physical species of) causal efficacy and affectability.

Its "actuality" is what he calls its availability *(Zuhandenheit)*—that is, its current, particular capacity to be so used. These two, role and availability, make up the *being* of equipment, in terms of which it is intelligible as equipment at all. Our primary mode of comportment toward equipment as equipment is, of course, using it as the equipment that it is, but there are other modes, such as making it, repairing it, looking for it, talking about it, and so on. The condition of the possibility of any of these modes of comportment is that the equipment make sense to us *as equipment*—which just is the disclosedness of its being (by lay or professional dasein).

Now, physical *being*—physical*ness*, we might call it—is clearly not itself a physical entity. It is not a physical particle, a physical property, a physical force, a physical interaction, or anything of the sort. Likewise, equipmental *being*—equipmental*ity*, we might call it—is not an item of equipment. Are physicalness and equipmentality *entities* of *any* sort? Heidegger insists that they are not—they are not *anything* that there *is* whatsoever. This is precisely the point of the ontological difference.

The idea that being "is" not anything *at all* can be hard to get used to. It is even hard to express: given the point, one strictly should not even use the copula "is" to talk about being—yet, the copula is built into the very structure of ordinary language (much as the quantifier is built into the structure of predicate logic). Accordingly, philosophers have tried to say that, although physicalness is not a *physical* entity (or equipmentality an *equipmental* entity), they—and with them various other sorts of being—must be entities of some further and somehow "special" sort. Perhaps the being of ordinary entities is an "abstract," "ideal," or even "divine" entity. But, then, what of the being of *these* entities (in terms of which alone they could be intelligible and accessible)? Nor is a possible regress the only problem with such traditional suggestions. Another that Heidegger is concerned to avoid is the implication that they make being somehow *eternal*. (It is no accident that the title of his book is *Being and Time*.) But the real payoff for recognizing the ontological difference and reawakening the question of being will lie in the insights it affords us into ourselves and our comportments toward entities as entities.

So far, I have mainly been introducing some Heideggerian terminology, including some of the relationships within it and between it and traditional terms. Now it is time to get down to business and see how these things really work.

2. DISCLOSING BEING AND THE GROUNDING OF ONTICAL TRUTH

We comport ourselves toward entities *as entities*. From one point of view, the whole question is what that means and how it is possible. Heidegger calls such comportments *ontical* comportments because they have to do with *entities*. This is to distinguish them from *ontological* comportments, which have to do rather with being. Disclosing being is an ontological comportment. Discovering entities is the corresponding term for ontical comportments. What we want to see is how disclosure makes discovery possible.

Discovery presupposes a species of truth—what we can call ontical truth (truth regarding entities—which is the only sort of truth most of us ever consider). This is implied in the pivotal qualifier "as entities": it means that ontical comportments must undertake to get the entities in some sense "right." The *feasibility* and *requirement* of ontical truth are what distinguishes human (ontical) comportments from the behavior of animals and inanimate things. Thus, in wanting to see how disclosure makes discovery possible, we want to see how it makes ontical truth possible. I will call this issue the *grounding* of ontical truth, and I will structure my exposition of Heidegger's transcendental philosophy as a three-stage response to it—that is, a three-stage grounding of ontical truth.

The first stage (the remainder of this section) spells out in more detail *why* discovery of entities presupposes disclosure of their being. In so doing, it shows also, though only in a preliminary way, how discoveries are *beholden* to the entities they discover (the "feasibility" of ontical truth). Stage two (section 3) shows how disclosure of being is inseparable from self-disclosure and thereby shows also, though again only in a preliminary way, how ontical truth is *binding* on dasein (the "requirement" of it). Finally, the third and deepest stage in the grounding (sections 4 and 5) will reveal why and how all of this depends on the so-called existentialist elements in *Being and Time*—especially the doctrine of death. In particular, it will fill in what is missing from the first two stages, in virtue of which they are each only "preliminary." (It must be conceded that Heidegger himself does not lay out the stages in quite this way or develop any of them quite fully. But he does say more as the stages get deeper and more difficult and is particularly fulsome at stage three).

In Heidegger's analysis, discovery and disclosure each have three moments—understanding, telling, and findingness. The fact that they each have this same structure evinces the fact that they are closely related phenomena; indeed, we could as well say (though Heidegger does not) that discovery just is *ontical* disclosure.

Heidegger's basic conception of *understanding* is *competence* or *know-how.* Thus, everyday ontical understanding is knowing how to use, manage, or otherwise cope with everyday entities and situations. For instance, understanding hammers is knowing how to hammer with them, understanding a language is knowing how to converse in it, understanding people is knowing how to interact and get along with them, and so on. Even everyday self-understanding is characterized as one's "ability-to-be" who one is—that is, to carry out one's various personal, social, and professional roles. This is not to deny that there can also be theoretical or intellectual understanding, but these are seen as dependent upon "practical" understanding in at least two ways. First, as many have pointed out, theoretical understanding is almost always derivative (perhaps via several intermediaries) from prior pretheoretical understandings, themselves rooted in practical mastery and difficulties. Second, even grasping a theory itself involves technical mastery of various formalisms, methods, vocabulary, models, and such.

"Telling" is my translation of *"Rede,"* a word which usually just means "talk." But Heidegger introduces *Rede* as the *foundation* of language and then explicitly defines it as the *articulation of intelligibility* (where "articulate" carries its original connotations of joints and separations between things). Now, "tell" comes from the same root as "talk" and often means much the same—as in telling others about something, telling them what to do, telling a story, and the like. But it also has other uses that have to do more with distinguishing, identifying, and even counting—such as telling apart, telling whether, telling what is what, telling one when you see one, telling how many, and so on. These latter senses clearly echo the image of articulation and are plausibly prerequisite to the possibility of putting things into words. So, for example, in skillfully hammering, I can *tell* whether I am swinging hard enough, whether the nail is going in straight, or whether the board is splitting, and these distinctions *articulate* what, in knowing how to hammer, I understand. They also underlie my ability to talk sensibly about hammering—at least insofar as I "know what I'm talking about."

"*Findingness*" is my contrived rendition of Heidegger's contrived word "*Befindlichkeit.*"[4] This bizarre term names the feature of human life that it is always responsive to what *matters* in its current, concrete situation—it *finds* the situation as thus mattering to it. For instance, if I am absorbed in hammering, I will be responsive to the heft and recoil of the hammer, the fit and integrity of the boards, the position and angle of the nail; these all matter to the hammering. But I am likely to be oblivious of the sawdust on the floor or the flicker of the lamp (unless, of course, they interfere with the work). Moods are Heidegger's favorite example of a response to what matters in a situation, at least in part because they are so pervasive, intrusive, and uninvited. A mood makes manifest not only (i) how things are going (here and now), but also (ii) the way in which this matters, and (iii) the extent to which it just has to be accepted (put up with). But I think that findingness must also include more than Heidegger explicitly mentions, such as the fluid, involved rapport of a craftsperson or athlete with the current work or play situation and even the attentive responsiveness that is prerequisite to "disinterested" observation.

These general characterizations of understanding, telling, and findingness have been neutral between discovery (ontical) and disclosure (ontological), but the examples have all been ontical. What would be examples of *ontological* understanding, telling, and findingness—that is, of disclosure properly so called? Heidegger is perfectly clear about the essential point: understanding, he says, always projects entities onto their *possibilities.* Ontical know-how masters entities as they are or are not *in fact.* Ontological know-how masters entities as they *could* or *could-not* be. In other words, disclosing the being of entities involves grasping them in terms of a distinction between what is possible and impossible for them.

This should not come as a complete surprise. After all, specifying what is possible and impossible for physical entities is precisely what the laws of physics do. (Indeed, they specify the possible relationships among the values of physical variables so precisely—that is, strictly—that it is often easier to think of them as specifying what is necessary, but that is just another way of saying the same thing). So, understanding physical entities in terms

---

4. In the book manuscript of *Dasein Disclosed* (part 2 above), Haugeland revised his preferred translation of *Befindlichkeit*, from "sofindingness" to "findingness." The former term was originally used in this paper, but the translation has been changed for consistency throughout the volume.

of these laws is projecting them onto their possibilities. Projecting entities onto their possibilities is the same as projecting them onto their being. (Heidegger uses both expressions.) So, the ability to project entities onto their possibilities is the ontological know-how that is the understanding moment of disclosedness.

Notice that, for sciences like physics, the essential connection between understanding and possibility is a commonplace in the philosophy of science even though it is expressed in a different vocabulary. The usual focus is explanation, but *explaining* something (perhaps something already known) is nothing other than a way of rendering it *intelligible*. And standard models of explanation always involve subsumption under lawlike generalizations—where "lawlikeness" amounts to some sort of modal force (necessity or possibility).

The possibilities and impossibilities for equipmental entities are not so strictly definable as for physical entities, but they are just as fundamental to understanding. What is possible for an item of equipment is how it *can* properly be used and how it *ought* properly to function in such use. Thus, stirring paint with a hammer is ruled out, and so is a hammer that shatters when it hits a nail. Of course, neither of these is "physically" impossible, but they are ruled out for this equipment as the equipment that it is. Clearly, equipmental possibilities and impossibilities are in some way normative. Yet, just as with the physical, the equipmental is intelligible as such in terms of—as projected onto—what is possible and impossible for it in the relevant sense. We can see, therefore, that standard accounts of scientific explanation are effectively special cases of Heidegger's more general formulation.[5]

Ontological understanding, like any understanding, is essentially integrated with a telling (articulation of intelligibility) and a findingness (responsiveness to what matters in the current situation). Manifestly, the articulation of ontological intelligibility is at least making the many determinate distinctions between the possible and the impossible for the entities of the relevant sort.[6] Without these distinctions, the ability to project would be

---

5. It is illuminating to consider how so-called functional explanations—say, of how mechanisms or organisms work—are another special case, partaking of elements from each of the foregoing examples, but that cannot be pursued here.

6. In *GP* (his summer 1927 lectures), Heidegger identifies and examines a deeper form of ontological articulation: the distinction, in the being of any entity (of whatever sort), between its that-it-is (existence or actuality, for instance) and its what-it-is (essence or reality,

vacuous. In effect, the ability to project is nothing other than the ability to "apply" these distinctions in particular and specified kinds of cases. Just as clearly, those distinctions would come to nothing—would not in fact be drawn—if there were in general no ability to "apply" them. So, the understanding and telling that belong to disclosedness belong essentially together.

Findingness is responsiveness to what matters in the current situation. What is it that matters for *ontological* findingness—the findingness that belongs properly to disclosedness? What *matters* is that the entities, as ontically discovered, be in fact *possible*—that is, not impossible—according to the understanding of their being. I will explain this point in a way that is not explicit in Heidegger's texts but lies, I believe, just behind the scenes. It is quite fundamental to the first stage in the grounding of ontical truth.[7]

---

for instance). Elsewhere he occasionally also includes a third member in this articulated set, corresponding to what the medievals called accidental-being. See, for instance, *GM* 476–81, an edited transcript of lectures delivered in 1929 and 1930. He calls these distinctions the articulation of being. And the question he always asks is: why is being articulated in just this way? But, so far as I know, he never succeeds in answering that question.

7. With this survey of the three moments of disclosedness we are in a better position to see some of the ways in which it differs from Kant's transcendental apperception. Most conspicuously, the architectonic is different. For Kant, there are two distinct faculties that *jointly* make knowledge possible: sensibility and understanding. The first is the capacity to be affected by objects, and the second is the capacity to make judgments that are about them and bound by them. But apperception is associated exclusively with the latter. For Heidegger, by contrast, there is only disclosedness. The closest thing to a "partner" for disclosedness, in the way that sensibility is the partner of understanding, would be the world itself. But even that is not quite right because disclosedness is the same as being-in as such, the "middle" element in the triune structure of being in the world. Disclosedness is "between" the self and the world.

But that implies a more particular—and particularly striking—difference. If disclosedness is "between" the self and the world in the structure of being-in-the-world, then it is no more to be identified with the self than with the world. Yet Kant explicitly identifies transcendental apperception with the "I that thinks" and the "transcendental self."

Closely related to this difference is a third. If understanding is basically skillful know-how, then, like comportment toward entities in general, it is not exclusively or even primarily mental (let alone intellectual). Rather, it is primarily a moment of skillful worldly activities—and the same goes for telling and findingness. (One might suppose that moods, at least, are somehow "mental" were it not for the fact that Heidegger explicitly disavows that as an implication of what he means: "Being-attuned [in a mood] is not re-

If ontical truth, "getting the entities right," is to be a distinctive possibility and aim of ontical comportments, then there must be a difference between those comportments that are true in this sense and those that are not, a difference that depends on the entities themselves and that the comportments undertake to be on one side of. The effect is that comportments must be, in a distinctive way, *beholden to* the entities toward which they are comportments. Thus, apart from all other questions of success or failure in a comportment, there is this *distinctive* question of success or failure: has the comportment "got the entity right"?

This will all seem less cryptic if we revert for a moment to more familiar territory. Suppose the comportment in question is a description of the state of some physical particle. Such a comportment (description) might succeed or fail in any number of ways: in impressing the graduate students, in securing a grant, in adhering to the grammar of English, or whatever. But there is a distinctive kind of success that descriptions *as such* must aim at—one that depends on the described entity itself. In our example, it depends on whether there is such a particle and whether it is in that state. This amounts to saying, of course, that a description as such undertakes to be correct or *true* (truth in the sense of correctness). Thus, truth, in the sense of descriptive correctness, is a special case of "getting the entities *themselves* right."

Heidegger uses the word "truth" for a more general phenomenon of which descriptive correctness is a special case. For example, using a hammer properly as a hammer is also true in this more general sense—it discovers the hammer as an entity and "gets it right." He also says of such true comportments (including but not limited to correct descriptions) that they "let entities be" and "let them show themselves" or "set them free." The idea is that entities first lie *hidden* either because they have not yet been

---

lated in the first place to the psychical and is not itself an inner state" (SZ 137). Clearly, disclosedness cannot be equated with consciousness (or the mind) in any familiar sense.

Finally, on my (controversial) reading, disclosedness is not even primarily private or individual. Rather, in the first place and usually, it is cultural and historical, hence *public*. Indeed, Heidegger's specific term for *unowned* disclosedness is *publicness (Öffentlich-keit)* (SZ 167). To be sure, particular instances of know-how, articulation, and responsiveness are found in individual people. But that is like pointing out that particular scientific experiments and speech acts are performed by individuals. Nevertheless, science and language themselves are clearly cultural/historical *public* phenomena, and that is the way I believe we should understand disclosedness. Needless to say, Kantian apperception is not public in this way.

noticed or because they have since been somehow disguised or even forgotten. *True* comportments bring them out of this hiddenness—out into the *open*. It is no coincidence that the terms "discover" and "disclose" both have connotations of unhiding and bringing into the open.

Now, if there is to be a significant distinction between "getting an entity right" and failing to do so, there must be some way—some feasible and nonarbitrary way—of telling it in particular cases. For instance, for a descriptive comportment (judgment or assertion), there must be some way of telling whether that description is true (correct) of the entity described—not in every instance, of course, but as a rule. Comportments in themselves, however, do not wear their ontical truth on their sleeves. Therefore, something else, some further comportment or comportments must be involved in telling whether they are true or not. So the question at this point resolves into these: how can some comportments impugn the ontical truth of others? And, supposing they can, how can the choice among them be nonarbitrary?

Comportments can impugn the ontical truth of others if their respective discoverings of entities as entities are mutually *incompatible*. Hence, such incompatibility must itself make sense and be tellable (identifiable) in practice. In general, discoverings of entities are incompatible just in case the entities themselves, as (ostensibly) discovered, would be *impossible*. And this, at long last, is why the difference between the possible and the impossible *matters*—matters, in particular, to the aim of ontical truth. Ontological findingness is *responsiveness* to ostensible impossibilities in the current situation as something that matters.

More specifically, the response must be a *refusal to accept* any current apparent impossibility. Impossibilities matter by way of being *unacceptable*. This is familiar enough: if you discover both that your son is now at school and now at home, then something must be *wrong*, for he *cannot* be two places at once. Likewise, if you discover that something is a hammer but *shatters* against a nail or that something is an electric current but generates no magnetic field. Since that would be impossible, *something* is wrong. So, you have to ask: what is wrong? You double-check, reexamine your means of discovery, find alternative ways to discover the same entities, seek confirmation from other people, and so on. Soon enough, other things being equal, it becomes clear which of your earlier *apparent* discoveries was wrong—was *merely* an appearance—and perhaps also why. By such perfectly ordinary procedures, the choice among the incompatible comportments becomes *nonarbitrary*. To put the emphasis another way, these procedures make feasible a nonarbitrary distinction between (mere) *appearance* and *reality*—that is, the ability to get the entities *themselves* right.

But that means we have shown how comportments can be beholden to *entities*—that is, can be comportments toward entities *as entities*. This, however, is just to show how they can undertake to be ontically true. Thus, ontological findingness, as the refusal to accept ostensible impossibilities, belongs together with ontological understanding (projecting entities onto their possibilities) and ontological telling (articulating the distinction between the possible and the impossible) in making true ontical comportments possible. And that is exactly what we wanted to show: disclosing the being of entities is a condition of the possibility of discovering them *as entities.*

In this first stage of the grounding of ontical truth it has been shown why any discovering of entities presupposes a disclosing of their being. In particular, it has been shown (though only in a preliminary way) how ontical comportments can be—feasibly and nonarbitrarily—*beholden* to the entities toward which they are comportments. This beholdenness belongs to the essential aim of any comportment toward an entity as an entity— namely, that it get the entity itself right. In other words, beholdenness to entities belongs to ontical truth as such, and it is *this* that has been grounded in the disclosing of being.

3. DISCLOSING DASEIN AND ONTOLOGICAL RESPONSIBILITY

Whenever any entities are discovered, they are discovered *by dasein*. It is dasein that, in comporting itself toward entities, undertakes to get them right. Thus, really, it is dasein that is "beholden" in any beholdenness to entities. This beholdenness *of dasein* must also belong to any adequate account of ontical truth. To avoid confusion, I will refer to this second essential side of beholdenness as the *bindingness* of ontical truth—namely, its bindingness *on dasein*. Explaining the essential bindingness of ontical truth is the second stage in its grounding.

As I mentioned at the outset, disclosedness is analogous to apperception in two ways: first, it is the condition of the possibility of comportment toward entities as entities, and second, it is *at once* a disclosing of the being of those entities *and* a self-disclosing. It is to the latter of these two parallels that we now turn. We have just seen what disclosing being means and how it is prerequisite to ontical comportments toward entities as entities. But what does that have to do with *self*-disclosing? In this section I will give an initial account of self-disclosing and then explain why it is and must be integral to disclosing the being of entities. And that will enable us to see (though again in only a preliminary way) how ontical truth is binding on dasein.

In the first place and usually, dasein does not "discover" itself by, say, using, observing, or measuring itself. Rather, in each case, it simply lives its life—mostly by taking care of its daily business. ("Dasein *in each case*" means each individual person, whether or not one accepts my controversial suggestion that dasein *as such* is not individual or personal.) As Heidegger says, we *are* what we *do* (SZ 126, 239). That is, in each case, we comport ourselves toward ourselves as ourselves (that is, as the entities that we are) by living our lives as *our* lives. As with any comportment toward entities as entities, we do so in terms of a disclosing of being—our being. This disclosing, too, has the form of an articulated sofinding understanding in terms of possibilities—our possibilities. In seeing what this means, we will see why dasein's self-disclosing is inseparable from a disclosing of the being of *other* entities.[8]

Dasein's possibilities are ways in which it can live—what Heidegger calls its *ability-to-be*. In the first place and usually, these are individual capacities that are governed and defined by social norms and practices, as further specified in each case by individual social roles. Thus, "we" (end-of-millennium Westerners, say) *can* use money to buy food and clothing of our choosing, *cannot* run around in public without clothing, *must* pay taxes, and *need* licenses if we are to operate automobiles. If we are academics, we can (and are "expected to") teach classes, assign work to students, and evaluate that work; on the other hand, we cannot issue traffic citations (unless we are also police officers). And I, in particular, can and am expected to teach particular classes (with a certain leeway in how I teach them) at particular times and with particular students. It is in such terms that we understand *ourselves* as entities and as the entities that we are—that is, as *who* we are.

---

8. Without putting it in the same way, what this paragraph describes (and so promises to explicate) is what Heidegger calls the three "priorities" of dasein (SZ 12ff).

These are all worldly possibilities. They are possibilities for an entity whose basic makeup is being-in-the-world, which means (among other things) being in the midst of entities and comporting ourselves toward them. I could not be a teacher, for instance, without comporting myself toward students, lessons, assignments, and the like. Thus, in knowing how to be me, I must know how to deal with the entities amidst which I work and live—indeed, these are often just two ways of looking at the same know-how. But that is not all: since what I can and am expected to do (in the roles onto which I project myself) depends on which entities there are and what they are, my comportments toward those entities must be ontically *true* (at least mostly). My self-understanding, therefore, *presupposes* that I understand the being of the entities amid which I live.

In fact, the connection is closer yet. My self-understanding is my ability-to-be who I am—the skillful know-how that enables me to project myself onto my own possibilities (as a teacher, for instance) and, in those terms, to live my life. But, if my self-understanding depends on my understanding of the being of other entities, then I must also *be able to* project those entities onto their possibilities. *This* ability, therefore, belongs essentially to my ability-to-be *me*. My ability to project those entities onto their possibilities is not merely another possibility onto which I project myself but is rather *part of* my ability to project myself onto my own possibilities at all. In other words, my *self*-understanding literally *incorporates* an understanding of the being of other entities. And since, conversely, there could also be no projection of any entities onto their possibilities if that were not something that someone is able to do, neither self-understanding nor understanding of being is possible except insofar as they are integrated with one another.

Obviously the same goes for articulative telling. Projection onto possibilities, whether possibilities for one's own living or possibilities for the entities around one, is for naught if the respective possibilities are not distinguished from impossibilities—that is, from something that is ruled out. Making such distinctions is the relevant telling, and there would be nothing to tell if there were no projections. Therefore, since the corresponding understandings are possible only as integrated, so are the tellings.

Findingness is more interesting. In understanding myself as a teacher, I project myself onto the possibilities that go with that role—possibilities that I distinguish from impossibilities. Moreover, I am responsive to that distinction as something that matters in each current situation, specifically in that impossibilities are not acceptable to me. That is the findingness that belongs to self-disclosing. But, since I am the entity that I am comporting myself toward, what matters is whether I am "possible" or not, which is to say, whether what I am *doing* is ruled out or not. For instance, in comporting myself toward myself as a teacher, it matters to me that, so far as I can manage, I do everything that is prescribed to me as a teacher and nothing that is proscribed. Stretching the terms a bit, we could even call such propriety the "ontical truth" of being a teacher.

Now, we saw earlier that comportments toward entities as entities *undertake* to be ontically true because impossibilities are *unacceptable*. In the context of self-disclosing, however, what I *undertake* is to *do* what I am supposed to—that is, never to *act* in a way that is ruled out; that is what matters in this findingness. But a responsiveness that finds what is ruled out in the responding entity's own actions to be unacceptable *to that entity itself* is *responsibility*. So, for instance, one can say of a hammer or other worldly entity that is found to be impossible (ruled out) that it is unacceptable, but one cannot say that it is irresponsible. By contrast, one can and does say exactly that of a teacher—or any other person—who is out of line in terms of his or her role. Therefore, the findingness that belongs to *self-disclosing* amounts to responsibility.

But, as we have also seen, performing as one is supposed to in a worldly role always involves comportments toward entities as entities, comportments that need, that is, mostly to be ontically true. I cannot carry out my responsibilities as a teacher, for instance, if I cannot reliably tell whether I have my notes with me, whether I am in the right classroom, and a host of other such things. Telling *reliably* means mostly truly. It follows that the responsibilities implied by self-disclosing *include* the responsibility to, in a broad sense, *tell the truth*.

This responsibility does not extend merely to everyday comportments toward, say, equipment or other people but also to all ontical comportments. Suppose, for example, a physicist discovered an entity that, according to certain experimental results, appeared to violate some law of physics (that is, was impossible according to that law). How should this physicist, *qua physicist*, respond to such a discovery? Well, in real life, there may be many reasonable alternatives, but nonchalant indifference is not among them. No one who simply did not give a damn whether experimental results accord with theory could be a proper scientist—it would be scientifically *irresponsible*. But this is just to say that every scientist as such must acknowledge the scientific responsibility (perhaps in concert with the larger scientific community) to see that such matters are cleared up, that is, to figure out what is true.

Since getting the entities right depends on the disclosure of their being, the ontological findingness that belongs to the disclosure of being is likewise not merely responsiveness but responsibility. That is, finding impossible entities unacceptable is not just a response but also a responsibility—a further part of the responsibility that dasein in each case has as self-disclosing. Moreover, there clearly could be no such responsibility except as part of dasein's self-responsibility. In other words, the findingness of self-disclosure and that of the disclosure of being are inseparable. Inasmuch as this responsibility is responsibility for ontical *truth*, it can also be called *ontological* responsibility. (Ontical responsibilities are just one's ordinary duties and the like.)

With this conclusion, we have shown for each of understanding, telling, and findingness that, as belonging respectively to *self*-disclosing and disclosing the being of other entities, they are inseparable. But, since these three moments are jointly constitutive of disclosing, to have shown that for each of them is to have shown it for disclosing itself. In other words, we have shown that disclosing as such is at once a self-disclosing and a disclosing of the being of entities. This was the first goal of the present section. (Among other things, it completes the justification of the analogy with transcendental apperception.)

The second goal now follows easily. Responsibility is intrinsically a kind of bindingness: one is "bound" by one's responsibilities. Therefore, in showing that dasein is *responsible* for ontical truth—for "telling the truth"—we have shown (at least in a preliminary way) how ontical truth is *binding* on dasein. And that completes the second stage in its grounding. What remains is first to see why these two stages have been only "preliminary" and second to supply what is still needed for a full grounding of ontical truth. That will take us into the thick of Heidegger's "existentialism."

4. OWNED DISCLOSEDNESS: RESOLUTE BEING TOWARD DEATH

The most pervasive and basic of Heidegger's "existentialist" concepts is that of *ownedness (Eigentlichkeit)*. The usual translation of *"eigentlich"* is "real" or "authentic" (as opposed, for instance, to fake or counterfeit). But

Heidegger explicitly warns that he has chosen his expressions *"Eigentlich-keit"* and its opposite *"Uneigentlichkeit"* in "the strict senses of the words" (*SZ* 43)—which I take to mean their etymological senses. The root word *"eigen"* is broadly equivalent to (and cognate with) the English word "own" (as in "a room of one's own"). This suggests that Heidegger's terms (neither of which is an ordinary German word) might better be translated "owned-ness" and "unownedness"—and that is how I will translate them (and cor-respondingly for the adjectives and adverbs). But the ultimate justification for this must be philosophical.

The first clue to a proper understanding is Heidegger's further remark (in the same passage) that ownedness and unownedness are *both* grounded in the fact that dasein at all is defined by *in-each-case-mineness* (*jemeinig-keit*). The point here is that each person's life *belongs to* the person whose life it is: each person can say "this is *my* life," "*my* decision," "*my* responsibility," and so on. It is not dasein *as such* that is "mine" (or can say "my . . ."); rather, dasein in each case is (respectively) "mine." Dasein *as such* is defined by this fact that in each respective case it is "mine." Ownedness and unownedness are modes of dasein's being, and they are both grounded in that fact about dasein as such, that it is in each case mine.

Thus, ownedness and unownedness are alternative *ways* in which das-ein, in any given case, can be respectively "its own" ("mine"). Dasein is in-variably *its own* (mine) in each case. But it may or may not be *owned*—ownedness is something over and above mineness that varies from case to case. (I think Heidegger should also have said that ownedness varies in degree from case to case and that, in any given case, its degree can differ in different respects, but he did not.) Unownedness is, so to speak, the de-fault: in the first place and usually, dasein is unowned. Ownedness, by contrast, is distinctive and special. But the *possibility* of ownedness is uni-versal (implicit in mineness) and is moreover, as we shall see, essential to dasein as the entity that comports itself toward entities as entities.

The difference between ownedness and unownedness is a difference in modes of disclosedness. Unowned disclosedness (the default) is called *pub-licness;* owned disclosedness (dasein's distinctive possibility) is called *reso-luteness.* But, given the way Heidegger uses the word "existential," it can also be called *existential* disclosedness. Thus, we will understand what this is all about—what it has to do with the transcendental question concerning the possibility of ontical truth when we understand resoluteness. It is in Heidegger's lengthy explication of resoluteness that all of the notorious existentialist notions—falling, anxiety, individuality, death, conscience, and being-responsible ("guilt")—come to the fore.

Falling is the basic characteristic of dasein that, in each case, it inevitably tends toward unownedness—specifically, unowned disclosedness (publicness). This is why publicness is the default. In the special case of scientific dasein, *fallenness* (unownedness) is exactly what Kuhn calls *normality* (as in *normal* science). So falling is a generalization of the tendency toward normality in science. Kuhn has a lovely explanation for *why* a dogged, even sometimes dogmatic, tendency toward normality is *essential* to science.[9] Heidegger, too, says that falling is not a derogatory concept and that it is essential to dasein, but he lacks Kuhn's developed explanation of why. Given this essential tendency toward unownedness or normality (what Heidegger also calls everydayness), there must also be some push in the opposite direction if there is ever to be anything else. Kuhn's and Heidegger's accounts of this opposing push likewise have much in common: the former is richer in historical example, while the latter is more general and more worked out philosophically.

Resoluteness, as a mode of disclosedness, has the same basic structure that we have already seen: a sofinding and telling understanding. Each of these three moments has an owned (existential) mode that belongs to resoluteness as owned disclosedness.

The owned findingness that belongs to resoluteness is *readiness-for-anxiety*. Anxiety is a mood that manifests a profound breakdown in an individual's way of life. Nothing makes any sense or means anything anymore—nothing matters except the overwhelming fact that nothing (else) matters. (Thus, anxiety is analogous to Kuhn's sense of crisis.) Heidegger says that anxiety *individualizes* dasein. This does not mean that dasein is not, in each case, already an individual but rather that, in anxiety, a person's individuality is "brought home" to the person in an utterly unmistakable and

9. The basic point is that, if scientists were not *tenacious* in their efforts to solve even highly recalcitrant puzzles (that is, in preference to giving up on their paradigm), then hard but solvable puzzles would seldom get solved. Yet it is precisely these solutions that are often the most valuable achievements of science. Moreover, if and when a paradigm shift does become inevitable, it will be largely driven and guided by those very intransigent puzzles which could have been identified as such only through persistent efforts to solve them and which, once so identified, can prove particularly revealing. See Kuhn (1962, 1970, 64f., 151ff.).

undeniable way. Falling back into public life (normality) is a way of escaping anxiety, and the public culture encourages this. Indeed, the culture offers "commonsense" interpretations that tend to minimize anxiety itself—turn it into (confuse it with) some weak-kneed or adolescent self-indulgence. Thus, the very possibility of genuine anxiety is publicly confused and covered up—disguised and forgotten.

Readiness-for-anxiety is not the same as anxiety, but it does run directly counter to this public (falling) tendency to disguise and forget anxiety. Readiness-for-anxiety is an individualized mode of findingness in which anxiety is held open as a constant possibility—a possibility that currently matters to that very individual. This does not mean that the person is hoping or striving for anxiety—far from it—but only that the person is determined not to hide or run away from it. (If we were to invent a Kuhnian analog for this, it would be openness to the possibility of scientific crisis.)

The owned telling that belongs to resoluteness is *conscience*—or, rather, that *reticence* (muting the public babble) in which conscience can be "listened for" and "heard." According to the common public interpretation, conscience is an "inner voice" that mainly warns and reproves—tells you when you would be or have been naughty. (A so-called good conscience merely reassures you that you have not been naughty). But, as with anxiety, Heidegger claims that this fallen interpretation disguises and forgets what conscience really articulates, which must be (Heidegger is not explicit here) the difference between one's whole life "working" and its breaking down or failing to "work"—the very difference that matters in readiness-for-anxiety.

What Heidegger *is* explicit about is that (in articulating this distinction) conscience *calls upon* dasein in each case to *take over responsibility* for its whole life—a call that the public interpretation likewise disguises and forgets. This is not the same as what I earlier termed *ontological* responsibility, which is perfectly intelligible in terms of public norms and expectations and which concerns only particular events. Rather, the responsibility that existential conscience gives dasein in each case to understand—namely, *existential* responsibility—is responsibility for its *own self as a whole*, for *who* it is. Thus conscience, like anxiety, individualizes.

Heidegger's formulation of this point takes advantage of some relationships among German word senses that cannot be reproduced exactly in English. The term that I am translating as "responsible" is "*schuldig.*" The two most common senses of this word are guilty/at-fault/culpable and obliged/indebted/liable. "Responsible," in English, is not as specific as either of these senses but is broad enough to cover them both. Clearly, the common theme is how one ought and ought not to behave. (It is helpful to remember that *"schuld-"* is cognate with "should.") Thus, Heidegger can say that, according to common sense, conscience mainly tells us that we are *schuldig*—guilty or obliged. But he can then go on to say that guilt and obligation are merely fallen public interpretations of being *schuldig*—interpretations that track only public norms and statuses, keeping score on everyone's credits and debits, points and infractions. As fallen, however, these "normal" interpretations are but forgetful disguises of a more originary *self*-responsibility—one that cannot be public but can be taken over only by an individual. Conscience, understood existentially, calls upon dasein in each case to take over and own *this* responsibility.

The owned, existential understanding that belongs to resoluteness is projecting oneself onto being-responsible. Thus, being-responsible, like anything onto which dasein projects itself, is a possibility for how it can live—an ability-to-be. Heidegger calls it dasein's ownmost *(eigenste)* possibility or ability-to-be. Now, dasein, as that entity that comports itself toward entities as entities, is *always* in each case responsible. (Irresponsibility is just a deficient mode of responsibility.) This was shown already in the second stage of the grounding. So the being-responsible (onto which owned dasein projects itself and which conscience gives it to understand) must be something over and above that invariable responsibility that always characterizes dasein—something that is a *possibility* for it but not necessary.

An individual's being-responsible is its *taking over* responsibility for its *whole self.* But what does that mean? Here we have "existentialism" in its full flower. Yet, according to the passage I quoted in my prologue, Heidegger does not want to preach an existentialist philosophy but rather to renew the question of being. Does that mean that being-responsible has something to do with the question of being? Yes, of course! Ultimately *everything* in *Being and Time* has to do with the question of being—and, with it, truth. The existential concepts are introduced for this reason and this reason only. Our task as readers is to understand how.

That task will take us through the most remarkable of detours—or, rather, what at first *seems* to be a detour—Heidegger's doctrine of death. As with anxiety, conscience, and guilt/responsibility, Heidegger claims that the understandings of death handed down to us by our culture are mostly fallen and forgetful disguises. He singles out two versions of these popular conceptions for particular attention so as to contrast them with his own and thus to set them aside. The first of these he calls *perishing*. This is the ubiquitous and all-too-familiar biological phenomenon that is the cessation of systematic biological function in an organism (and, typically, the onset of organic decay). All organisms eventually perish: plants, animals, fungi, and what have you, including all specimens of *Homo sapiens*. But *dasein never perishes*—not because it is immortal or everlasting but because it is not a living organism in the biological sense at all.

The second popular conception of death Heidegger calls *demise*. Unlike perishing, demise is not a biological phenomenon but pertains exclusively to dasein. It is instead a social-cultural phenomenon. Roughly speaking, demise is that social event upon which you cease to be countable in the census, your spouse becomes a widow or widower, your property ceases to be yours and passes to your heirs, criminal charges against you automatically become moot, and so on. Although demise typically coincides with the perishing of an organism, these are not at all the same. The relationship between demise and perishing is loosely analogous to that between marriage and mating (which likewise are not at all the same).

What is important about these is only that neither is to be identified with death, *existentially* conceived. Without attempting a full account, I will relate a few of the most salient and significant things that Heidegger says about death (as opposed to perishing and/or demise):

- Death is *not an event:* it is not something that happens—*ever* (SZ 240, 250, 257).
- Death "is" only in *being toward* death; that is, death is intelligible only as a certain sort of being-toward (SZ 234, 245, 259).
- Death is a *way to be* (dasein is *constantly* dying); in other words death is a way of life (SZ 245, 251, 259).
- Death is dasein's *ownmost possibility*—a possibility that it is called upon to take over in each case and so one that *individualizes* dasein (SZ 250, 263f.).
- More specifically, death is the *possibility of the impossibility* of dasein's existence at all—that is, of any comportment toward entities as entities—and is thus the possibility of giving itself up (SZ 250, 262, 264).

- In its being toward death, dasein *decides* or *chooses to choose* itself (*SZ* 259, 264, 384; see also 188, 268, 287ff.).
- Death is dasein's *finitude* and *ability-to-be-whole*, that is, in being toward death, dasein exists *finitely* and as a *whole* (*SZ* 264, 309, 329ff., 384–86).

It is clear from the wording of several of these (especially the fourth) that death is related to resoluteness. But Heidegger makes the connection explicit and even stronger. On the one hand, at the conclusion of his existential interpretation of death (*SZ* 266), he acknowledges that, as so far described, being toward death remains a "fantastic exaction" and that it has not been shown how dasein is *capable* of it. On the other hand, following his initial account of resoluteness, he suggests (*SZ* 302ff.) that it has not yet been "thought through to its end." The solution is that each discussion fills the lacuna in the other: thought through to its end, resoluteness must be resoluteness *toward death*, and it is as thus resolute that dasein is *able to be* toward death.

Accordingly, he offers (*SZ* §62) a further elaboration of resoluteness. As resolute, dasein projects itself onto its ownmost being-responsible—that is, understands itself as responsible for its whole life by *owning* that responsibility and "taking it over." *Owning* responsibility, however, means taking it over not as something occasional or incidental but rather as constant and essential; that is, it projects *itself* onto being-responsible *as a whole.* To put it another way, it understands itself as responsible *no matter what.* But, *as finite,* dasein simply *cannot* project itself "no matter what." The "whole" as which it projects itself must be a *finite* whole—which is to say, the projection must be in some way limited and must project itself as thus limited. (Resolute dasein does not hide or run away from its finitude.) As Heidegger puts it, resolute dasein projects itself as self-responsible "right to its end" (*SZ* 305).

Such whole-but-finite resolution means resolution toward death. Death—which is intelligible only as being toward death—is dasein's ability-to-be-whole and its finitude. Conscience and anxiety exact this resolute responsibility of dasein (*SZ* 307ff.); so, while indeed an "exaction," being toward death is not "fantastic."

The word "resolute" means firmly and unwaveringly determined or decisive. Heidegger expresses as much by saying that resoluteness resolves to "repeat itself"—that is, to keep at it or stick to it by, as it were, constantly "reresolving." But he makes this point in the context of making another:

resoluteness cannot become rigidly set in its ways about its situation but rather must be held open and free for whatever its current possibility is. In particular, it must hold itself free for a possible—and, in each case, necessary—*taking it back*. Taking a resolution back means retracting or withdrawing it—that is, giving up on it. These two points are made together and as belonging together (SZ 307ff., 391). Resoluteness *as such* resolves to repeat itself (stick to it) *while also* holding itself constantly free for the possibility of taking it back (giving it up). Clearly (and as Heidegger immediately makes explicit), the possibility of "taking it back" refers to death. This is what is meant by saying that resoluteness is resolute being toward death.

But building this into the structure of resoluteness as such—as something it "holds itself free for"—sounds incoherent. Sticking to it is, of course, a possibility onto which dasein projects itself—which just means that it rules out the contrary, not sticking to it, as unacceptable to itself. But this seems flatly incompatible with holding itself free for the possibility of taking it back. Including them both in the definition makes being "resolute" sound like making a promise with your fingers crossed—which is not to make a *promise* at all.

So we have to ask: how can resoluteness be *resolute* if, as such, it must be resolute *toward death?* What kind of *responsibility* could that be? And, in the meantime, what can it have to do with the question of being and the grounding of ontical truth?

5. TRUTH AND FINITUDE

We are not, after all, unprepared for a connection between resoluteness and the questions of being and truth. Resoluteness is a mode—the owned, existential mode—of disclosedness. Disclosing is at once a disclosing of the being of entities and a disclosing of dasein itself. We have seen not only how these can be described separately but also how they are essentially united. As thus unitary, disclosedness is the condition of the possibility of comportment toward entities as entities—hence of ontical truth. That was the substance of the first two stages of the grounding. Resoluteness, as a mode of disclosedness, is likewise at once a disclosing of being and of dasein. What we have focused on so far is resoluteness as the owned disclosing of dasein. Therefore, in order to complete the story, we must see how, as the owned disclosing of dasein, resoluteness is essentially also an owned disclosing of being.

In *Being and Time* as we have it, Heidegger does not fully work out this crucial chapter of the account. But it is implied in everything that we do have. So the omission cannot be mere negligence, nor can it be that he thought it unimportant. I conjecture, therefore, that it is one of the topics to have been addressed in the never-published third division of part one. (The *main* topic to have been addressed in that division is temporality as the "sense of being," which might have amounted to a fourth stage in the grounding of ontical truth.) Accordingly, I propose to sketch out in the remainder of my chapter how resoluteness is an *owned* disclosing of being. That will complete the third—and for now final—stage in the grounding of ontical truth.

A moment's reflection shows that the possibilities onto which entities are projected—hence, their being—is cultural and historical. Physicists learn the theory and practice of physics at school and from their peers as part of their cultural heritage, and what they learn today is not what they learned a hundred or a thousand years ago. After all, except in times of crisis, the standards for scientific investigation and getting the entities right are established by normal science, and what is *normal* is cultural and historical. Though less dramatically obvious, the same is true for the possibilities and being of ordinary, everyday entities.

Heidegger emphasizes that dasein is essentially historical *(geschichtlich),* not merely in the sense that it always "has" a history but rather, and more basically, in the sense that its being (existence) is constituted by historicalness (SZ 382). Accordingly, insofar as dasein is owned, it is owned as historical. This means, among other things, that resolute dasein discloses its current possibilities from out of a heritage that it *takes over*—that is, takes responsibility for (SZ 383). In responsibly handing possibilities down to itself from out of its heritage, it *explicitly* chooses them for itself *(chooses to* choose them), and this explicit handing down is *repetition*— the repetition that belongs by definition to resoluteness (SZ 384ff.). (Heidegger adds that this repetition of an inherited possibility is not mere reiteration but also makes a "reciprocative rejoinder.")

As we saw in the second stage of the grounding, since dasein's basic makeup is being-in-the-world, its self-disclosing is inseparable from its disclosing of the being of the entities toward which it comports itself. Therefore, resolute dasein, in handing down possibilities to itself from out of its heritage, is handing down *at once* the possibilities onto which it projects itself *and* the possibilities onto which it projects those entities. Though the wording is peculiar, the point is easy to see: physicists, in becoming physicists, inherit *both* the possibilities for working as physicists and the possibilities for the physical entities with which they work. Neither makes sense without the other. In other words, the being of the physical is just as historical as the practice of physics. And a resolute physicist takes responsibility for both.

How can a physicist take responsibility for the *being* of the physical? Heidegger, unfortunately, declines to say. After briefly discussing the scientific projection of entities (especially in mathematical physics) and concluding with a quick invocation of resoluteness, he remarks: "The origin of science from out of owned existence will not be pursued further here" (SZ 363). Whether he intended to pursue it further later is not made clear. Be that as it may, I think we can pursue it further now, and moreover we must if we are to complete the grounding of ontical truth, which is so strikingly and thoroughly prepared in the text we have.

Resoluteness not only repeats itself but also holds itself free for the possibility of taking it back. But this freedom is not irresponsible license—precisely not. It is the freedom of *responsible* decision. To *what* is this free decision responsible? Cryptically, yet not incorrectly, we can say that it is responsible to *itself*. Less compressed, this says it is responsible to that very disclosing of self and being that, as a resolute decisiveness, resoluteness as such is. How that can be will come into focus if we think again about disclosedness and responsibility.

In the first stage of the grounding, disclosing the being of entities makes intelligible a nonarbitrary distinction between appearance and reality via the entailed refusal to accept apparent impossibilities in entities as discovered. That refusal stands behind all the double-checking and so on that ferrets out which apparent discoveries are wrong and so vindicates those that are right. In the second stage, in which that same disclosing is seen instead from the side of self-disclosing, that same responsive refusal manifests itself as ontological responsibility—that is, responsibility for ontical truth. For unowned dasein, that is as far as responsibility for the truth goes.

There is, however, and can be no antecedent *guarantee* that all that double-checking and whatnot, no matter how assiduous, will ever actually succeed. That is, no matter how hard the relevant individuals and community try, they may not find a way to reconcile their apparent discoveries with what they know to be possible. What then? Well, of course, there can be appeals to magic, miracles, and mysticism. There can be denial, disinterest, and decline. In the meantime, everybody is busy: if the impossibility is remote or arcane, maybe the best thing is to ignore it and see if it goes away. But, what is the *responsible* response? Notice that this question cannot be about *ontological* responsibility. What that responsibility requires—the double-checking and ensuing corrections—has already been exhausted. So we are looking for another and *further* responsibility—"further" because it comes up only after wholehearted ontological responsibility has exhausted itself. This further responsibility, too, must take the form of a *refusal to accept* any discovered impossibilities. ("Accepting" them is simply irresponsible.) A discovered impossibility rests on two factors: what is in fact discovered and what is ruled out by the projection onto possibilities. The careful and persistent double-checking has eliminated the discoveries as the culprit. That leaves the possibilities—in other words, the *being* of the entities discovered. So, our further responsibility must be responsibility for the projection onto those possibilities, which is to say, for the disclosing of that being.

Taking responsibility for something is not only taking it as something that matters but also *not* taking it for granted. Taking the disclosure of being for granted—whether explicitly or tacitly—is characteristic of fallen dasein and normal science. *Owned* dasein, as taking over responsibility for its ontological heritage, no longer takes it for granted. It reawakens the question of being—as its *ownmost* and sometimes *most urgent* question. In other words, it holds itself free for taking it back. That does not mean it *does* take it back, still less that it does so easily or casually. The freedom to take it back is not a liberty or a privilege but rather a burden— the most onerous of burdens. That is why everyday dasein runs away and hides from it and even denies that there is any such freedom. Hence, conscience and anxiety must *exact* it of dasein, and resolute dasein must *hold* itself free.

Giving up on a disclosing of being is not a matter to be taken lightly, and the reason is not hard to see. Heidegger, like the early Kuhn, concentrates on extreme cases—maybe even more so (it is hard to be sure since, unlike Kuhn, he does not offer examples). An extreme case is one in which a disclosing is given up more or less wholesale or, as is sometimes said, radically. The trouble with giving up the roots is that you forfeit also the branches. Put less figuratively, the point is that the means of discovering entities—what Heidegger calls "modes of access" and Kuhn calls "experimental procedures" and "puzzle-solving techniques"—themselves *depend on* the disclosure of the being of those entities.

The design of scientific instruments and experiments and the interpretation of their results depend *essentially* on the very laws and theories they sometimes test. Without a great deal of accepted physics, for instance, no cloud-chamber image or statistical pattern from a cyclotron could so much as make sense, let alone reveal anything. But this means that, if intransigent discovered impossibilities undermine a disclosure of being, they pull the rug out from under themselves as well—and along with them, any other discoveries and abilities to discover in that region. The disclosure, the discoveries, and the abilities to discover all stand or fall together—as a *whole*. So, giving up on a disclosing of being is, in effect, giving up on *everything*—including the self-disclosing, which makes possible that way of life.

This is why Heidegger speaks of death—or, rather, of resolute being toward death. Taking responsibility resolutely means living in a way that explicitly has everything at stake. Heidegger's way of saying this is as follows: dasein is the entity for which, in its being, that very being is an issue (*SZ* 12, 191, 240, 263). This is the most basic definition of dasein; all the others follow from it. It follows, for instance, that dasein's basic makeup is being-in-the-world because its being could not be an issue for it if its life were not essentially at risk, and this risk presupposes the potential intransigence of intraworldly entities. And it follows that dasein is the entity that discloses entities in their being since entities could never be intransigent if they were not projected onto *possibilities* or if impossibilities were not unacceptable. *Existence*, in Heidegger's proprietary sense, is the *being* of dasein; hence, it means all of these.

Fallen, everyday dasein runs away and hides from the issue of its being (though it can never escape it); resolute dasein faces up to it by taking over responsibility for itself—that is, by resolving to repeat itself while holding itself free for taking it back. "Refusing to accept" intransigent impossibilities has a double meaning. One way of refusing to accept is bullheadedly refusing even to *see*—blinding oneself. *Existentially*, that kind of refusal—running away and hiding—is *irresponsible*. Thus, holding itself free for taking it back belongs just as essentially to existential responsibility as does sticking to it as long as one reasonably (responsibly) can. The existential *understanding* that belongs to resoluteness—self-projection onto being-responsible—just is perseverant being toward death.[10]

It is crucial, therefore, not to lose sight in this context of the other clause in the formula for resoluteness as a responsible way of life: it resolves to *repeat* itself—that is, to *stick to it.* Since most apparently discovered impossibilities are *merely* apparent, it would be wavering and irresponsible ("irresolute") to give up too soon—that is, so long as there is any way that it might *responsibly* be avoided. Thus, double-checking and ontological responsibility are entailed by resoluteness. Resolute Dasein, too, is responsible for getting the entities right—indeed, as we shall soon see, all the more so.

What differentiates owned from unowned disclosedness is its holding itself free for the possibility, *in extremis*, of taking it back. In so doing, it takes over responsibility not only for ontical truth itself but also for that disclosedness that is the condition of its possibility. Since this disclosedness is the projection of those entities onto the possibilities that determine their *being,* we can, in parallel with the phrase "ontical truth," call it *ontological* truth. Heidegger himself calls disclosedness *originary* truth, and he calls the owned mode of disclosedness (that is, resoluteness) *owned* truth and the *truth of existence* (SZ 220ff., 297–99, 307, 397). Thus, in these terms, resolute Dasein takes responsibility not only for *ontical* but also for *ontological* truth. But, in what sense can disclosedness be called a sort of *truth* at all? What could be counterposed to it as a sort of "falsehood," and what are the feasible and nonarbitrary responses that tell them apart?

Falsehood is a *failure* of truth, a *fault* of it, not merely in the sense of an error (waywardness) but more in the sense of a breach or lack. So the "opposite" of ontological truth would be a failure, breach, or lack of disclosedness. That is exactly the sort of breakdown that manifests itself in anxiety, is told by conscience, and for which owned understanding projects itself onto the responsibility for facing up to it. Therefore, resoluteness, as both resolving to repeat itself and holding itself free for the possibility of taking

---

10. In other words, owned dasein faces up to and takes over the ultimate riskiness of its life as a whole—it lives resolutely as and only as ultimately vulnerable. According to this interpretation, then, it is ironic (to say the least) that the character of religiousness B that Dreyfus and Rubin specifically identify as omitted from ownedness is risk and vulnerability (1991, 298, 335ff.). Their concluding critical observation that the position they attribute to Heidegger "makes no sense" strikes me as telling.

it back, takes responsibility—*existential* responsibility—for the difference between *ontological* truth and falsehood while undertaking to stay on the side of the former.

Ontical truth and the responsibility for it presuppose a disclosing of the being of *entities* because the need for responsible double-checking arises *only* in the face of apparent impossibilities and only so are ontical comportments feasibly and nonarbitrarily beholden to entities. But there can be no comparable account for *ontological* truth and the responsibility for it because there is no "metadisclosedness" for them to presuppose. The possibilities for entities are not themselves projected onto "metapossibilities" in terms of which there could be apparent "metaimpossibilities." How, then, and to what is ontological truth *beholden?*

Ontological truth is beholden to *entities*—the very same entities that ontical truth is beholden to and via the very same means of discovery. The difference lies in the character of the potential failure and the required response. A failure of ontical truth is a misdiscovery of an entity, such as a factual mistake. With more or less work, it can be identified and corrected, and life goes on. A failure of ontological truth is a systematic breakdown that undermines everything—which just means a breakdown that *cannot* be "fixed up with a bit of work." So the only responsible response (eventually) is to take it all back, which means that life, *that* life, does *not* "go on." But this response, too, is a response to discovered entities and only to them—a refusal to accept what we might paradoxically call *"real"* impossibilities among them. Intransigent impossibilities can show up *only* among entities as ostensibly discovered. To be sure, they may turn out in the end not to have been discovered entities after all, but that eventuality *presupposes* ostensible discoveries of entities.

This is an important result, for it means that ontological truth, though historical, is not arbitrary. Therefore, Heidegger's (and Kuhn's) "historicism" about being does not imply relativism. Discovery of entities does indeed presuppose—hence is "relative" to—dasein's disclosure of their being (or a "paradigm"), which is historical. But whether a way of life with its ontical comportments works or not is not ultimately up to dasein either individually or historically. So that disclosure itself, in turn, is *beholden* for its "success" to those very entities as discovered—entities that are independent of it in the concrete and inescapable sense that they are out of control. And that beholden disclosure is *binding* on dasein in that its very life depends on it. Resolute dasein *takes over* that beholden bindingness—binds *itself*—in existential responsibility. Therefore, resolute being toward death is the condition of the possibility of ontological *truth*.

The first and second stages of the grounding showed in a preliminary way how ontical truth is feasible and nonarbitrary and how, as such, it is beholden to entities and binding on dasein. Those demonstrations were only preliminary, however, because the status of the presupposed possibilities for those entities was left out of account. If those possibilities themselves (the disclosed being of the entities) were to remain arbitrary and therefore neither beholden nor binding, then the achievement of the first two stages would be hollow at best—even ontical truth would not be a sort of *truth* after all. The demonstration that ontological truth (disclosedness) is itself feasibly nonarbitrary and, as resolute, also bound and beholden closes that gap. It constitutes, therefore, the third and most fundamental stage in the grounding of ontical truth. The existential conception of finitude—death—that is its crux is accordingly *transcendental.*

Kant understands human knowledge as *essentially finite*. Only in terms of this finitude does a transcendental grounding of its objectivity so much as make sense. But the finitude of knowledge is itself grasped only in contrast to and as falling short of infinite knowing. The relationship between any knowing and what is known in it can never be merely arbitrary. Infinite (divine) knowledge is perfect in itself in that it is not in any way *limited* by what it knows. Infinite just means unlimited: unbounded and unbound. Such knowledge is therefore originary or creative; that is how the relationship to what it knows is nonarbitrary (in effect, what is known is bounded and bound by the knowing of it).

Finite human knowledge, *by contrast,* is *not* perfect in itself. Since it is not originary, it can be knowledge only insofar as it is bounded and bound by what it knows. But that means that whatever it knows must stand over against it as an *object (Gegenstand).* So, finite knowledge can *only* (at best) be *objective*—it falls short of being creative. In order to be objective (bounded and bound), it must be responsive to objects, which means it needs a passive faculty of receptivity. But since mere passivity does not suffice for objectivity (it suffices for boundedness but not for bindingness), finite knowledge also needs an active faculty of spontaneity—a faculty that can somehow *bind itself* to what is accessible in receptivity. The entire problem of the transcendental analytic is to delineate the conditions under which this *self*-binding is possible—an issue that arises only because human knowledge is only finite.

Heidegger calls his analysis of dasein and disclosedness an *existential* analytic not because the grounding of ontical truth is not transcendental but because it can *be* transcendental only *as* existential. Death, as dasein's finitude, plays, as we have seen, a starring role in this drama—not, however, as the antagonist who makes the dramatic resolution necessary but rather as the protagonist who makes it possible.

Temporality

(2002)

1. The declared, official aim of *Being and Time* is to reawaken the question of the sense of being—everything in the book should be read as bearing on this aim and this question.[1]

> —Temporality *(Temporalität)* is Heidegger's concise name for what he also calls dasein's "ekstatic-horizonal unity," which is the most basic structure of any understanding of entities and their being.
>
> —What I hope to do is make a start on explaining what this means and why it is plausible.

We can begin by setting out as "beacons" two of Heidegger's most fundamental theses.

> —First, *being, dasein,* and *time* come as a package—no one of them makes any sense without the other two.
>
> —Second, all three of them are *finite.*

2. By way of preview, the essential connection between dasein and being goes via the *understanding* of being.

---

1. This talk was delivered, virtually as written here, as the keynote address to the July 2002 meeting of the International Society for Phenomenological Studies in Pacific Grove, CA. The numbering and indentations were in Haugeland's original text and have been preserved both to recognize the relations they express between primary and subordinate points and to indicate that the text was prepared for oral presentation rather than as written prose.—*Ed.*

—For, on the one hand, dasein is, *by definition,* the entity that understands being—or rather, and more pointedly, dasein is the entity that *is* an understanding of being.

—On the other hand: no understanding of being, no being.

—As Heidegger himself puts it: "only so long as dasein (that is, the ontical possibility of an understanding of being) is, 'is there' ['*gibt es*'] being"—which he underscores a few lines later by emphasizing "the dependence of being (not of entities) on the understanding of being" [SZ 212].

Similarly, the essential connection between dasein and time goes via originary time.

—For, on the one hand, originary timeishness [*ursprungliche Zeitlichkeit*] is the sense of the being of dasein (that is, the sense of care).

—In other words, it is that wherein the intelligibility of care maintains itself.

—On the other hand, no originary timeishness, no time at all.

—That is the point of the word 'originary' and likewise of all the derivations of world time, vulgar time, and so on (that Bill Blattner 1999 has so splendidly expounded).

Finally, the essential connection between time and being was to have been the topic of division III—the one that Heidegger never got around to.

—Somehow it must be implicit in the first two (by transitivity of essential connections), but it would be much more satisfying to have it spelled out explicitly.

—In fact, I think, 'temporality' (as opposed to 'timeishness') is approximately a name for this connection since it establishes that being (as understood in dasein) is not arbitrary.

—At any rate, that is what I'm going to try to show—at least as far as *Being and Time* got.

3. Before getting down to business, I need to lay some groundwork by summarizing a thesis about dasein which, though it has cost me a bit of trouble over the years, I have yet to recant.

—According to me, though dasein and people "coincide" in a way, the respective terms are not coextensive—in part because their referents are individuated differently.

—Very roughly, it is something like a checkerboard and the sixty-four squares: people are the squares, and dasein is the board.

—Or, somewhat better: *being-in-the-world* is the whole board, and dasein is its essential structure qua checkerboard.

I say that dasein is a *living-understanding-of-being*—by which I mean: an understanding of being that is concretely embodied in the lives of the people who live a living-way-of-life (that is, it is embodied in their living that way).

—("Living-way-of-life" is my gloss on being-in-the-world as dasein's "basic makeup").

—This is why Heidegger can say that sciences and languages have the being of dasein.

—For they, like all dasein, are understandings of being concretely embodied in the living of certain ways of life.

—(It follows, by the way, that dasein itself is individuated roughly as sciences and languages are.)

—So, the term 'living'—in 'living-way-of-life'—means basically what it does when we speak of a "living" (as opposed to a "dead") language.

—That is: currently "being lived"—or "practiced"—by some community of people.

—(Likewise, of course, there can be living and dead sciences—chemistry is a living understanding of being, alchemy a dead one.)

Individual people, on the other hand, are what I call *cases* of dasein.

—They are the ones whose concrete ways of living embody the understandings of being.

—Thus, no people, no dasein, and vice versa—but, even so, they are not identical.

—One way to see the distinction is in the terminology of one of Heidegger's basic formal indications: dasein as such is characterized by *Jemeinigkeit*—in-each-case-mineness.

—But individual people are not characterized by *in-each-case-mineness*—they are just "mine"—each of them, respectively (*je meines*).

—'Mineness' and 'in-each-case-mineness' name the same phenomenon, but they name it, so to speak, from two different perspectives—hence the need for distinct terms.

—The relation of dasein to "cases" of it is not the same as that of a species to its specimens, a whole to its parts, a type to its tokens, or any other traditional "level" relation.

—Rather, dasein is to cases of dasein as the understanding of being embodied in the concrete practice of chemistry is to the chemists who practice it.

4. Since this is (still) a controversial reading—approximately, me against
everybody else—it may be worth saying a few more words in its defense.
Perhaps the clearest *textual* basis for it is Heidegger's account of being-
in-the-world, which, as he says, is dasein's basic-structural-makeup
[*Grundverfassung*].

> —Though this structural-makeup is a *unitary* phenomenon, it has
> three constitutive moments that can be brought out for analysis: the
> world, the who, and being-in as such.
>
> —The analyses of the world and the who closely parallel one another
> and are particularly revealing.

Each begins with an account of the relevant intraworldly entities and
their being and then moves "up a level" to the phenomena that constitute
being-in-the-world.

> —So, the world chapter begins with a discussion of intraworldly equip-
> ment, the that-being of which is availability (*Zuhandenheit*) and the
> what-being of which are their respective equipmental roles
> (*Bewandtnis*).
>
> > —Only after he has finished the discussion of equipment does
> > Heidegger "move up" to the phenomenon of the world (which the
> > possibility of equipment presupposes).
>
> —Likewise, the who chapter begins with a discussion of the intra-
> worldly entities that he calls "the others."
>
> > —It is important to remember that (despite the term) "the others"
> > does not mean "everybody else but me" but always includes "one-
> > self" as well.
> >
> > —The that-being of the others is co-dasein (*Mitdasein*), and their
> > what-being is "what they do"—which is to say, their respective
> > professional and interpersonal roles.
> >
> > —And, again, only after this discussion of the others does Hei-
> > degger "move up" to the phenomenon of the "who" of everyday
> > dasein—which is the anyone (*das Man*).

Now, I think it is perfectly obvious that "the others" (including each of us
ourselves) are people—individual users of equipment and members of
society.

—And so, lacking any clear alternative, I take it that 'other' is Heidegger's official term for an individual person—what I prefer to call a
case of dasein.
By contrast, the world and the anyone—which, along with being-in as such,
constitute being-in-the-world—are a "level up" from either individual
equipment or individual others.

—Indeed, both of them are public and "common" in a way that is
surely incompatible with individuation at the scale of people.

—I conclude, therefore, that being-in-the-world itself is "a level up"
from individuals.

—But, insofar as it is the "basic makeup" of dasein, dasein, too, must
be (at least) a level up.

—(I say "at least' because dasein strictly-so-called is not being-in-
the-world—that is, a living way of life—but rather the understanding of being that is concretely embodied in the living of it.

—So maybe, in some sense, it is two levels up.)

All that notwithstanding, however, it cannot be denied that Heidegger also
often uses 'dasein' to denote individual people.

—Thus, I have to maintain that he uses it in two different ways without consistently distinguishing them—a lamentable practice that I
recommend none of us follow him in.

5. Having said a bit about dasein, it will be helpful also to add a few remarks about being before turning to the main topics of dasein's timeishness and the temporality of being.

—What is perhaps most surprising about being is that it has a lot of
structure—two dimensions of which will matter here.
First, the regionalization of being is its subdivision into different "regions"
for ontologically different sorts of entities—entities that are in different
senses of 'are.'

—For instance, most philosophers would agree that the sense in which
numbers are is different from that in which physical objects are, and
many would argue that the senses for biological organisms, social institutions, and/or mental events are different again.[2]

---

2. Most Anglo-American philosophers nowadays would *not* agree with this claim; for
discussion, see McDaniel 2009 and van Inwagen 2009.—*Ed.*

—All of these are distinctions among *regions* of being.

Second, the *articulation* of being is what is marked by the traditional distinctions among actuality, essence, and accidents—or, as Heidegger calls them: *that-being, what-being,* and *thus-being.*

> —What these respective "articulata" mean, exactly—their *sense*—varies from region to region (that is what makes the regions different).
>
> —But the threefoldness of the articulation—that/what/thus—is common to all regions.
>
> > —So the two dimensions of structure are orthogonal to each other.
>
> —In particular, the sense of 'that-being' ought to be different for each region.

But one of Heidegger's main complaints about the history of ontology is that, though the differences among regions are recognized, they are all tacitly assigned the same sense of that-being—namely, the one that he calls being-occurrent *(Vorhandensein).*

> —In effect, the regional *differences* are all relegated to the moment of what-being.
>
> —Descartes, for instance, drew an ontological distinction between *res extensa* and *res cogitans*—a classic example of two different regions.
>
> —But the sense of *that*-being for entities from either region is the same—reality = actuality = being-occurrent—the regional distinction residing instead in the respective essential attributes (extension versus thinking).

Heidegger, by contrast, insists that the senses of the that-being of equipment (being-available) and of (mere) things (being-occurrent) are fundamentally different.

> —Even more important, the sense of the that-being of dasein (existence) is profoundly different again.

6. So, what is it to *exist?*

For an understanding of being to exist is for a distinctive sort of *ability*—what Heidegger calls the ability to comport toward entities *as entities*—to be embodied in somebody's concrete way of living.

> —Notice: to exist is not to *have* this understanding or this ability but rather to *be* it.
>
> > —(It is *cases* of dasein who "*have*" the understanding and the ability—by embodying them in the way they live.)

—Nevertheless, an understanding of being (in other words, dasein) is itself an *entity*—something determinate that there is (here
and now, for instance).

    —(There was not always dasein, and presumably there will
    not always be.)

—The *what-being* of dasein is its "*specificity*"—that which makes one
understanding of being different from another.

    —So: understandings of being that go with different regions differ
    in their what-being.

—The *thus-being* of dasein is the particular ("concrete") comportments toward entities as entities that it manifests itself in—in other
words, *exercises,* by cases of dasein, of the ability that the understanding is.

Heidegger has names—indeed, two different names—for each of these
articulata for dasein.

    —The that-being of dasein is called not only existence but also its
    being-forward-of-itself.

    —Its what-being is called both its facticity and its being-already-in-
    a-world.

    —And its thus-being is called both its falling and its being-amidst-
    entities.

These three together, as a unity, are the being of dasein—which is also
called *care.*

7. We can get a better idea of what all this means and how it is supposed to
work by focusing first on dasein's concrete being-amidst-entities (= falling)
and then seeing how the other two moments are needed to fill it out.

Being-amidst, as embodied in the living of a way of life, is dasein's particular comportments toward entities *as entities*—which is a kind of generalized notion of intentionality.

    —(The generalization is such as to include various "noncognitive"
    comportments like skillful rapport with equipment, genial rapport
    with other people, and so on.)

    —The appended and emphasized qualifier "*as entities*" is crucial,
    however, for it makes explicit that the comportments in question
    are all and only those that involve dasein (that is, an understanding of
    being).

—Thus, it excludes not only reflexes and many habits but also the broader range of "intentionality-like" phenomena that are exhibited by animals and some machines.

—The point of the exclusion, of course, is not to argue about words but to focus in on a narrower class of phenomena in order to characterize them more precisely).

What is distinctive of comportment toward entities *as entities* is that it has built into it an issue of something like *truth*.

—This applies not only to familiar varieties such as belief, desire, and perception but also to the kind of "rapport" I mentioned earlier in comportments like hammering with a hammer or coordinating with a teammate.

—A skilled carpenter, for example, even if she does not have to "think about" what she is doing, still has to hit the nail on the head, have a "feel for" the wood and the hammer she is using, stop when the nail is in, and so on.

—All of these are a function of the particular entities involved, such that in her skillful adjustment to them she has to be getting those entities "right."

—This "getting the entities right" is what I mean by "something like truth."

But the account of it so far is fundamentally incomplete.

—After all, a hawk closing in on a mouse or a mosquito closing in on a capillary will not get its dinner if it does not get the location of its target "right."

8. The essential reason for this incompleteness—it turns out—is that we have yet to bring in the other two moments of care: dasein's being-already-in a world and its being-forward-of itself.

Let us look first at being-already-in a world (= facticity).

—A *world*, in Heidegger's sense, is not a collection of things distributed in space but rather an integrated totality of roles—or, more generally, of possibilities—for intraworldly entities.

—We can see the relevance of this by taking a brief detour through empirical science.

As everybody knows, even apparently well-conceived and well-executed experiments do not always give correct results.

—That is why they are typically duplicated or corroborated by related experiments.

—But such corroboration makes sense only if it is antecedently determined how *correct* results could and could not *possibly* be related.

> —In established sciences, these constraints are typically formulated as laws of nature.
>
>> —To take the simplest example, *correct* measurements of the speed of light in a vacuum all *have to* give the same value because it is a law of physics that that speed is a constant.
>>
>> —Measurements of other magnitudes may be mutually constrained via laws in more complicated ways, but the upshot is the same: if the *combination* of observational results would be *impossible*, then at least one of them must be *wrong*.

And, though the details are less crisp, the same goes for the carpenter.

—In an ordinary case of driving a nail into a board, it is *impossible* that the hammer bend, the nail refuse to budge, or the board shatter at the first blow.

> —What 'impossible' means here is: *ruled-out* by the normal and proper roles of the respective equipment.
>
> —So, if such a thing *were* to happen, something in the carpenter's skilled rapport with that equipment must have been *wrong*—that is, she was not "getting it right."

The lesson of both examples is that comportment toward entities *as entities*, as presupposing a distinction between the true and the false about them, *also* presupposes an *antecedent* distinction between what is possible and impossible for them.

—And "having" that antecedent distinction—that is, its being embodied in the living of a *specific* way of life—is what Heidegger means by dasein's being-already-in a world.

9. But that is still not enough since just "having" the distinction would be effectively inert.

The distinction must actually be *drawn in practice*—that is, in concrete comportments—and drawn, moreover, *as a distinction between the possible and the impossible.*

—But to draw *that* distinction (not just in word but also in deed) is nothing other than to hold the impossible *unacceptable*—that is, as something that *cannot be right*.

 —(Sherlock Holmes notwithstanding, anyone who purports to hold the impossible true fails to grasp *either* concept.)[3]

—In other words, the very ability to *draw* the distinction between the possible and the impossible—hence, between the true and the false— requires a *refusal to accept* (as true) anything that would be impossible.

—But, to say that a refusal is *required* in living a certain way can mean only that those who live that way *require it of themselves* (and each other) in a kind of *stand* or *commitment*.

So, the third essential factor in dasein's comporting toward entities *as entities* must be a *standing refusal* to accept the impossible—which is to say, a commitment to reject it.

 —And, this standing commitment, as embodied in living a certain way, is what Heidegger means by dasein's being-forward-of itself (= existence).

 —Note that what is here called a 'commitment' is just a fuller characterization of what I earlier called an *ability* to comport toward entities *as entities*—an ability which, as we *also* now know, must include an ability to distinguish the possible from the impossible.

 —Making this distinction, with that commitment, is called projecting entities onto their possibilities.

  —(Needless to add, hawks and mosquitoes have no such abilities.)

10. This articulated but essentially unitary phenomenon—being-forward-of itself, being-amidst-entities, and being-already-in a world—is *care*, the being of dasein.

 —It amounts (when fully spelled out) to a remarkably rich and general account of the conditions of the possibility of comportment toward entities *as entities* (a generalization of intentionality) and its essential connection with truth.

---

3. Haugeland implicitly gets the Sherlock Holmes reference wrong. The phrase for which Holmes was famous was "When the impossible has been eliminated, what remains, however improbable, must be the truth." Thus, Holmes endorses Haugeland's point rather than denying it.—*Ed.*

But that achievement—supposing it is acknowledged—raises an awkward question:

—Why are we not *done*? Why is *Being and Time* not finished at the end of division I?

—To be sure, a few incidentals—like ownedness, time, finitude, and history—have yet to be discussed.

—But what do *they* have to do with comporting toward entities *as entities?*

11. One way to frame an approach to these questions is to invoke—in a way that Heidegger himself does not—the traditional problems of skepticism and relativism.

—Assuming that we can dismiss (as a pseudoproblem) the old metaphysical riddle of how we can ever get "outside the closet of consciousness," then what remains of modern skepticism reduces to the question: How can we *make sense* of intentionality and especially the prerequisite ability to distinguish the true from the false?

—As we have just seen, division I can be read as a general answer to this question.

The challenge of relativism, on the other hand, is different (and harder).

—Given that any ability to distinguish the true from the false *presupposes* some definite vocabulary and repertoire of skills—in other words, some contingent historical culture—how can we *justify* adopting any one such set of resources over any others?

—Division I does not answer this question but at most focuses it.

—In particular, the *specific* antecedent possibilities, in terms of which the true and the false are distinguished, are simply *taken for granted* in the foregoing account.

—(For everyday dasein, these possibilities are the everyday world of *das Man*.)

So I am going to organize my exposition of division II—and especially the doctrines of timeishness and temporality—as a response to this challenge of relativism.

12. The second division begins with a long, difficult, and thoroughly amazing account of what Heidegger calls *owned* (*eigentlich*) dasein.

—The story progresses from being-toward-death and anticipation through wanting-to-have-a-conscience and readiness-for-anxiety, to being-responsible [*Schuldigsein*] and resoluteness.

—Although the basic point of this account is essential for what follows, all we will actually need to mention are a few of the high points, and only as they come up along the way.

13. First, though, we have to lay out a daunting array of terminology.

    —It comes in two main groups—in effect, one for timeishness and one for temporality—each of which has a threefold articulation (mirroring that of care).

    —Altogether, we have to absorb something like a dozen new technical terms—all intricately interrelated—so bear with me.

Timeishness, which is not discussed until §65 (immediately following the treatment of ownedness) is introduced as the *sense* of dasein's being—that is, the sense of care.

    —That care has a "timeish" character is adumbrated (surely not by accident) in the names of its structural moments: forward-of, amidst, and already-in.

    —And the three structural moments of timeishness correspond to these—namely, as follows:

        —Dasein's *coming-toward* (itself)—is the sense of its being-forward-of itself;

        —Its *enpresenting* (of entities)—is the sense of its being-amidst-entities; and

        —Its *coming-back-to* (itself)—is the sense of its being-already-in a world.

    —Generically, these moments are referred to as the "ekstases of timeishness."

        —(We will be able to see what all these terms mean when we see how they fit together in the larger structure of temporality.)

Temporality itself, however, is scarcely mentioned in *Being and Time*—though the few promissory notes that there are (e.g., *SZ* 19, 147) make clear that it has to do with *being as such* (that is, being as *understood* by dasein) as opposed just to dasein's own being.

—Fortunately, the last chapter of *The Basic Problems of Phenomenology* says a little more.

—Though it is still pretty sketchy, two important points do emerge distinctly:

>—First: temporality just *is* timeishness, but considered in a further way—namely that, as the sense of care, it is *also* the condition of the possibility of any understanding of being at all (e.g., *GP* 324, 388ff., 429, 436ff., 443ff.).

>—And second: this further way of considering timeishness consists in appreciating that its ekstases have *horizonal schemata* (see, e.g., those same pages and *SZ* 333).

>—So, as we might put it, timeishness considered narrowly (as the sense of care) is *ecstatic*.

>—But considered more fully (as also making the understanding of being possible—which is to say, as temporality), it is *ekstatic-horizonal*.

Finally (and predictably), the horizonal schemata of the ekstases also have names, which are (according to *SZ* §69c):

—the *for-the-sake-of-itself*;

—that which is defined by the *in-order-to*;

—and the *in-the-face-of-which*.

And that completes the basic terminological lineup—which we now have to interpret.

>—(A person might be forgiven, I think, for being reminded here of the emperor's complaint to Mozart: "Too many notes!")

14. It is easiest to begin with the horizonal schemata and work back to the ekstases since the terms for the former are independently explained in *Being and Time*.

So, first: dasein's for-the-sake-of-which is its *ability-to-be* (*SZ* 298, 334, 359, 364)—which is, as we know, its committed ability to be toward entities *as entities* by discerning and rejecting the impossible—and that just means the understanding of being that it is.

>—Accordingly, in the ekstasis of coming-toward itself, the horizonal schema that dasein "comes toward" is *itself as* this ability-to-be (= that understanding of being).

—Such an ability can be a "for-the-sake-of-which" because—as we will see shortly—it is essentially *vulnerable*.

> —(It is worth noting that this same ability is the *"issue"* in the thesis that dasein's being is an issue for it—and therefore also the issue that *being-toward-death* is all about.)

Second: what is defined by the in-order-to is *equipment*.

—But this must be just a special case—the horizonal schema of enpresenting entities has to be *entities* in general.

> —(Alternatively, one might suggest that there is a single horizon of enpresenting with several schemata—different ones for different sorts of entities—but the text is silent.)

And, third: the schema of the past is spelled out more fully as that in-the-face-of-which it has been *thrown* and to-which it has been *abandoned*.

—But that is just the world and the situation in which it has (up to this point) "ended up."

> —It is the 'here' in the resigned sigh: "*Well*, I guess we'll just have to go on from *here*."

—But what dasein, as an understanding of being, always has to "go on from" is its (mostly inherited) repertoire of ways to distinguish the possible from the impossible (on the basis of which, in turn, it can distinguish the true from the false).

—So, in the ekstasis of coming-back-to itself, what dasein comes back to is *itself* as this antecedent repertoire—which might be a nexus of social and equipmental roles or, perhaps, the natural laws of some scientific region.

> —Either way, it is the *world* in-the-face-of-which dasein is thrown and to-which it is abandoned.

15. Now, with this preliminary interpretation of the individual horizons on the table, we are in a position to ask what the point of it all is—and that will illuminate the ekstases.

—*Why* does Heidegger go beyond care to this elaborate ekstatic-horizonal unity?

—Why, indeed, do we *care* about the *sense* of care?

The most obvious difference between the care-structure and the ekstatic-horizonal unity is that the latter has a sixfold articulation rather than just three.

—In particular, it has two triples, somehow juxtaposed to one another.

—The second most obvious difference is, as it were, "grammatical":

—The terms for the moments of care (forward-of/amidst/already-in) are all static, whereas those for timeishness (coming-toward /enpresenting/coming-back-to) are dynamic—they suggest some kind of motion or action.

These two differences, moreover, are a perfect match: the "motion" of the ekstases is "toward" the horizonal schemata.

—And this clearly is the basic point—if only we can figure out what to make of it.

—For the Greek word *'ekstasis'* just means a *displacing* (it derives from a verb meaning "to put something out of its place").

—Further, lest anyone miss the etymology, Heidegger glosses *'ekstasis'* as *'Entrückung,'* which is a being-carried away (of someone from something) (e.g., *SZ* 338ff., 350, 365).

—(It should perhaps be mentioned that each of these words also has connotations of being "carried away" psychologically—as in ecstasy, trance, or rapture.

—But I cannot see that this does any work—and, in any case, I do not like it a bit.)

—Finally, the horizonal schemata themselves are introduced as the "whither" or "where-to" (*'Wohin'*) of the being carried away (*SZ* 365).

—The schemata are, so to speak, where the ekstases are "going."

16. But the real clue to what this is all about lies in the word 'horizon.'
The Greek verb *'horizō"* means: to bound, delimit, determine, or even define (e.g., a word).

—(Thus, even in its ordinary sense, a horizon is a limit—namely of visibility.)

—So, the *horizonal* character that temporality adds to timeishness is that, in being carried-away, dasein is carried *to* some *limit* or *terminus*—and that means that it is *finite*.

And, we can get a start on the significance of that by remembering how Heidegger explains *Kant's* account of our (cognitive) finitude (*KPM* §§4&5).

—For Kant, the finitude of human knowledge is understood by way of its difference from the in-finitude of God's originary intuition.

—Divine intuition is nonfinite because it is not constrained—not limited—in any way by that which it is an intuition of.

—And it is not so constrained because, as originary, it is creative in the sense that whatever is intuited in it comes into being from and in accord with that intuiting.

—(Hence, also, there is no intelligible possibility of falsehood.)

Human knowledge, by contrast, *is* constrained (limited) by the objects known.

—Those objects are prior to and independent of our knowledge of them, and so our knowing must, via its receptivity, *adjust itself to them* (on pain of being false).

—(That is why the entities we know are *objects, Gegenstände:* they "stand over against" our knowing of them.)

—And this constrainedness of our knowledge *by its objects* is precisely its *finitude*.

—By the same token, that constrained finitude is what makes sense of there being—for us—a difference between cognitions that are true and those that are false.

Now, Heidegger is not interested in any invidious comparisons between us and God.

—But, as I have argued, he is very interested in what makes possible the difference between truth and falsehood.

Insofar as this Kantian account of our finitude bore on Heidegger's, it would have to be in regard to the horizon of the present—for the schema of enpresenting is *entities*.

—But comporting toward entities *as entities*—as *requiring* accepting the true and rejecting the false—just is *bound* (that is, constrained or limited) *by those entities*.

—So the horizonal finitude of the present essentially *is* the Kantian finitude, generalized from perceptual knowledge to comportment toward and from objects to entities.

17. What, then, of the past and the future?
The schema of dasein's coming-back-to—the "limitedness" to which it comes back—is dasein itself *as* world.

—I have interpreted this as its antecedent (mostly inherited) ways of distinguishing the possible from the impossible—as embodied in a way of living and fixed, for instance, in roles or laws—which are prerequisite for its comporting toward entities *as entities.*

—These roles and laws, however, are not only enabling but also *constraining.*

—Indeed, they are enabling only *because* they are constraining.[4]

—So it makes perfect sense—more than that: it seems to me clearly *right*—to say that the world, as such roles and laws, is the essential *finitude* of the ekstasis of the past.

The schema of dasein's coming-toward (the "limitedness" toward-which it "comes") is dasein itself as that ability-to-be for-the-sake-of-which it is.

—I have interpreted this as its ability to comport toward entities *as entities*—which entails: a committed *requiring of itself,* as embodied in each case in a way of living, that it reject the impossible.

—What is less clear, however, is how such a commitment, as a *self-requiring,* could be any sort of *limitation* or *finitude.*

Solving this puzzle will take us all the way to the end—including the answer to relativism.

18. So far, I have been scrupulously vague about the *status* of the possibilities that are dasein's world—mentioning only that they are mostly inherited.

Likewise, I have been conspicuously mute about dasein's *owned being-toward-death*—mentioning only that the account of timeishness begins immediately after it in the text.

—These two omissions are connected.

Death (in Heidegger's "existential" sense) is not an event that "happens" (*ever*) (SZ 240, 250, 257) but rather a possible way to be (that is, a way of living) (SZ 245, 251, 259);

—Death "is" only in *being-toward* death (SZ 234, 245, 259);

—This being-toward is dasein's *ownmost* possibility—a possibility that it is called upon to *take over* in each case and so one that *individualizes* it (SZ 250, 263ff.);

---

4. Elsewhere in the volume ("Dasein's Disclosedness," p. 19n2), Haugeland cites Brandom 1979 as the classic exposition of this point.—*Ed.*

—More specifically, it is the possibility of the *impossibility* of dasein's existence at all—that is, of any comportment toward entities as entities—and is thus the possibility of *giving itself up* (*SZ* 250, 262, 264).

—And, last but not least, death is dasein's *finitude* (*SZ* 264, 329f, 384–86).

The interplay between dasein and cases of dasein in these passages is delicate and important.

—It is only *cases* of dasein that can live in the way that is being-toward death.

—Moreover, it is only these *cases* who are called upon to "take it over" and only they who could "give it up."

—Yet this being-toward is *dasein's* ownmost possibility, and it is *dasein* that gets individualized in it.

—And, of course, it is *dasein's* existence that is at stake, and this being-at-stake is *dasein's* finitude.

The key to this complicated relationship is the "taking over" that "individualizes" dasein.

—Taking-over being-toward-death is taking over *responsibility* for dasein as finite.

—More specifically, it is taking responsibility for the possibilities onto which entities are projected and therewith for dasein's ability-to-be as an understanding of being.

—Heidegger calls the way of living in which that responsibility is taken *resoluteness,* and he says that the dasein for which that responsibility is taken is *individualized* in it.

Only *cases* of dasein are resolute, but it is *dasein as such* that is individualized in them.

—The official term for dasein that is individualized in this way is *owned* dasein—owned, of course, by the individual cases of dasein that it is individualized in.

—(By the way, the ability to explain ownedness in this way strikes me as another compelling reason for the basic distinction between dasein and cases of dasein.)

This possibility of resolute responsibility—that is, of owning dasein—will now bring us to the heart of the matter.

19. *Normally,* when some combination of discovered entities is found to be collectively impossible, one or more of those discoveries must be rejected.

—That, too, is a kind of responsibility—*routine* responsibility, we might call it—for it makes possible all routine distinctions between the true and the false and therewith all comportment toward entities *as entities*.

> —(This is the *only* sort of responsibility the anyone—dasein's bastion of normality—ever recognizes.)

Routine responsibility, moreover, is not easy—for it is not always obvious *which* discovery or discoveries should be rejected or even how any of them *could* be.

> —Thus it can be the case that each of those discoveries is well checked and separately corroborated, such that there are, in effect, multiple incompatibilities that are not well localized.

> —Most often, of course, even such pervasive problems are eventually resolved—typically with a bonus of unexpected new knowledge.

But not always.

> —Sometimes—usually only after a fair struggle—it becomes thinkable that the problems may lie not in the discoveries but in the possibilities onto which they are projected.

> > —In other words, they may lie not in the entities as discovered but in the understanding of being those discoveries presuppose— which is to say, in dasein itself.

> —To take this alternative seriously is to take *responsibility*—now not routine but *resolute* responsibility—for that understanding of being and therefore that dasein.

To *own* dasein is to take responsibility in this way for the possibility that the understanding of being that it is may not be viable—to take responsibility for it as *essentially vulnerable*.

> —*Resoluteness*, Heidegger says, resolves to *repeat* itself (that is, to remain resolute), while, at the same time *holding itself free* for the possibility—that is, the possible *necessity*—of *taking itself back*.

> —This vulnerable holding-itself-free is *owned being-toward-death*.

> —And the possible necessity that it holds itself free—for the possible nonviability of an understanding of being—is the *finitude* of dasein's coming-toward itself.

In other words, it is the horizon of the ekstasis of the future.

20. The challenge of relativism is that the possibilities onto which entities are projected and in terms of which truth and falsehood about them can be distinguished seem historically contingent and ultimately arbitrary.

—But the possible *necessity* of taking those possibilities back means that they *are not* arbitrary—far from it.

—Some understandings of being turn out *not* to be viable—and, when this is shown, it is shown in the crucible of empirical investigations that cannot be made to cohere.

—Thus, the possibilities that are the specificity of any understanding of being are in fact—though indirectly—themselves also under empirical control.

And that, at long last, is how division II gives the lie to relativism—the corrosive "postskepticism" of "postmodern" philosophy.

21. As a reading of *Being and Time*, however, it raises again the awkward question: Why are we not done?

—Well, first, of course: if (by any chance) I have said one or two things tonight that are not actually *in* the text as we have it, *they* would certainly have been made fully explicit in division III.

—Beyond that, however, we must remember that division II has answered only the question of the sense of dasein's being—not the sense of being *tout court*.

—But reawakening *that* question must await another occasion.

FOUR

Papers on Heideggerian Themes

Social Cartesianism

(2004)

I begin with brief, critical overviews of three well-known arguments in the philosophy of language due respectively to Nelson Goodman, W. V. O. Quine, and some amalgam of the later Wittgenstein and Saul Kripke.[1] I then maintain that the failings in these three arguments have a common origin. And I conclude by suggesting that this common origin is a modified legacy of Cartesianism—a legacy that Heidegger, by contrast, managed to overcome.

I. THE NEW RIDDLE OF INDUCTION

In *Fact, Fiction, and Forecast,* Goodman (1954) considers two problems concerning induction. The first is the traditional logical/epistemological problem of justifying our formal canons of good inductive inference. This problem he "dissolves" by treating it as a matter of defining a general term— namely, 'good inductive inference'—by a process of accommodation between theoretical considerations and intuitively clear positive and negative instances (§§ 3.2 and 3.3). Given that approach, the issue reduces to "the constructive task of confirmation theory," which can be addressed with standard syntactical tools with reasonable expectation of progress.

1. *Acknowledgments:* I am grateful for discussions of this paper at Michigan State University and Bates College and for detailed critical comments from Michael Kremer, Jason Bridges, and, above all, Joan Wellman.

The second problem, which Goodman dubs "the new riddle of induction" (§§ 3.4 and 3.5), has to do not with the legitimacy of formal inference rules but rather with the legitimacy of the inductive hypotheses and predicates to which those rules are applied. Some hypotheses and predicates are, as he puts it, "lawlike" and "projectible" respectively, whereas others are not, and only the former are suitable for use in inductive inferences. For example, the observation that one piece of copper conducts electricity does support the inductive hypothesis that other pieces of copper also conduct electricity, but the observation that one member of a lecture audience is someone's third child does not support the general hypothesis that the other members of that audience are also third children. The former hypothesis is *lawlike,* and its predicates *projectible,* but the latter are not.

So far, however, these are still just names. The difference between the two examples may be clear enough at an intuitive level, but providing a general philosophical account of it is another matter. *That* is the new riddle of induction.

We can see why this riddle is new—that is, not just a variant of the traditional problem—by turning to Goodman's most famous illustration: the choice between the familiar predicates '*blue*' and '*green*' on the one hand and the contrived alternatives '*grue*' and '*bleen*' on the other. The latter are defined in terms of the former and some specified time, *t* (no earlier than the present), as follows: Something is *grue* just in case *either* it has already been examined by *t* and is green *or* it has not yet been examined by *t* and is blue (and, contrariwise, for '*bleen*') (1979, 74). It is essential to be clear about how these alternative predicates work. To project the predicate '*grue*'—by adopting, for instance, the hypothesis that all emeralds are and will be grue—is not to predict that the emeralds we already know and love will turn blue at *t*. No, for them to be (and stay) grue just is for them to be (and stay) green—because it will always be the case that they were *first* observed *before t*. The '*grue*' prediction diverges only for "new" emeralds, ones that have never been seen before *t*. To predict that they, too, will all be grue—"just like" their predecessors—is to predict that *they* will all turn out to be blue (and presumably were blue all along, even before they were observed). That is a *loony* prediction, of course. Nobody denies that. But the philosophical question is: *Why?* What, *exactly,* is loony about it?

The question arises because, given the definitions, it would seem that, at or before *t*, every confirming instance of "All emeralds are green" is *equally* a confirming instance of "All emeralds are grue." So induction itself is neutral between them. To be sure, the 'grue' hypothesis is not *really* confirmed by old green emeralds—even though, by definition, those old emeralds are also all grue—because the predicate 'grue' is not projectible, and the hypothesis is therefore not lawlike. But that is merely a fancier formulation of the same issue. In this context, 'nonprojectible' is just a big Harvard word for loony, and that is what we want to understand.

Now, what makes this a *new* difficulty is that—unlike the difference between good and bad inference rules—the difference between these two hypotheses and their putative relations to instances cannot be drawn *syntactically*. Their *logical* forms are all exactly the same. In other words, what is new about the "new riddle" is that syntactical methods are powerless against it. Accordingly, we need some nonsyntactical criteria for projectibility (and hence lawlikeness).

Goodman's own proposal is subtle and ingenious. What distinguishes legitimate (projectible) inductive predicates, he says, lies in *the history of actual projectings*—that is, actual adoptions of hypotheses containing the predicates in question (or synonyms of them). Thus, to the question of what rule will "make the proper choice" between "All emeralds are green" and "All emeralds are grue," he replies as follows:

> [W]e must consult the record of past projections of the two predicates. Plainly 'green,' as a veteran of earlier and many more projections than 'grue,' has the more impressive biography. The predicate 'green,' we may say, is much better *entrenched* than the predicate 'grue.' // We are able to draw this distinction only because we start from the record of past actual projections. (1979, 94)

As this suggests, and as becomes explicit in the following paragraphs, the idea is that a predicate is more projectible to the extent that it is better entrenched, and, to a first approximation, a predicate is better entrenched to the extent that there have been more projections in the past of hypotheses containing it.

This first approximation, however, needs—and receives—considerable refinement. Predicates do not, in fact, garner entrenchment from *all* prior projections containing them but only from those that are *supported* (by some positive instances), *not violated* (by any negative instances), *not exhausted* (by having all their instances checked), and *not overridden* (by incompatible hypotheses projecting still better entrenched predicates). What is more, predicates can inherit entrenchment from other well-entrenched predicates by being related to them in various logical and theoretical ways and so on. The upshot is that the degree of entrenchment of a predicate reflects and encodes a good deal of actual prior *experience*—in the social history of empirical practice.

But it is important to appreciate how this social/empirical pedigree works. The fact that a given predicate has been successfully used in the past (along with other pedigreed predicates) is not taken as *evidence* that it is legitimate. For that would amount to establishing its legitimacy inductively, which would be out of order for at least two reasons. In the first place, there would clearly be something fishy about *using* induction in an account of inductive legitimacy, but second, and more to the point, the aim is not to *ascertain* or *establish* the legitimacy of inductive predicates but rather to explain what such legitimacy *consists in*. Entrenchment does not *show* or *confirm* the legitimacy of a predicate but rather *constitutes* it.

That Goodman understands entrenchment as constitutive of legitimacy and not just as a sign or manifestation of it is made explicit in his answer to a pair of rhetorical questions a few pages later:

> Must we not explain why . . . the really projectible predicate happens to have been the earlier and more often projected? And in fact wasn't it projected so often *because* its projection was so obviously legitimate, so that our proposal begs the question? I think not. . . . The reason why only the right predicates happen so luckily to have become well entrenched is just that the well entrenched predicates have thereby become the right ones. (98)

Distressingly, however, this passage runs together two quite different issues, implying that the same response addresses both. One question is why only the right predicates get entrenched, and the constitutive answer that entrenchment is what *makes* predicates "right" is at least to the point. But the other question is why some predicates "happen" to become entrenched, whereas others do not, and the reply does not speak to that issue at all.

This is not a minor quibble, for, were it to emerge that *some further factor* systematically explained which predicates get entrenched and which do not, then this further factor might well offer a *deeper* account of predicate legitimacy itself, even *granting* the constitutive point. To see how such a story might go, return to the opening gambit with 'grue' and 'bleen.' A natural objection is that they—*unlike* 'blue' and 'green'—are defined in terms of a specific, arbitrary time. But Goodman counters that the situation is perfectly symmetrical: 'green' and 'blue' can be formally introduced and explained in terms of 'grue,' 'bleen,' and that same arbitrary time just as easily as the other way around (74, 79ff.).

The trouble is: that reply does not work. The symmetry Goodman invokes is *merely* formal; the situation is not really symmetrical at all. For it is *simply not true* that—in the real world—'grue' and 'bleen' could ever be *introduced* or *explained* in terms of 'grue and 'bleen.' No one could ever first come to understand the words 'blue' and 'green' on the basis of a prior understanding of 'grue' and 'bleen' (plus some formal definitions), for the obvious reason that no one could ever come to understand the words 'grue' and 'bleen' (in the intended senses) *except by* already understanding 'blue' and 'green' and then being given those definitions.

Though I take that to be self-evident, sketching an argument for it may still be useful as a step toward seeing what underlies it. So imagine trying to *teach* the words 'grue' and 'bleen' to a child old enough to learn color words but *not* old enough to understand the concept of when something was or will be first observed. If you proceed in the ordinary way—how else?—by showing the child various examples and coaching her on which ones to call what, then, if it is before *t*, she will certainly learn the words, but she will just take them to mean green and blue. (They are the same lessons, after all.) After *t*, on the other hand, the task is hopeless. If you start with 'grue' and show her both old and newly discovered samples, she may take the word to mean a blue-green range of colors or perhaps a disjunction. But when you introduce the bleen *contrast* set (also with old and new samples), everything falls apart. One emerald is grue, but another—that looks just the same to her—is not; likewise for sapphires and so on. (In fact, unless they are distinguishable on other grounds, *you* cannot tell the grue from the bleen stones, either.)

An essentially similar point can be made about measuring instruments. There are many ways to build a machine that can reliably distinguish green things from blue ones without any information about what time it is or when the samples were first observed. But there is no way to build a machine that, after *t*, could reliably distinguish grue from bleen, subject to the same constraints, for it can no more tell an old stone from a newly discovered one (without extra information) than can you or your young pupil.

It seems to me that these simple facts about learning and instrumentation are not only a likely explanation of why predicates like 'green' and 'blue' (as opposed to 'grue' and 'bleen') are entrenched but also the key to developing a more basic insight into predicate legitimacy itself.

2. THE INDETERMINACY OF TRANSLATION

In sections 12 to 16 of *Word and Object,* Quine (1960) argues for an ineliminable empirical indeterminacy in the translation of what he calls "terms of divided reference" (91–95) and the concomitant "apparatus of objective reference" (53, 61, 70). The former, now often called "sortals," are words like 'rabbit,' 'chair,' 'emerald,' and 'person' that (as we ordinarily understand them) denote distinct, enduring individuals—entities that we can keep track of, count, distinguish one from another, and reidentify later (in the sense of "the very same one"). Correlatively, the apparatus of objective reference comprises the pronouns and quantifiers, along with various devices for expressing unity, plurality, number, numerical identity, distinctness, and the like.

The alleged indeterminacy can be introduced as follows. Suppose we have a way of translating some language (call it the "away" language) into our own ("home") language that is fully satisfactory by all empirical criteria, and suppose further that our translations often use sortal nouns and the apparatus of objective reference. Then there are also *other* ways to translate that language into ours—systematically related to the first but intuitively quite different—that are *equally* satisfactory by all empirical criteria. But if they are all equally satisfactory, then there can be no *empirical* grounds for choosing among them. Quine concludes that, although the translations are different, there is no fact as to which of them is the "right" one because there is no "objective matter to be right or wrong about" (73), and *that* is the indeterminacy.

Before considering the argument for this conclusion, it is important to be clear about when and where it is supposed to apply. The indeterminacy of translation has nothing to do with how "different" or "alien" the away speakers or their language might be (as compared to us and our own). On the contrary, "home" and "away" can be as close as Minneapolis and St. Paul, the "strangers" as familiar as the people next door. Keeping that firmly in mind, then, here is the general argument strategy. Insofar as we have an empirically satisfactory translation scheme that uses sortal nouns and the apparatus of objective reference, we can generate an intuitively different scheme by systematically altering how those nouns and that apparatus are used, but in such a way that the alterations "cancel each other out"—at least as far as empirical adequacy is concerned. Thus we get alternative translations that are intuitively different but empirically equivalent.

So, adopting the famous example, suppose a rabbit scurries by, and (while pointing at it) the away speaker says *"Gavagai."* According to one translation method (which, by hypothesis, is systematically satisfactory across the board), this means "Lo, a rabbit." But, as Quine notes, no one can point at (or see, touch, stuff in a bag) a rabbit without *also* pointing at (seeing, touching, stuffing in a bag) a temporal stage of a rabbit, an undetached part of a rabbit, a portion of the spatiotemporal fusion of all rabbits, *and* a concrete manifestation of the abstract universal rabbithood—and likewise, of course, for apples and emeralds, ducks and people (cf. 51ff.).

Thus, it seems, we could adopt an alternative—equally good—translation method according to which our sample utterance means "Lo, a temporal-rabbit-stage" or "Lo, an undetached-rabbit-part." Those substitutions alone, however, would not quite work. If Inge goes to market and says something that means (according to our first method) "Please give me two rabbits," this could *not* be rendered equally well as "Please give me two temporal-rabbit-stages" or ". . . two undetached-rabbit-parts." For a *single* rabbit could satisfy either of those requests—yet we can be confident that Inge herself would not be satisfied. Still worse, asking for two rabbit fusions or two rabbithoods would not even make good sense.

But these show only that our alternative methods have to be a little fancier. In particular, if we use a different type of noun, we must also use (in compensation, as it were) a correspondingly different apparatus of objective reference. Thus, if 'rabbit' is to be replaced with either 'temporal-rabbit-stage' or 'undetached-rabbit-part,' then 'two . . . s' must be replaced with something like 'two standardly coherent-concrete-units-of . . . s.' On that method, then, Inge's request becomes: "Please give me two standardly coherent-concrete-units-of temporal-rabbit-stages" or ". . . undetached-rabbit-parts"—which does, at least, convey what she wants. Finally, if the replacement noun were 'the rabbit-fusion' or 'rabbithood,' the required compensation would again be the same but without the final 's.'

It is immediately striking that, in all four of Quine's alternative translations, the needed "compensatory adjustments" are essentially the same. On reflection, however, it is not hard to see why this should be so. What Quine's alternative nouns are alternatives *to* is *sortals* ("terms of divided reference"). But these are just those nouns the denotata of which come in something like "standardly coherent concrete units"—which is to say, distinct, durable *individuals*.

When Inge says (something equivalent to) "two rabbits," she means, of course, two of these standard rabbity individuals. In English, that intention is implicit in the sortal noun 'rabbit' (especially when used with a numeral and a plural ending). But Quine is surely right that not all languages have to express this intention in the same way. What is common to his four alternative renditions of 'gavagai' is that, unlike 'rabbit,' they do not have any standard mode of individuation built into their senses as nouns. Accordingly, whenever such individuation is important to what's being communicated—such as in a request for two rabbits—it would have to be indicated in some other way. That is what an auxiliary construction like "standardly coherent-concrete-units-of" (or, more likely, some equivalent particle or inflection) would provide. And that provision is what is meant by a compensatory adjustment in the apparatus of objective reference.

What are we to make of this? It is well known that, although all natural languages have ways of indicating tense, case, aspect, and so on, the surface structures of these indications can differ quite widely. What Quine has shown, in effect, is that the surface structures for indicating reference to standard wholes or units—concrete individuals—can differ as well. What is particularly noteworthy, however, is that both the argument and its conclusion *take for granted* that all the languages in question do have *some way or other* for indicating reference to individuals. Thus, insofar as this new variability in surface structure is like the others, we can also say that affording reference to individuals is itself a linguistic *universal*—at least for *human* languages. The discovery of this deeper universal, which Quine evidently presupposes, would seem to be at least as important philosophically as the surface variability in how it can be manifested.

3. PRIVATE LANGUAGE

In *Wittgenstein on Rules and Private Language*, Kripke (1982) interprets Wittgenstein's (1953) *Philosophical Investigations* as posing a "sceptical paradox" and then proposing a "sceptical solution" to that paradox. A sceptical paradox is an argument to the effect that we do not (or cannot) have something without which we could not live as we do. (It is paradoxical because we obviously do live as we do.) There are two possible ways to re-solve such a paradox: what Kripke calls a *straight* solution refutes the argu-ment that we do not have the something in question; a *sceptical* solution, on the other hand, accepts that we do not have it but then shows how we can perfectly well live without it. According to Kripke, what Wittgenstein argues we cannot have but ultimately do not need is privately determinate meanings or (what comes to the same thing) privately determinate rules for the correct use of our words.

I will not be concerned with whether Kripke's interpretation of Wittgen-stein is satisfactory, nor will I pay much attention to the argument that leads to the sceptical conclusion. Rather, I will focus mostly on the proposed scep-tical solution to the paradox—and that, indeed, only in connection with the example that Kripke discusses most fully—namely, arithmetic terms. Even within these limits, however, it is necessary to be clear about what the para-dox is supposed to be.

Though Kripke does not introduce it quite this way, the difficulty can be seen as arising from the following plausible line of thought. A person can use his words in any way he wants to. If he decides to use the word 'duck'—in his own private way—to mean bucket, he is free to do so, and no one can stop him. ('Private,' here, does not mean secret or covert; it just means be-longing to a single person—like "private property.") If that much is right, however, then, even in the ordinary case, an individual's meanings are ul-timately up to that individual. Thus, if I use the word 'duck' to mean what everybody else means by it, that just shows that I have chosen—tacitly and unconsciously, perhaps—to go along with the crowd. Since I *could have* decided to mean something else by that word, my not doing so still amounts to a choice—by default, so to speak. Therefore, *all* meanings must rest, in the end, on individuals' decisions, deliberate or otherwise, and are, in that sense, *private*.

The sceptical argument, however, shows that this is impossible. The meaning of a word does not merely determine how it is used or likely to be to be used but how it *ought* to be used. If 'duck' means duck, then calling a bucket a duck is not just odd; it is *wrong*—a misuse of the word 'duck.' In other words, meanings, by their very nature, are *normative rules*. And the essential problem is that individuals cannot impose norms *on themselves*. For that would be like taking a dictator, with absolute legal authority, to be bound by her own law. But she cannot really be *bound* by her own law since, given her authority, if she changes her mind and does something different, that just changes the law—which is equivalent to saying that the law did not bind her in the first place. Similarly, but on a smaller scale, an individual cannot, on his own authority, bind himself by his own private norm.

In sum: if meanings must be normative, but individuals cannot impose norms on themselves, then private, individual meanings are impossible. That is the sceptical conclusion. But if, as the preceding "line of thought" seemed to show, all meanings must rest, in the end, on private decisions, then the two arguments together imply that there can be no meanings at all—which is paradoxical. According to Kripke, Wittgenstein accepts the sceptical conclusion but denies the paradox because meanings and linguistic norms are not private at all. Rather, they are both essentially *social*.

Kripke illustrates the point with an extended discussion of arithmetic terminology—in particular, the word 'plus.' He invites us to imagine that he (Kripke), an experienced and competent adder, happens never to have added any integer larger than 56. (Certainly, *some* integer *is* the largest he has ever added.) So, by hypothesis, if he is now given the problem "68 plus 57 equals . . . ," this will be completely new to him in the sense that he has never actually computed it before. And the question we are to address is: how *ought* he to respond to this new problem, given what *he himself* has hitherto always *meant* by the word 'plus'? The question is not about arithmetic itself, of course, but about meaning. More specifically, it is about how Kripke's own private mental history (understandings, intentions, decisions, etc.) can determine how he *ought* to respond now in order to remain consistent in what he means by 'plus.'

We did allow, of course, that he is an experienced adder, and we can allow further that, in consequence of that experience, he has quite definite dispositions, such that he will reliably and confidently respond to the aforementioned problem with "125." But how he will and would respond to various problems is a different matter from how he *should* respond—and it is the latter that we are asking about. Obviously, that depends on what 'plus' has *meant* to him, but that is just where we came in.

To make the issue vivid, Kripke introduces a "bizarre sceptic" who suggests that maybe his response to the new problem *ought* to be "5." To facilitate discussion, he also introduces a new integer function, called *quus*, which has the same value as 'plus' for all argument pairs both members of which are less than 57 but has the value 5 for all other pairs. So, by our hypothesis, every time Kripke has computed the plus function *so far*, he has *also* computed the quus function—because, for all the problems he has actually solved, they coincide. Given that, the sceptic's suggestion can also be put this way: maybe what Kripke has meant all along was not plus but quus. Certainly the mere fact that he used the *word* 'plus' cannot, by itself, settle what he *meant* by it.

Well, then, what *does* settle it? The short answer (after a long argument) is that *nothing* about Kripke *himself*—mental or dispositional, past or present—suffices to settle what the words he uses *mean*. That is, nothing about him as an individual—nothing *private* in that sense—determines how he *ought* to use or understand words. Rather, as has already been mentioned, the norms that govern correct usage are, and can only be, *social.* Hence, in particular, the norm governing the correct use of 'plus,' such that the correct evaluation of '68 plus 57' is 125, is social. This does not mean, of course, that the values of integer functions are determined by society—mob rule in arithmetic, as one might put it—but rather that, by determining what our words mean, social norms determine which functions we have words for.

This account, however, cannot be satisfactory as it stands. For the quus example raises not only the issue of how meanings can be determinate but also the issue of how they can be nonarbitrary. The social-norms account may well address the former, but it does not speak to the latter at all. Thus, for all Kripke's Wittgenstein says, there could perfectly well be a *community* in which there is a norm-governed word meaning "quus" and none meaning "plus"—an implication Kripke even seems to endorse:

> The set of responses in which we agree, and the way they interweave with our activities, is our *form of life.* Beings who agreed in consistently giving bizarre quus-like responses would share in another form of life. By definition, such another form of life would be bizarre and incomprehensible to us. . . . However, if we can imagine the abstract possibility of another form of life (and no *a priori* argument would seem to exclude it), the members of a community sharing such a quus-like form of life could play the game of attributing rules and concepts to each other as we do. (96)

I do not know what to say about abstract possibilities for unspecified "beings," but I do not believe we *can* imagine, concretely, any "quuslike" *human* civilization here on Earth. And I am encouraged in this negative opinion by the historical fact that, although the numerous known civilizations have differed widely in many ways, they nevertheless all had systems of arithmetic, and they *all agreed exactly* on every single sum, difference, product, and quotient that they had numerals to express. This, I suggest, cannot be mere coincidence.

4. WHAT'S MISSING IN THESE PICTURES?

I now propose to show that the three arguments just reviewed are all deficient in the same way: in discussing language and meaning, they all leave out of account the same essential factor. That factor is the world itself—the real world that we all live in.

Consider first the predicates 'grue' and 'bleen.' No one ever has or ever will sincerely project those predicates. Why is that? It is not beside the point that—apart from the odd philosopher—the very idea would never occur to anyone. But why would it not? The earlier remarks about teachability are surely relevant: it is simply not possible to *learn* the predicates 'grue' and 'bleen' except by *first* learning 'green' and 'blue' and then grasping the switchover at t. But notice: this is not a claim about how the mind works or about language or semantics. (The companion point about machines shows that much—since they do not have any minds or language.) The indistinguishability, after t, of old grue emeralds and newly discovered bleen ones is not a fact about the mind or language; it is a fact about the *world*.

It may seem that this begs some question by taking it for granted that 'green' is projectible and 'grue' is not. I *do* take that for granted, of course—we all do—but it *does not* beg any question. The issue was never *whether* 'green' is a legitimate inductive predicate, as opposed to 'grue,' or even whether we can tell but rather *why*. Goodman was not asking how we *know* that the one is projectible and the other not but rather what *makes that the case*. This is the only question that the constitutive, entrenchment account could so much as address.

What is wanted is not a vindication but an explanation. And the real answer to that explanatory "Why?" question is that no genuine kind of thing will be consistently grue (for any given t), whereas many kinds of thing—emeralds, chlorophyll, copper chloride—are and will be consistently green. It does not matter for the explanation whether we *know* this general fact about genuine kinds; it matters only that it is *true*. It is this fact—whether we know it or not—that makes 'green' a legitimate inductive predicate and 'grue' a loony one. (Or, if it is not a fact, then some other predicate is the legitimate one, and we will have to find out the hard way.)

The reason that there are projectible predicates, the reason that induction works at all, is that worldly entities—at least many of them—instantiate genuine kinds. To a first approximation, a genuine kind is a consistent and reliable collocation of structures and properties and/or combinations thereof. Emeralds are a genuine kind because a certain crystal structure, composition, color, hardness, heat capacity, and so on are reliably collocated in them. Our own perceptual organs and the sorts of measuring instrument I mentioned earlier also depend on genuine kinds in their own internal components. (The molecules in our retinal cones that enable them to respond selectively to different colors are instances of genuine kinds.) Finally, given that there are such kinds, there can be consistent and reliable kinds of interaction—including, for instance, those that make perception, measurement, and science possible.

All of this has to do with the actual things themselves. It does not depend at all on the social history of language use. Accordingly, and *contra* Goodman, predicates are not legitimate because they have become entrenched; at best, they become entrenched because they are legitimate. And they are legitimate—to the extent that they are—because they track the real world.

The indeterminacy of translation, in the (1960) version considered earlier, turns out to be a less startling thesis than it might at first have seemed. It can be seen as a new variation on the familiar theme that unrelated languages can serve the same ends—provide the same communicative facilities—in notably different ways. And, given that way of seeing the point, the underlying assumption that the end or function in question is a linguistic universal can begin to look like the more important discovery. Quine himself does not actually discuss the matter from this point of view, but we can.

Why is it that all natural human languages afford ways of referring to and talking about concrete individuals? No sooner is the question asked, I think, than the answer is obvious. Individuals are everywhere, and they are important to all human forms of life. In the first place, individuating *people* is prerequisite to the social training (and nouns) that make public language possible. (*Word and Object* begins with this sentence: "Language is a social art.") But further, the example of Inge and the two rabbits is clearly representative of countless transactions, commercial and otherwise, that we all engage in every day. And, as we have seen, this presupposes a standard *individuation* of those rabbits that is both mutually understood and unambiguously invoked in the verbal request. Inasmuch as such social training and transactions are ubiquitous in human life, every natural human language must facilitate them—in, as Quine points out, one way or another.

It is important to realize that this significant prevalence of individuals is neither a consequence of individuative language nor a necessary truth. If, for instance, we were slimes, living out our amorphous lives in some semi-liquid goo, with no sharp boundaries or stable forms, we would have neither use nor opportunity for any terms of divided reference. Even if, somehow, factual communication were possible and worthwhile under such conditions, it could be nothing like any actual human language—and precisely *because* the relevant facts are so different.

By the same token, the *real reason* that divided reference is both feasible and valuable in all human languages is ultimately not a fact about language as such at all. Rather, it is a contingent fact about the world we live in and what matters to us in it.

It is not hard to see why there has never been a civilization that did not do arithmetic in basically the way that we do—at least as far as they got. You cannot build or maintain a city without a good deal of arithmetic calculation, and it will not work if you do not get the right answers. What we need to consider, therefore, is what *makes* those answers the *right* ones. Arithmetic calculation is initially important in connection with counting and measurement.

Only three simple points need to be made about counting. First, what we count, in the most primitive and fundamental case, are the same distinct, durable individuals that we refer to with terms of divided reference. Second, in order for counting and arithmetic to make sense, you have got to be able—in practice—to delineate sets of individuals and also a few relations like disjointness, subsets, and unions. And, third, once you have got those things, along with counting itself, the addition function—the one that is worth having—is already determined. If you have got a basket of 68 apples, and you add 57 more, you are just going to get 125 apples—no matter what anybody's norms are.

Measurement is similar but more interesting. First, of course, once measurement of lengths, weights, volumes, and the like is well defined (in terms of standard, iterated units), measurements of relevant combinations are just as predetermined by those of their components as are the counts of the apples. For example, 68 inches end to end with 57 just is 125 inches—again regardless of anybody's norms.

What makes this more interesting than counting is that the additivity of measurements depends on what is being measured. Not all measurements—not even all those expressed numerically—are additive. A pH value of 8, for instance, is not twice as acidic as a pH value of 4; nor is a hardness of 8 on the Mohs scale twice as hard as 4. But the most revealing case is temperature: 8 degrees Celsius is not twice as hot as 4 degrees in any useful sense. But, with Lord Kelvin's discovery of absolute zero, it was also *discovered* that there are scales on which temperature *is* additive: 8 degrees *Kelvin* is indeed twice as hot as 4 degrees. What this relatively recent discovery reveals—and precisely because it is not lost to history—is that the possibility of additive measurement scales is a *contingent fact*, depending on what is being measured.

Ancient peoples must have discovered this fact pretty early about distance and perhaps time, and they would have needed to know it also for weight, volume, and maybe area before they could build and manage cities. Two conclusions matter here. First, like the prevalence of durable individuals, the additivity (given the right scale) of some measurable phenomena (but not others) is not a fact about society or language but a fact about the world. And, second, once the relevant facts were discovered, it was—as history attests—clear to everyone that there is *only one right way to add.*

It remains only to say what 'right' could mean in that conclusion. I certainly do not deny that social norms are prerequisite for all human languages or that these norms support and explain an essential right/wrong distinction in regard to usage. My point is rather that this does not go far enough. In addition to the issue of what is right or wrong according to a given body of social norms, there is an issue of the right or wrong norms *for a society to have.* In connection with arithmetic, at least—and quite possibly other things—having any norms other than the ones we in fact have would quite clearly be a mistake. And this, I have argued, follows from the determinate, contingent character of the world we actually live in.

5. DIAGNOSIS AND CONCLUSION

When Descartes more or less launched modern philosophy in 1642, his most fateful move was not the evil demon hypothesis and hyperbolic doubt or the ontological proof and the argument that God is not a deceiver or even the *cogito* and the criterion of clarity and distinctness. No, the fateful move was an unstated assumption on which all of these depend. That assumption is that, if our ideas exist at all, they are fully determinate in and of themselves quite apart from anything else that there may or may not be. The determinacy that matters here concerns not the formal reality of those ideas (roughly their ontological character as modes of thinking substance) but rather their *objective* reality (roughly their intentional content as representations). Taking the latter to be "internally" determinate in this way is the defining assumption of classical internalism.

No one could accuse Goodman, Quine, or Kripke's Wittgenstein of being internalists in this classical sense. Quite the opposite: they are among its most incisive and effective critics. Important differences notwithstanding, they are alike in arguing that society and public language are prerequisite to the possibility of any distinctively human meaningfulness or intentional content at all. And society is certainly not internal in the way that Descartes meant.

Insofar as there is an element of scepticism in these later positions— only Kripke frames the issue with that term—it is not traditional scepticism about the possibility of knowledge but a new-fangled scepticism about the possibility of legitimate, determinate meanings for individual people considered in isolation. Thus, it is scepticism about the very assumption that made *Cartesian* scepticism possible. In other words, the common conclusion that meanings are legitimate and determinate—to whatever extent they are—only in a historical, communal setting makes Cartesian scepticism in its original form not just false but unintelligible as well. That is why none of these authors is a classical internalist.

Yet, if I am right, there is a peculiar irony in what actually results. For I have argued that each of them still neglects an essential element in the determinacy-cum-legitimacy of these admittedly public meanings. That further essential element is the world itself. The irony is that, inasmuch as they systematically deny the world a role, they do not so much demolish the Cartesian barrier as merely shift it "outward" a notch. That expanded inner/outer perimeter now encloses not only private thoughts and feelings but also public language and social norms, but it still *excludes* the real things and happenings that those thoughts and conversations are primarily about.

Commitment to remaining within this enlarged *cordon sanitaire* when considering questions about meaning is what I mean by "*social* Cartesianism." As I have argued in the preceding sections, its effects are still philosophically distorting and pernicious. It still amounts to a kind of immanence/transcendence distinction, privileging a new social-linguistic version of "subjectivity." In other words, "social" though it may be, it is still Cartesianism—and the epithet is still pejorative.

In a famous footnote (*Kritik der reinen Vernunft:* Bxxxix), Kant (1975) calls it "a scandal of philosophy and human reason in general" that there is no proof of "the existence of things outside us." Referring to this passage, Heidegger says the following:

> The "scandal of philosophy" is not that this proof is still missing but *that such proofs are expected and attempted again and again....* Dasein, properly understood, defies such proofs because, in its being, it in each case already *is* what subsequent proofs hold must first be demonstrated for it. (SZ 205)

Although it is now the legitimacy and determinacy of meaning that are held questionable, the scandal is still with us and still essentially the same. For what dasein in each case already is, in its being, is *being-in-the-world* as a *unitary* phenomenon. That means that individual people, everyday social living (including talking), *and the everyday world* are first intelligible only as a unity—that is, as an integrated whole. Only on the basis of that prior whole can those three respective moments be singled out for even relatively focused attention. Since there is no possibility of adequately understanding any of them apart from *both* of the others, there is no more prospect of a philosophically defensible *cordon* around two than around just one.

Authentic Intentionality

(2002)

I. COMPUTATION AND INTENTIONALITY

Once upon a time, we "knew" what computation is: it is whatever it is that Turing machines do—generalized, of course, to include von Neumann machines, production systems, Lisp machines, and all the other provably "equivalent" architectures. By these lights, so-called analog computers were not really computers in the strict sense but only devices that had that name for historical reasons. Now, however, things do not seem so clear— hence the reason for this book.[1] I will mention in passing just two of the numerous issues that have clouded the idea of computation in the last decade or two.

The first is the emergence and mathematical analysis of systems with totally different architectures and very powerful capabilities, of which it is hard to say that they are not computing (in some pretheoretical sense). The most conspicuous among these are connectionist networks, artificial life (A-life) systems, and some dynamical models (including some that make essential use of chaotic attractors). It is enough to make one rethink the dismissal of old-fashioned analog systems. So, the question arises: what might it be that makes all of these (but not everything) computing devices?

And the second is the idea that maybe semantics is essential to computation as such. This is encouraged by the easy thought that, to count as

1. This paper was originally published in a collection of essays titled *Computationalism: New Directions.—Ed.*

260

computing at all, a device must be computing something (and not just some "function" because, in some sense everything does that). But there are also two more important motives for bringing semantics into the picture. One is the hope that semantics might be what is needed to answer the question raised by the first issue I mentioned: what makes all of these systems computers? And the other is the long-sought assimilation of computation to cognition—for cognition surely presupposes semantics.

I will not try to address either of these issues directly but rather engage in what might be thought of as necessary spadework preparatory to a resolution of either of them. In particular, I want to formulate a thesis about what is required for semantics—or, as I prefer to call it, *intentionality*—especially insofar as it is prerequisite to cognition. As I formulate it, this requirement will be neutral as to the various possible "architectures" for computation, but I do not know whether it really is neutral. That is probably an empirical question to which no one can yet know the answer.

2. SPECIES OF INTENTIONALITY

Almost twenty years ago, John Searle (1983, 1992) and I each introduced a pair of contrasting terms for two different species or types of intentionality. His distinction and mine are often confused, but they are not equivalent.

I distinguished what I called derivative intentionality from original intentionality. Derivative intentionality (or meaning) is the intentionality that something has only by virtue of having it conferred on it by something else that already has it. A common example is the intentionality of words and sentences, which (according to this view) they have only because it is conferred on them by thoughts, which already have it.

Original intentionality, by contrast, is any intentionality that is not derivative. I offered no positive account of original intentionality—what it requires or what makes it possible—but only the observation that there must be some for the simple reason that not all intentionality could be derivative. My purpose was only to make it clear that original intentionality is the real problem and to be able to raise the question of what has it and what it takes to have it.

Searle, on the other hand, distinguished what he called *observer-relative* intentionality from intrinsic intentionality. Observer-relative intentionality, at least insofar as it also means user-relative, turns out to be much the same as derivative intentionality, and, more recently, Searle has often adopted the latter term. Searle's original term, however, does have the following advantage: it suggests, correctly, that derivative intentionality is intentionality only to or for something else—a user or an observer, for instance—never to or for whatever has it itself.

But intrinsic intentionality means much more than just original intentionality. Intrinsic intentionality is understood by Searle as an intrinsic, higher-order property that some physical structures have just in virtue of their (intrinsic) physical structure. So it is supposed to be analogous to the wetness of H_2O (water) or the hardness of tetrahedrally crystalline carbon (diamond). I, like many other philosophers and cognitive scientists, have had a hard time taking the notion of intrinsic intentionality seriously. But it does have one important merit that the notion of original intentionality lacks: it is intended as a positive account of the source ("origin") of all other intentionality. The fact that Searle's discussions of it are sorely lacking in plausible detail about what makes it possible does not cancel out this merit.

What I now want to do is offer *my own* positive account of what original intentionality requires and what makes it possible. My account will be profoundly different from Searle's and will include significantly more detail. But one way in which it will not differ from his is that it will not contain any hints at all about exactly what it takes to implement it. Thus, though more detailed in various ways, it is like Searle's in being, in effect, a challenge to empirical science: go figure out what it would take to implement *this*.

To explain my proposal, I will need to introduce a new classification of types or species of intentionality (or "intentionality-like" phenomena). This is a three-way classification, for which I will use the following terms:

1. *Authentic* intentionality
2. *Ordinary* intentionality
3. *Ersatz* intentionality

None of these is equivalent to any of original, derivative, intrinsic, or observer-relative intentionality. The relations among the old and new types go like this: either authentic or ordinary intentionality can be either original or derivative (yielding four possible subtypes, if you like). I will refer to all of these subtypes generically as genuine intentionality. Ersatz intentionality is none of the foregoing but rather, as the name suggests, not genuine intentionality at all; it is only an imperfect analogue that is in some ways "intentionality-like"; finally, there is no such thing as intrinsic intentionality.

The relation between authentic and ordinary intentionality is more complicated. In general, only systems that are in some sense capable of authentic intentionality are capable of ordinary intentionality. (I say "in general" because there may be deficient or partial cases that would call for tedious qualifications.) But actually having ordinary intentionality does not require actually having authentic intentionality. One of my main aims here is to make the reasons for this complicated claim clear.

Before proceeding to that, however, let me explain briefly what I mean by ersatz intentionality (and then be done with it). Ersatz intentionality is the so-called intentionality that can be attributed in what Dennett calls "the intentional stance." I do not mean that all intentionality attributable in the intentional stance is merely ersatz but rather that the most that such attributability suffices for is ersatz intentionality. In other words, in my view, the intentional stance by itself is not useful at all for explicating the difference between genuine and ersatz intentionality.

In particular, I maintain that the intentionality-like character of various states attributable to (subhuman) animals or (so far as I know) to any actual or concretely envisioned robots is not genuine intentionality but merely ersatz. Examples like thermostats and flowering trees are just ludicrously extreme cases. I will not explicitly defend either of these claims (about the intentional stance or about animals and robots), but my reasons for them should become obvious as the story unfolds.

3. INTENTIONALITY AND OBJECTIVITY

The first point I want to make about genuine original intentionality, whether ordinary or authentic, is that it presupposes the capacity for objective knowledge. Indeed, since derivative intentionality presupposes original intentionality, the argument will apply to *all* genuine intentionality. In the present context, I mean by 'objective knowledge' beliefs or assertions that are true of objects nonaccidentally. That the intentionality of beliefs and assertions presupposes the possibility of some of them being objectively true—that is, true of objects as they actually are—is obvious. For, if none of them could even possibly be true of actual objects, it would make no sense to say that any of them were about or intended any objects at all (or, therefore, to call any of them beliefs or assertions at all).

It is equally obvious that beliefs or assertions that are genuine knowledge must be not only true but also true nonaccidentally. What this means, however, and how it is achieved scientifically is not so obvious and will emerge in what follows in several stages. But that the capacity for such knowledge is prerequisite for genuine intentionality is true by stipulation: it is what I mean by "genuine." The point of the term, after all, is to mark a distinction—a distinction that is philosophically important and that goes missing in those discussions that indiscriminately run together the "intentionality" of people, animals, and (current) robots (not to mention flowering trees and thermostats). The aim of the arguments to follow is not to defend this stipulation but rather to show how much it involves—that is, how deep a gulf the distinction it marks really is.

(In the case of other propositional attitudes and speech acts—such as desires, doubts, commands, questions, and so on—the connection between intentionality and the possibility of objective truth is less direct but just as essential. I expect this claim to be uncontroversial, but, in any event, I will take it for granted without argument. I believe that an analogous case could also be made for nonpropositional intentional states—if there are any—such as mental images or internal emulations or simulations, but this, too, I will leave aside here.)

So, the fundamental question is this: what is required for the possibility of nonaccidental objective truth—that is, knowledge? I am going to argue that it requires the taking of *responsibility* on the part of the person (or "system") who is capable of such objective knowledge. Indeed, it will turn out that two levels of responsibility are involved, and it will be the difference between these levels that accounts for the distinction between ordinary and authentic intentionality. But first things first.

4. OBJECTIVITY AND RESPONSIBILITY

In order to make out the case for this essential relevance of responsibility, I will focus on a distinctive species of objective knowledge, namely, scientific knowledge. The reason is not just that scientific knowledge is especially explicit and compelling but rather that it has been much studied, so its features and factors are fairly well known. But I am convinced that (perhaps with more work and less clarity) basically the same case could be made for commonsense knowledge. Thus, though I do not agree with Quine that science is "continuous with" common sense, I do agree that they have the same fundamental character. Accordingly, I maintain that examining the conditions of the possibility of scientific intentionality is a suitable entry point for examining those of any genuine intentionality. The advantage of the focus on science is purely expository.

One conspicuous fact about reputable scientists is that they are always highly trained and highly disciplined. Hand in hand with this conspicuous fact goes another: scientific research is always and inherently self-critical—not only individually but also interactively. Such self-critical discipline is quite visible, for instance, both in how scientists perform experiments themselves and in how they evaluate each other's performances.

So we see here, what is obvious anyway, that scientific research is fundamentally communal and, in particular, that it is governed by *communal norms of proper performance*—that is, of proper procedure and technique—in terms of which particular performances can be critically judged. These norms effectively define the *discipline* of normal scientific research. At the same time, they provide the basis for what I will call *first-order* scientific self-criticism. Disciplined science is self-critical in that it carefully scrutinizes actual procedures to ensure that they are in accord with its norms of proper performance.

This critical self-scrutiny is manifestly a crucial factor in the ability of scientific research to discover the truth about the objects it investigates since it weeds out experimental results that are compromised by sloppy or improper procedures. Such results are, of course, unreliable—in the specific sense that they are either false or, if true, only so by accident ("dumb luck"). Therefore, first-order self-criticism is also essential to the fact that scientific results can be not only true but also nonaccidentally so—that is, objective knowledge. Hence it is prerequisite to genuine intentionality.

There is also, however, a second sort of self-criticism in normal experimental practice. This comes into view when we remember that, unless a result is utterly routine, it usually will not be accepted until it has been replicated by other teams in other laboratories. But what does it mean to say that a result has been replicated, and why does it matter? Why, exactly, is there anything wrong if replication efforts fail? These questions may seem trivial, but I think they cut pretty deep.

Note first that replication of an experimental finding is seldom simply a duplication of the previous experiment. On the contrary, it is much better if the same result can be obtained by other means. So, our first question comes to this: how can a different experiment amount to a replication of (or a failure to replicate) the same result?

The answer is that (except, perhaps, in times of crisis) scientists always have pretty determinate convictions about what the objects they are investigating must be like. The most basic of these convictions are expressed in scientific laws and principles. These laws (and their more specific implications), in determining the objects, sharply constrain how the results of various different experimental procedures would have to be related.

To take a contrived example, suppose an experiment were performed to measure the electric charge on some newly isolated particle. This experiment will rely on certain laws about how charged particles interact with various other particles, fields, and so on. But there are lots of such interactions and combinations thereof. So another team could proceed in quite a different way and still be confident that it was measuring the same property of the same particle—that is, the same object, as determined by the same laws. In this way, the constraints expressed in the laws make it possible for two quite different experiments to produce the same result—or, as the case may be, a conflicting result.

In the light of all of that, however, it is also clear why replication—or, more to the point, a failure of a replication—matters. Inasmuch as the norms of proper performance, together with the laws governing the objects under investigation, effectively promise that the results will agree, any disagreement means there is something wrong somewhere. Of course, the most common upshot is that, on closer examination, one or the other of the experiments was not properly performed after all. Most apparently conflicting results are actually due to experimental error.

But the more interesting case is when no such error can be found. Then scientists turn their scrutiny not on individual performances but on the very norms that determine procedural propriety for all performances of that sort. This is not as drastic as it sounds: the business of refining observational technique in the light of experience is bread and butter to any thriving experimental practice.

In other words, empirical science is inherently self-critical in a second and deeper way: it critically scrutinizes not only individual performances but also the very practice itself. I call this second and deeper scrutiny *second-order* self-criticism. And, as with first-order self-criticism, this, too, is obviously a basic factor in the ability of scientific research to discover—nonaccidentally—the truth about its objects. Hence it, too, is prerequisite to the possibility of scientific knowledge and hence genuine intentionality.

So far, I have spoken about how scientific research as such is inherently self-critical, and I have distinguished two "orders" of that self-criticism. Further, I have pointed out that both the impetus and the need for this self-criticism arises out of the relation between scientific results and their objects—namely, the objects as what are determined and constrained by the basic laws and principles. In particular, it arises from the fact that certain combinations of results can show that something is wrong somewhere and so needs to be found and corrected. It is by giving content to the idea of being wrong that this basic structure contributes essentially to the possibility of being correct. Finally, I have drawn the obvious conclusion that whatever is prerequisite to getting the relation to objects correct is prerequisite to objective knowledge and hence to genuine intentionality.

What I have not yet done is say anything about what scientists themselves must be like. Of course, it is the scientists who must "respond" when something is wrong, and a corrective response is required—it is they who must be "self-critical." But what must they be like, qua scientists, if this "requirement" is to get a grip on them and move them to action?

Clearly, it must be something like this: scientists qua scientists will not and cannot tolerate a body of results in which there is something wrong in the way that I have been discussing. For such tolerance would undermine the process of weeding out unreliable results and thereby also the ability to settle nonaccidentally on one truth about objects—that is, to discover it. Incompatible results, as determined by the laws and principles governing the objects under investigation, must be unacceptable to scientists qua scientists. Thus, in order to be a scientist, a person must be such that she will not—because she cannot—accept or tolerate results that are incompatible, hence somehow wrong.

Two clarifications are needed to ensure that this point is not misunderstood. First, the refusal to accept the results in question cannot simply be a matter of denying or suppressing them. Rather, it must take the form of an effort to find out what went wrong and then correct it. Second, the "cannot" (in "cannot accept or tolerate") must have a normative rather that an alethic force. That is, it is not that the scientist is unable to tolerate such results (as in an inability to tolerate pain or pomposity) but rather that such tolerance would be impermissible in a scientist—incompatible with being a *genuine or honest* scientist.

But as soon as the point about unacceptability is understood in this way, it becomes clear that it can also be expressed as follows: being a scientist entails a certain kind of responsibility. In particular, it is the responsibility of any scientist, qua scientist, not to accept results in which something has been shown to be wrong and, moreover, to regard finding and correcting whatever is wrong as incumbent on the scientific community.

5. RESPONSIBILITY AND COGNITIVE SCIENCE

If you gather up (and swallow) everything I have said so far, then this conclusion about science and responsibility has important implications for cognitive science. For I have argued that:

- genuine intentionality presupposes the capacity for objective knowledge;
- scientific knowledge is an exemplary case of objective knowledge;
- scientific research, as a route to objective knowledge, is inherently self-critical in at least two ways; and
- in order for research to be thus self-critical, scientists themselves must accept a certain kind of responsibility.

But those together imply that any system capable of genuine (original) intentionality must be capable of accepting that kind of responsibility. Hence any system capable of genuine cognition must have that same capacity for responsibility.

It is my impression that cognitive science—and especially cognitive science inspired by the idea of computation—has been effectively oblivious to this essential connection between cognition and responsibility. I suspect that an inkling of this oblivion is what lies behind various ill-formed (and often annoying) "intuitions" to the effect that AI (artificial intelligence) systems (of whatever stripe) cannot really mean anything, cannot understand their own inputs and outputs, cannot really be *conscious,* and so on. It is not that I think these intuitive judgments are false but rather that they do not get at the underlying problem and hence remain mere intuitions, with regard to which "arguments" (pro and con) can be, at best, aggravatingly inconclusive.

Correlatively, I believe that this same oblivion also enables a profoundly misguided and misleading assimilation of human cognition to so-called animal cognition. This assimilation then encourages the perverse supposition that, insofar as robot capabilities approach those of animals, they thereby also approach those of people. So far as I know, no (subhuman) animal or any current or envisioned robot is capable of accepting any responsibility on its own. Therefore, by the earlier argument, none is capable of any genuine intentionality or cognition. This is why I have coined the term "ersatz" intentionality for those aspects of animal and/or robot behavior that are, in certain superficial ways, undeniably intentionality-like.

I believe that the foregoing argument suffices to show that at least most of contemporary cognitive science seriously underestimates its own essential field and that it cannot fully succeed in its own goals unless it rectifies that underestimation. For, in being oblivious of personal responsibility as prerequisite to the possibility of original intentionality, which is acknowledged as prerequisite to genuine cognition, it denies itself the possibility of adequately understanding the latter.

Moreover, insofar as it is held that at least some species of computation presuppose genuine intentionality (a view on which I will voice no opinion), current approaches to understanding computation suffer from the same debilitating underestimation. (Such a view of computation would be required of anyone who held that cognition just is computation of a certain sort.)

All the same, I also believe that the discussion of intentionality so far remains essentially incomplete. In beginning to address this incompleteness, I will, to be sure, be raising the bar still higher for cognitive science (and perhaps for computer science). But I would like to reemphasize something that I indicated at the outset: it is no part of my aim to argue that the requirements that I am setting cannot be met. They are not intended as showstoppers, still less as refutations, but rather as serious scientific challenges to fundamental research. Of course, I am also in no position to claim that these challenges *can* be met—nor do I have any clear sense of what it would take to meet them. The best I can do as a philosopher is to try to articulate some of the boundary conditions.

In characterizing the second-order self-criticism that belongs to science, I observed that the norms of scientific practice *together with* the laws governing the objects under investigation "promise" that properly obtained scientific results will all agree about those objects. It is the breach of this promise, when results conflict, that shows that *something* is wrong. But then I considered only one of the two obvious options for *what* might be wrong—namely, something in the norms governing the practice (that is, proper procedures). Scrutinizing and refining these is what I called second-order self-criticism.

Clearly, however, there is no guarantee that any way of refining and improving the practice (the norms) will actually eliminate all conflicts among properly obtained results. In other words, there may be no way to make this field, as presently constituted, "work." Thus, eventually, if the conflicts prove serious and persistent enough, then—and only then—will scientists begin to take their last option seriously: that there is something wrong with the basic laws and principles in terms of which they understand the objects in their domain.

This process I will call—predictably—*third-order* scientific self-criticism. It is always the *last* option because it raises the stakes in a fundamental way.

6. AUTHENTIC RESPONSIBILITY

Revising the laws that a scientific community takes to govern the objects in its domain is a far more radical undertaking than merely revising the practices for investigating them. The reasons for this can be summarized in three closely connected points.

First: the laws and principles tend to be interdependent, forming a coherent whole or "package" such that you cannot revise just one or two at a time, leaving the others as they were. Thus, any such revision is likely to have to be more or less "wholesale." By contrast, revisions in the norms for proper experimental procedure can usually be managed roughly at "retail"— that is, one or a few at a time.

Second: the experimental procedures, as we have seen, are themselves intelligible only in terms of the laws governing the objects. So, although you can refine procedures without revising laws, you cannot revise laws without revising procedures—or at least reconceiving them. What is worse, since the law revisions are apt to be wholesale, the required procedural revisions will have to be more widespread as well. In other words, a whole lot of things have to be reconceived at once, which makes the space of alternatives much larger and the number of "fixed points" to guide the search much smaller.

But finally, and most fundamentally: the laws governing the objects are crucial to the very intelligibility of those objects as what they are. The point is most easily seen by example: how could one possibly understand what mass, force, momentum, and energy—not to mention electrons, orbiting planets, springs, and gases—are, apart from how they figure (in relation to one another) in the relevant laws of motion, gravity, elasticity, thermodynamics, and so on? The connection between laws and intelligibility is conspicuous as well in the fact that scientific explanation, which is the context in which scientific understanding is made explicit, standardly appeals to laws and principles (or something like them).

Of course, the intelligibility of the objects also depends on the (various) empirical procedures by which they can be observed and measured—a truism that once lent plausibility to verificationism, operationalism, and their ilk. But, without the laws, even the procedures would make no *systematic* sense, and all that would remain would be a traditional craft (and perhaps some mythology). It is because the laws and principles *collectively* determine the intelligibility of the objects that they cannot be revised piecemeal or without also revising the practice.

In sum, when it turns out (after long struggle) that a scientific discipline cannot in fact be made to work—too many of the results that it itself deems proper are, by its own lights, impossible—then that discipline as a whole comes into question. This is why I said that third-order self-criticism raises the stakes in a fundamental way. Often enough, the eventual changes are so radical that it makes as much sense to say that the old discipline died out and got replaced by a successor (or successors) related only by a pattern of family resemblances to what preceded. Hence the appeal of grand phrases such as "paradigm shift" and "revolution." Yet, however radical and however described, if a discipline just does not work, pursuing such transformations (or replacements) can sometimes be the only responsible response to the actual situation. Accepting this responsibility is peculiarly personal not merely because it is so risky but also because what is at stake in it is the individual's own professional self-understanding. Who, after all, are you, professionally, if your professional specialty dies?

However, even though the ability of *some* scientists to accept this responsibility is essential to science—lest it degenerate into a dogmatic and unempirical orthodoxy—it is not essential that *every* scientist actually be able to accept it. As Kuhn argued, on historical grounds, most scientists will not actually jump ship until they can clearly see a plausibly better vessel on the horizon. Revolutions, as everyone knows, always need their heroes.

Since this responsibility is, in some sense, for the whole, and yet peculiarly personal, I call it (not ordinary but) *authentic* responsibility.

7. AUTHENTIC INTENTIONALITY

Intentionality is directedness to *objects*—objects as they *are*. It therefore presupposes not only the distinction between objective truth and falsity but also the ability to discover the former nonaccidentally—that is, to *know* it. We have already seen this structure in the conditions of the possibility of ordinary intentionality (first- and second-order self-criticism and ordinary responsibility).

But what are *objects?* What does it mean to say "objects as they *are*"? In speaking to these questions, I will rely on an approach to metaphysics that is far from universally endorsed. Accordingly, my conclusions will presuppose some controversial premises. But, since I endorse this approach, I think the conclusions are valid. Your mileage may vary.

This is not the place to spell out my approach to metaphysics in detail, let alone defend it. I will mention only one (familiar but tendentious) claim that motivates it and then the basic shape of an accommodation of this claim. The claim is that "absolute" or "capital-R" Reality—Reality as *God* describes it—is a notion that cannot be made sense of. Note: this is not the claim that we can never come to know "capital-R Reality" but rather the claim that the notion of such reality does not make sense and that therefore neither does knowing it or not knowing it. The philosophical challenge, then, is to make sense of objectivity, truth, and knowledge without appealing to any notion of "capital-R Reality."

The basic shape of the response is to relativize reality not to God's descriptive resources but to our own—the only ones we can ever have or understand. Then, of course, the demon to be exorcised is mere or capital-R *Relativism,* which is incompatible with any robust conception of objectivity. What is so upsetting about such relativism is that, according to it, our descriptive resources are ultimately arbitrary—in effect, accidental—the results of personal taste, historical happenstance, extraneous cultural influences, and the like. This is really just the flip side of capital-R Realism since it accepts the same basic assumption that the only alternative to arbitrariness is capital-R Reality. Therefore, what any more satisfactory relativizing must do is show how the descriptive resources in question are not ultimately arbitrary.

But that, after all—showing how descriptive resources are not ultimately arbitrary—is exactly what *authentic* responsibility is all about. It is authentic in that it is personal—one's own—responsibility for the science as a whole, including in particular the basic laws and principles in terms of which the objects—hence the terms for them—are understood. In other words, it is responsibility for the basic descriptive resources of the field. But, inasmuch as it is genuine *responsibility*, it is not arbitrary. Third-order self-criticism is driven—neither easily nor happily—by two factors. It is driven by an overarching insistence on maintaining a discipline that actually works by its own demanding lights—that is, a discipline that reliably produces stringently constrained results that are consistently possible according to its own defining laws and principles. And it is driven by a persistent empirical recalcitrance in those results—results that have themselves all survived careful first- and second-order critical scrutiny.

In other words, it is driven by a persistent empirical failure to make the discipline work despite assiduous and often ingenious efforts on the part of many. Whether a discipline can be made to work is not up to the scientists (or history or fads or culture). There is nothing *arbitrary* or *accidental* about it. That is why I can say that, in the end, giving the whole thing up is not just a matter of personal preference or social trends but rather of the highest scientific *responsibility*.

Accordingly, the ability to accept this responsibility—*authentic responsibility*—on at least some occasions by at least some scientists is prerequisite to scientific objectivity. Hence, by my earlier argument, it is prerequisite to genuine intentionality and cognition. I call the intentionality of someone who does accept authentic responsibility *authentic intentionality*.

And that is why I said earlier (in section 2) that the *capacity* for authentic intentionality is prerequisite to the *capacity* for ordinary intentionality, but *actually having* the former is not prerequisite to *actually having* the latter. But even this somewhat complicated dependency shows that cognitive science will not have understood the conditions of the possibility of intentionality—hence of cognition at all—until it has understood the possibility of authentic responsibility and intentionality.

8. DRAMATIC CONCLUSION

It used to be said—perhaps reassuringly, perhaps defensively—that the aims of artificial intelligence are limited in a certain way. The goal, it was said, is not to construct a machine (or "system") capable of the full gamut of human experience or of the human mind, but rather only a system capable of humanlike *intelligence* and hence cognition (so far as it is required for intelligence).

The intended contrast (what **AI** is not concerned with) included things like emotions (love, anger, fear, . . .), feelings (pleasure, disgust, embarrassment, . . .), and perhaps nonintellectual evaluations (this is fun, fascinating, beautiful, . . .). I am inclined to think that none of these separations—topical quarantines, in effect—will ultimately prove defensible. But here I want to broach just one such doubt.

I have argued that the objectivity and intentionality of scientific thought—and, by extension, all thought—depends essentially on a certain rather rich structure of self-criticism and responsibility. The deepest and most fundamental layer of this structure—authentic responsibility—can be characterized generically as follows: it is an *honest commitment*—in the sense of resolve or dedication—to making something work, on pain of having to give the whole thing up. Such honest commitment is "double edged"—it cuts both ways—in that, first, it requires honest and dedicated effort to making it work, and yet, second, it also requires the honest courage, eventually, to admit that it cannot be made to work—if it cannot—and then to quit. These two edges are ordinary and authentic responsibility, respectively.

But I think that this structure of double-edged commitment is widespread in human life—not just in science but also in many (and in some sense all) areas of the greatest human import. In particular, I believe that it is the basic structure of love and also freedom and that love and freedom are its most basic forms. Therefore, I close with the following dramatic—but also perfectly serious—claim: cognitive science and artificial intelligence cannot succeed in their own essential aims unless and until they can understand and/or implement genuine freedom and the capacity to love.

REFERENCES

ACKNOWLEDGMENTS

INDEX

References

LIST OF ABBREVIATIONS FOR HEIDEGGER'S WORKS
CITED IN THE TEXT

GM   *Die Grundbegriffe der Metaphysik*
GP   *Grundprobleme der Phänomenologie*
ML   *Metaphysische Anfangsgründe der Logik im Ausgang von Leibniz*
PG   *Hegels Phänomenologie des Geistes*
PIK   *Phänomenologische Interpretation von Kants Kritik der reinen Vernunft*
SZ   *Sein und Zeit*

LIST OF REFERENCES FOR HAUGELAND'S TEXT AND
THE EDITORIAL NOTES

Blattner, William. 1999. *Heidegger's Temporal Idealism.* Cambridge: Cambridge University Press.

Brandom, Robert. 1979. Freedom and Constraint by Norms. *American Philosophical Quarterly* 16: 187–96.

———. 1983a. Asserting. *Nous* 17: 637–50.

———. 1983b. Heidegger's Categories. *Monist* 66: 387–409.

———. 1994. *Making It Explicit.* Cambridge, MA: Harvard University Press.

———. 2002. *Tales of the Mighty Dead.* Cambridge, MA: Harvard University Press.

Carnap, Rudolf. 1950. Empiricism, Semantics and Ontology. *Revue Internationale de Philosophie* 11: 20–40.

Davidson, Donald. 1970. Mental Events. In *Experience and Theory*, ed. L. Foster and J. W. Swanson, 79–101. Amherst: University of Massachusetts Press. Reprinted in Davidson 1980, 207–227.

———. 1974a. Belief and the Basis of Meaning. *Synthese* 27: 309–23. Reprinted in Davidson 1984, 141–54.

———. 1974b. Psychology as Philosophy. In *Philosophy of Psychology,* ed. S. C. Brown, 41–52. London: MacMillan. Reprinted in Davidson 1980, 229–244.

———. 1975. Thought and Talk. In *Mind and Language,* ed. S. Guttenplan, 7–23. Oxford: Oxford University Press. Reprinted in Davidson 1984, 155 –170.

———. 1980. *Essays on Actions and Events.* Oxford: Oxford University Press.

———. 1984. *Inquiries into Truth and Interpretation.* Oxford: Oxford University Press.

———. 1986. A Nice Derangement of Epitaphs. In *Truth and Interpretation,* ed. E. LePore, 433–446. Oxford: Blackwell. Reprinted in Davidson 2005, 89–108.

———. 2005. *Truth, Language, and History.* Oxford: Oxford University Press.

Dennett, Daniel. 1971. Intentional Systems. *Journal of Philosophy* 68: 87–106.

Descartes, René. 1983. *Principles of Philosophy,* trans. V. Miller and R. Miller. Dordrecht: D. Reidel.

Dewey, John. 1925. *Experience and Nature.* La Salle, IL: Open Court.

Dreyfus, Hubert. 1991. *Being-in-the-World.* Cambridge, MA: MIT Press.

Dreyfus, Hubert, and Jane Rubin. 1991. Appendix: Kierkegaard, Division II, and Later Heidegger. In Dreyfus 1991, 283–340.

Goodman, Nelson. 1954. *Fact, Fiction, and Forecast.* Cambridge, MA: Harvard University Press.

Hanson, N. R. 1958. *Patterns of Discovery.* Cambridge: Cambridge University Press.

Heidegger, Martin. 1963. *Sein und Zeit.* Tűbingen: Niemeyer. English translation 1962. *Being and Time,* trans. J. Macquarrie and E. Robinson. New York: Harper and Row.

———. 1975. *Grundprobleme der Phänomenologie.* Frankfurt am Main: Klostermann. English translation 1982. *Basic Problems of Phenomenology,* trans. A. Hofstadter. Bloomington: Indiana University Press.

———. 1977. *Phänomenologische Interpretation von Kants Kritik der reinen Vernunft.* English translation 1997. *Phenomenological Interpretation of Kant's Critique of Pure Reason,* trans. P. Emad and K. Maly. Bloomington: Indiana University Press.

———. 1978. *Metaphysische Anfangsgründe der Logik im Ausgang von Leibniz.* Frankfurt am Main: Klostermann. English translation 1984. *The Metaphysical Foundations of Logic,* trans. M. Heim. Bloomington: Indiana University Press.

———. 1980. *Hegels Phänomenologie des Geistes.* Frankfurt am Main: Klostermann. English translation 1988. *Hegel's Phenomenology of Spirit,* trans. P. Emad and K. Maly. Bloomington: Indiana University Press.

———. 1983. *Die Grundbegriffe der Metaphysik.* Frankfurt am Main: Klostermann. English translation 1995. *Fundamental Concepts of Metaphysics,* trans. W. McNeill and M. Walker. Bloomington: Indiana University Press.

———. 1991. *Kant und das Problem der Metaphysik.* Frankfurt am Main: Klostermann.

———. 1997. *Being and Time,* trans. J. Stambaugh. Albany: State University of New York Press.

———. 2002. *Grundbegriffe der Aristotelischen Philosophie.* Frankfurt am Main: Klostermann. English translation 2009. *Basic Concepts of Aristotelian Philosophy,* trans. R. Metcalf and M. Tanzer. Bloomington: Indiana University Press.

Kant, Immanuel. 1975. *Critique of Pure Reason,* trans. Norman Kemp Smith. New York: St. Martin's.

Kripke, Saul. 1982. *Wittgenstein on Rules and Private Language.* Cambridge, MA: Harvard University Press.

Kuhn, Thomas S. 1962. *The Structure of Scientific Revolutions,* 2nd enlarged ed., 1970. Chicago: University of Chicago Press.

Lewis, C. I. 1929. *Mind and the World Order.* New York: Scribner's.

Lewis, David. 1969. *Convention.* Cambridge, MA: Harvard University Press.

McDaniel, Kris. 2009. Ways of Being. In *Metapmetaphysics,* ed. D. Chalmers and D. Manley, 290–319. Oxford: Oxford University Press.

Okrent, Mark. 1988. *Heidegger's Pragmatism.* Ithaca, NY: Cornell University Press.

Quine, W. V. O. 1953. *From a Logical Point of View.* Cambridge, MA: Harvard University Press.

———. 1960. *Word and Object.* Cambridge, MA: MIT Press.

Ryle, Gilbert. 1950. *The Concept of Mind.* New York: Harper and Row.

Searle, John. 1983. *Intentionality.* Cambridge, MA: MIT Press.

———. 1992. *The Rediscovery of the Mind.* Cambridge, MA: MIT Press.

Sellars, Wilfrid. 1997. *Empiricism and the Philosophy of Mind.* Cambridge, MA: Harvard University Press.

———. 2007. *In the Space of Reasons,* ed. Kevin Scharp and Robert Brandom. Cambridge, MA: Harvard University Press.

Van Inwagen, Peter. 2009. Being, Existence, and Ontological Commitment. In *Metametaphysics,* ed. D. Chalmers and D. Manley, 472–506. Oxford: Oxford University Press.

White, Carol. 2005. *Time and Death.* Burlington, VT: Ashgate.

Wittgenstein, Ludwig. 1953. *Philosophical Investigations,* trans. G. E. M. Anscombe. New York: Macmillan.

Acknowledgments

The acknowledgments for this book are in three distinct sections, with different authorial voices. The opening section, including these remarks, are written by the editor, acknowledging the many contributions that made the publication of this volume possible. The second section is written on behalf of John Haugeland by his surviving spouse and literary executor, Joan Wellman. These remarks anticipate some of what John might have said had he lived to complete *Dasein Disclosed* in its intended form. The final section is written by Joan Wellman in her own voice, as her acknowledgment of those whose efforts enabled the book to appear in this form.

John Haugeland was an extraordinary philosopher, teacher, friend, and mensch. Bringing this book to press on his behalf was a labor of love and gratitude. The publication nevertheless could not have come to pass without the enthusiastic encouragement and support of Joan Wellman, John's widow, partner in all things, and literary executor. I am grateful to William Blattner, Steven Crowell, and Rebecca Kukla for their willingness to provide suggestions and critical commentary on my editorial efforts at multiple points during the process of compiling and editing the volume. The project has greatly benefited from their constructive critical support, although they must be absolved of responsibility for any remaining errors or infelicities in the editorial choices and commentary. The participants in the 2011 meeting of the International Society for Phenomenological Studies provided helpful responses to an earlier version of the editor's introduction. Special thanks go to Mark Lance, whose comments on that occasion led to a substantial reconfiguration of the introduction. Lindsay Waters and Shanshan Wang of Harvard University Press have provided enthusiastic support and invariably constructive assistance in bringing the manuscript to publication.

Permission from the following copyright holders to reprint previously published papers by John Haugeland is hereby gratefully acknowledged:

From Wiley-Blackwell:

"Heidegger on Being a Person," *Nous* 16 (1982): 16–26.

"Dasein's Disclosedness," *Southern Journal of Philosophy* 28 supplement (1990): 51–74.

"Reading Brandom Reading Heidegger," *European Journal of Philosophy* 13 (2005): 421–28.

From MIT Press:

"Truth and Finitude: Heidegger's Transcendental Existentialism," in *Heidegger, Authenticity, and Modernity: Essays in Honor of Hubert Dreyfus*, vol. 1, ed. Mark Wrathall and Jeff Malpas, 43–77. 2000.

"Authentic Intentionality," in *Computationalism: New Directions*, ed. Matthias Scheutz, 160–74. 2002.

From Stanford University Press:

"Letting Be," from *Transcendental Heidegger*, ed. Steven Crowell and Jeff Malpas, 93–103, 150. Copyright © 2007 by the Board of Trustees of the Leland Stanford Jr. University. All rights reserved.

From De Gruyter:

"Social Cartesianism," in *The Externalist Challenge*, ed. Richard Schantz, 213–26. 2004.

Joseph Rouse

Had John Haugeland lived to finish and publish *Dasein Disclosed*, he surely would have included sincere acknowledgments of influence, help, and support. I will try to do at least some of that on his behalf.

I expect that John would have begun by thanking Hubert Dreyfus, who introduced him to Heidegger and whose input and philosophical friendship was important to John throughout his career. I don't have to put words into John's mouth to do this properly.

In the acknowledgments John wrote for *Having Thought*, he says: "I would like above all to thank Bert Dreyfus for first teaching me what philosophy is and much of what I will ever know about it."

John's thinking about *Being and Time* was shaped by his thinking about Kant's *Critique of Pure Reason*. And his thinking about Kant was deeply influenced by an extended reading group and discussions with James Conant and John McDowell in Pittsburgh. He counted those conversations among the most searching and productive of his philosophical career.

Jonathan Lear read and taught Heidegger with John in Chicago. Their conversations were important and provocative for John. He respected Jonathan's insight, candor, and creativity. He found talks with Jonathan enormously useful and deeply gratifying.

Thanks belong to regular participants in the meetings of the International Society for Phenomenological Studies ("the Asilomar group"), especially William Blattner, Taylor Carman, David Cerbone, Steven Crowell, Rebecca Kukla, Mark Lance, Leslie MacAvoy, Mark Okrent, Joseph Rouse, Joseph Schear, Iain Thomson, Katherine Withy, and Mark Wrathall. Their annual gatherings exhilarated John. Their feedback on his work was particularly appreciated.

John worked on his "Heidegger book" (as he always called it in conversation) for many years. He had countless conversations with many philosophers, both about its general trajectory and purpose and about various particular questions surrounding his interpretations. Participants in *Being and Time* reading groups, course assistants for Heidegger classes, and the students in those classes also helped him develop and articulate his views. I am, sadly, not in a position properly to thank many of you by name. But you know who you are. He was abidingly grateful to, and frequently humbled by, his colleagues and students.

Thanks as well for support from the Faculties and Departments of Philosophy at the University of Pittsburgh and at the University of Chicago. A year of leave to work on this manuscript was made possible by a 2003 Fellowship from the John Simon Guggenheim Memorial Foundation.

Joan Wellman on behalf of John Haugeland

John spent much of his adult life reading, thinking about, talking about, and writing about Heidegger's *Being and Time,* but he didn't publish much. He was a slow and careful writer who let go of a manuscript only when he was satisfied that he'd expressed himself as well as he possibly could. His early death prevented his completing what he envisioned as a clear and concise presentation of his global interpretation. That would have been *Dasein Disclosed.*

When we lost him so early, therefore, it was certain that none of the previously unpublished material in this volume came up to his rigorous standards. He wasn't done with it yet. But it was also certain, to those of us who knew him, that John was deeply committed to an ongoing conversation with other Anglophone Heidegger scholars.

So the task with which I was confronted was to identify material that might be interesting and useful to his students and colleagues while also meeting standards that merited inclusion in the body of his published work. I could not have done that on my own. I am therefore personally grateful to those who helped me sift through his manuscripts and decide what to include in this volume.

Many thanks to William Blattner, Steven Crowell, David Finkelstein, Clark Remington, Matthew Shockey, Lindsay Waters, and Emma Wellman. Each of you encouraged me at various crucial times and helped me think through how best to approach the work. I've been fortunate in having such wise advisors.

For undertaking all the reading, for helping to select, for editing, for serving as contact person with the Press, for composing an insightful and enlightening Introduction, for soliciting and responding to feedback from colleagues, for impeccably good judgment and unfailing generosity: deepest thanks to Joseph Rouse, philosopher and friend.

I believe John would be very pleased.

Joan Wellman

Index

Milton Keynes UK
Ingram Content Group UK Ltd.
UKHW010118280923
429503UK00002B/11/J